ENDORSEMEN

"*Where the Colors Blend* invites the reader into ⟨...⟩ ⟨...⟩ story or God. Stephen's thought-provoking, raw words of soul/spirit seeking invite the reader to thirst for overflowing streams of God, not sips; to strain to hear/feel the heartbeat of God, not settle for whispers; to see the face of God, not grab erratically for glimpses soon forgotten; to grasp the life of God, not skirt the boundary of His presence; to ponder the depths of God's redemptive work in the stories of others and how those stories intersect and impact our individual stories. Stephen's writing masterfully draws us into his spiritual journey and, by so doing, invites the reader to take her own bold steps of discovery."

Christine M. Browning, Ph.D., LPC/MHSP, NCC,
Associate Professor of Counseling, Milligan College

"In *Where the Colors Blend*, Stephen paints a beautiful—yet difficult—picture of his own faith journey by taking the reader inside the lives of those who helped him discover his true self. Stephen's spiritual vulnerability is a welcome change from those who always seem to have it together and never once question their belief structures. And in working out the complexities of his realization that he is truly beloved by God, Stephen gives the reader permission to doubt, scream, curse, cry, be still, and then find hope all over again. This book has moved me and helped me to remember that no matter where my current faith stands, I'm not alone, and I'm going to be OK. As Stephen says, 'Doubt, I'm finding, is actually a gateway to transformation, wisdom, and knowledge.'"

Chad Michael Snavely, Founder and Executive Producer, CMStudio

"As a guy, we are raised to be tough, unfazed by challenges, and we think we should have all of the answers to life's problems. We hate talking about our feelings and hate asking for help even more. *Where the Colors Blend* allows the reader to join Stephen on his spiritual journey as we see that it's healthy to question, struggle, and face giants in life, as he masterfully ties in an entertaining story about the impact of a men's softball tournament on the country of Paraguay. Stephen and I became close friends during the Charlotte chapter of his life, and I've come to love his authenticity and transparency, which comes out in this book."

Cody Zeller, Charlotte Hornets Center

"Stephen gives us a candid look into his journey—from faith deconstruction to reconstruction—that is vivid and resonates. In this refreshing memoir, he demonstrates that doubt and questions aren't a cliff we leap from to our spiritual death. Rather they are a divine alert notifying us that it is time to upgrade our operating systems. Hopefully his courage to share how he embraced his doubts will inspire others to do the same and discover that they now have a palette not of black and white, but of beautiful, vibrant colors."

Cedric Lundy, Pastor, Writer, and Activist

"Stephen has written a book that reads with amazing ease as he brings the reader from place to place and into the depths of his own life and the lives of others. Stephen has done the hard work of following his spiritual journey and now opening it up to those who are privileged to read this, his first memoir. From the front piece on this text rings the bell of truth as he tells of others' lives and as his own life grows and emerges in these wonderful and sometimes painful life stories. I am struck by the beauty and variety of emotions that he brings before us and that the reader can carry with the writer. His gift of narration and the fact that he clearly is a natural storyteller—par excellence—brings you and I into a multi-layered journey into a young life that helps us to know something more about our own journeys as well. Coming to know Stephen and now to read this helps me again to believe that our young in America today want to journey, find friends and mentors along the way, and then offer to us and others the fruits of finding their way in the world."

Father Daniel Riley, O.F.M.

"What I've always known and valued in Stephen is his deep commitment to an inner personal journey. I've watched his journey alter the course of his own life and have real impact in the lives of others. What makes *Where the Colors Blend* work—and work so well—is Stephen's deep commitment to naming the different theological and psychological aspects of his journey and speaking their existence into print. Something the world needs more of from the generation Stephen represents."

Matt O'Neil, Watershed Charlotte Co-Pastor

"Steve's journey from a faith that was filled with striving and constriction to an authentic spirituality rooted in love, oneness, and divine union will speak hope to anyone struggling with finding their way in religion. *Where the Colors Blend* is dripping with beautiful imagery, metaphor, and poetry as he walks the labyrinth to find an authentic faith. The universal themes of tension and struggle as one grows in his understanding of himself and the divine are filled with laughter, candor, and raw honesty. I felt more alive and understood after reading Steve's story and getting to know his friends along the way."

Brooke Lehmann, Poet, Sacred Feminine Writer and Teacher

"Vulnerability has a way of opening us. Let Stephen's words land in that fertile place where change and hope can grow alongside one another and produce in us a robust faith."

Jamie George, Journey Church Lead Pastor,
Author of Love Well *and* Poets and Saints

"Stephen writes like a pilgrim on a journey, and his transparency and vulnerability are refreshing and powerful, like the primal cry of one of the Psalmists! I am grateful that he ended up with the key theology of union with and abiding in Christ. Authors like Brennan Manning and Henri Nouwen have done a great service to the church (yes, Protestants, too) with their insights and focus on intimacy with Jesus."

Jeffrey A. Gill, D.Min., Ph.D., Vice President and Dean Professor of
Leadership Studies, Grace Theological Seminary

Where the Colors Blend

Where the
COLORS Blend

*An Authentic Journey Through Spiritual
Doubt and Despair ... and a Beautiful
Arrival at Hope*

Stephen Copeland

NEW YORK

LONDON • NASHVILLE • MELBOURNE • VANCOUVER

Where the Colors Blend

An Authentic Journey Through Spiritual Doubt and Despair ... and a Beautiful Arrival at Hope

Published in New York, New York, by Morgan James Publishing. Morgan James is a trademark of Morgan James, LLC. www.MorganJamesPublishing.com

The Morgan James Speakers Group can bring authors to your live event. For more information or to book an event visit The Morgan James Speakers Group at www.TheMorganJamesSpeakersGroup.com.

ISBN 9781683509677 paperback
ISBN 9781683509684 eBook
Library of Congress Control Number: 2018935510

Cover Design by:
Rachel Lopez
www.r2cdesign.com

Interior Design by:
Chris Treccani
www.3dogcreative.net

In an effort to support local communities, raise awareness and funds, Morgan James Publishing donates a percentage of all book sales for the life of each book to Habitat for Humanity Peninsula and Greater Williamsburg.

Get involved today! Visit
www.MorganJamesBuilds.com

To my family, for always accepting me as I am, not as I should be.
To Coach, Marcos, and Norberto, for inviting me into a story.
To Paraguay, my heartbeat.

Contents

The best way to tell a story is by entering into another.
To enter into another story is the best way to find yourself.

FOREWORD
By Dave Hickman
M.Div. Gordon-Conwell Theological Seminary
Author, *Closer Than Close: Awakening to the Freedom of
Your Union with Christ*

I'll never forget the first time I met Stephen Copeland. I was agonizing over the manuscript of my first book at a random Starbucks in Charlotte, North Carolina, when a tall, lanky, disheveled-looking guy walked in balancing a stack of books atop two three-inch binders filled with paper. "Dear Lord, let this kid be an author or a writer of some sort!" I whispered selfishly. I had labored (and I mean labored) for months trying to push words out of my gut onto paper and was in desperate need of help—even from a complete stranger.

"Hey, are you an author?" I blurted awkwardly.

"Yeah, sort of," Stephen responded while struggling to maintain his grip on his many books and binders filled with paper.

As we shared conversation over coffee black, one thing became crystal clear: We needed each other. I needed help outlining a book I hadn't written, and Stephen needed help to discover the person he had always been. I needed someone to help me organize my thoughts about God, and Stephen needed someone to help him to deconstruct his view of God. Looking back, I'm absolutely convinced that our meeting wasn't happenstance or random but was by divine appointment.

For nearly three decades, I suffered from religion-induced guilt. I lived most days under the perpetual frown of a God I could never seem to please. My identity was based on my performance for God plus other people's perception of my performance. This venomous equation led to a life riddled with anxiety, depression, and deep despair. Deviations and distortions of the "gospel" from my conservative fundamental background blinded me of the reality of my belovedness until one morning, in the darkness of my shame and anguish, I awakened to the Jesus I never knew—a Jesus who wasn't interested in simply being "close" to me, but one who longed to be "perfectly one" with me instead. After a lifetime of "chasing hard after God" and trying to have a "healthy and growing relationship with Jesus," I was shocked to discover, in the fiery words of the late Brennan Manning

> that the living God seeks **more than** an intimate relationship with us. The reckless, raging fury of Yahweh culminates, dare we say it, in a symbiotic fusion, a **union** so substantive that the apostle Paul would write: IT IS NO LONGER I WHO LIVE, BUT CHRIST LIVES IN ME." (Brennan Manning, The Furious Longing of God (Colorado Springs: David C. Cook, 2009), 30. Capitalization in the original, per Brennan's bold spirit.)

While some would never dare claim to be "one" with God for fear of sounding "new age" or something worse, there is a rising generation of young people, like Stephen, heralding the scandalous (and historic, mind you) truth that the transcendent God united himself with the fullness of our humanity in the person of Jesus so that we might become "partakers" of His divine nature (2 Peter 1:4). In the words of Athanasius, "He (the Son) became what we are so that we might become what He is"—true sons and daughters of a loving and engaged Father. For those who somehow insist that God is unwilling (or incapable) of uniting human beings with the fullness of His divinity need look no further than the suffering, compassionate face of Jesus Christ, our forever brother in the flesh.

Where The Colors Blend paints a painfully beautiful picture of the real Jesus—the One who is closer to us than we are to ourselves. The One who stopped at nothing until He became "one" with the object of His affection. Unfolding over the course of six years, Stephen invites the reader into his life (our shared lives) to taste and know that God is good, even when all seems lost. Through the stories of ordinary people like Coach Briscoe, Norberto, and Marcos, Stephen, with child-like wonder, guides the reader on a spectacular journey into the quick of life—that sensitive, often overlooked area of our lives, where, when touched, we feel deeply and are reminded that we are alive.

The pages that follow are an open invitation into intimacy. They proclaim the glorious truth, that the transcendent God, while powerful (and mysterious) as a thunderstorm, is as gentle as a soft mountain breeze—if we dare enter into the torrent of His love.

It is true that the best way to tell a story is by entering into another. For to enter into another story is the best way to find yourself. As you enter into Stephen's authentic journey through spiritual doubt and despair, I pray that you, too, will arrive at a beautiful place of hope where kisses fall by the thousands.

NOTE TO THE READER

It's interesting to go back through a project that took nearly seven years to write and color in your subconscious, now able to see where the story was moving all along. Though the book unfolds in present tense, it was this "coloring in" that made these events into a *story*.

When an agent first signed onto this project, the then-150,000-word convoluted horror of a purge I sent him was met by an understandable "I have no idea where this is going, and it reads more like a woeful journal." He apologized for the massacre he performed on its pages, but it was exactly what I needed. I went back to the drawing board, nearly chopped the manuscript in half, and—while leaving much of the language from those old journals in the manuscript to maintain its emotional honesty and, at times, quite provocative dissection of my faith in its present-tense unfolding—I tried to give language to the subconscious realm of my journey. Language that I might not have had then but do now. I suppose I'll always be searching for better language to describe my experience.

Beyond writing, this exercise of "subconscious linguistics" has become somewhat of a spiritual and psychological practice for me. If I can attempt to give language to the experiences of my past, the thoughts and emotions that I struggled then to explain, then perhaps I can be more present with those same thoughts and emotions when they resurface—less blindsided by them and therefore less reactive to them. Awareness is key.

Perhaps the most revealing—and, at times, admittedly shocking—revelation of my subconscious in this book is the "poetry" at the end of some of the chapters. I put *poetry* in quotation marks because I do not consider myself a poet. Nor do I consider most of what is in here poetry. Some of those closing lines have somewhat of a spoken-word feel, whereas others seem more like songs. But I'm not a musician either, other than playing Taylor Swift songs on my acoustic guitar. Nonetheless, these lines add to the authenticity of the manuscript because they encapsulate what I was feeling and wrestling with at the time I wrote them.

Last, whereas some of the language I stumbled upon deals with my psychological journey, much of it pertains to my spiritual journey—which, if we're honest, are often one and the same. Though I have tried to find language for my own spiritual journey in these pages, I in no way claim to have found the answers to the eternal realm. The second I think that I can adequately describe the Absolute is the second I've made an idol out of my language. In my experience, that kind of arrogance usually isn't well received. I have tasted something of grace but will always be tasting. I have seen something of love but will always be waking up to that reality. And I need those whose stories are most different than my own to help me see what I couldn't see before.

This book encapsulates my own transformative journey—as I was confronting my doubts, deconstructing my faith, wading through spiritual despair, and opening myself up to a new kind of hope and faith. My struggles in these pages aren't necessarily unique. Loss, heartbreak, transition, and grief are as natural as the seasons. But I hope that perhaps my dissection of these struggles will be helpful in some way. That maybe we can journey inward together. Though you'll find some doctrine and dogma in these pages, I'm less concerned about those types of conversations these days if they're just about "being right." What's most important to me is exploration and transformation. Wrestling with theological ideas has helped to evolve my view of God, self, and others, and that's what makes it important. As Richard Rohr writes in his book *The Divine Dance*, "What I believe, and have dedicated my life to reversing, is that we have not moved doctrine and dogma to the level of inner experience."

Incarnation is where faith—and life—become downright fun.

YEAR I

1

THE FIRST DRIVE

I am excited to see Coach Briscoe in Roanoke, Virginia. That's where I'm heading now. I think he'll help reassure me that I made the right decision. It has only been a month since I left, but it is a strange thing to go where you know you need to go—to do what you know you need to do—yet still be confronted with such confusion and loneliness and angst. One might think that such darkness would not accompany something so freeing as a call, something so mysterious as a voice within, but in my experience, it always does.

Am I in the right place?

Did I make the right decision?

I don't know.

I already miss Winona Lake, Indiana, with its brisk falls and white winters, and all the professors and students walking through Grace College's campus in coats and scarves with cold noses and cherry cheeks, past the brick buildings with snow-covered roofs and the bell tower tolling of your tardiness. My best friend, Josh, and I once broke into the bell tower as undergraduates, a very undergraduate thing to do, only to find there was no bell at all, which made us want to find the hidden disk-changer and swap the hymnal bell music with an album of some profane punk band that sang about getting high and pleasuring themselves and hating George W. Bush, which we never did, thank goodness, because we might have been expelled—since the college was also a seminary and since Christians, by and large, are fond of George W. Bush.

There was a magic, a romance, to those falls and winters, but what made Winona Lake a utopia of sorts were its springs and summers, when people would boat or kayak, or relax at the park on the canal, or walk down the hill from campus to the quaint, Craftsman-style village that wrapped around the east side of the lake, and visit one of its many artisans, galleries, or shops. That entire summer before leaving, I would often sit down by the lake on the coffee shop's screened-in porch, beneath the clerestory with a clock, and find solace there as I wrote, as I contemplated my future and tried to navigate through my emptiness. One evening, not long ago, I remember sitting on that porch as dusk fell upon Winona, and as the colors danced on the surface of the lake, the sun sinking once more into its hammock, I could not help but wonder what an odd thing it was to experience such deep-seated discontentment in such a seemingly perfect place.

Yes, there was discontentment in my soul that I struggled to pinpoint, but if I were to take an overall assessment of my life, I would have to conclude that things, on the outside at least, couldn't have been better. I had an enjoyable job working in the sports information department at my alma mater with my best friend, Josh, for the best boss I ever had, Coach Chad Briscoe. What more does one need? I went to school to be a sportswriter, and, considering how scarce journalism jobs are, I felt blessed to have the job that I did. It didn't involve as much creative writing and storytelling as I wished—I wanted to write books— but believe me, I had no complaints. Plus, how does a person start writing such a thing as a book? Anyway, all I can say is that I just had a general feeling that I wasn't in the right place, that I wasn't doing the right thing. There was something outside of me that kept calling me elsewhere, out of that perfect place. There was a voice, a groaning, rising up from a mysterious space deep within me that kept urging me to depart. And eventually the voice became a scream and the groan became a stinging ache, and I had no choice but to leave the place I loved.

So I did.

I left.

That was nearly a month ago, but I often find myself re-living that fateful Tuesday in August. The day I left Winona Lake.

I remember Josh walking with me out into the parking lot that morning, helping me carry my box of belongings from the office we shared. As I loaded up my trunk and rambled on and on about something that did not matter, fumbling around on the shoreline of reality, trying not to get wet, I stupidly said something like "Well, I'll see you soon," and I remember finally looking up from my trunk at Josh and noticing that his eyes were red and puffy. So I looked back down at my trunk, then back up at him, then back down. I had never seen Josh like this before, and I admit I was confounded. The next exchange—my "goodbye"—is blurry in my memory, and all I can conclude is that Josh plunged into reality and I did not, that he was drenched and I was not, that he was alone and I still for some reason assumed that I'd see him tomorrow, and that, as we hugged, I was in a stupefied state, in utter denial that this chapter of my life was really closing.

And after leaving Josh there in that parking lot on that poignant midmorning in Winona Lake, and driving along the lake for good measure, I drove south to Indianapolis, where I was raised, straight to a golf course on the west side where my girlfriend was working, for she was the only person in the world I wanted to see. When I saw her, we embraced, and I told her I loved her, and I thought about what a strange thing it was for a guy like me, as noncommittal as my friends tell me that I am, to be so smitten.

Then we went to my parents' house for dinner, and as Dad cooked lemon-marinated chicken on the grill, and Mom sat there next to him, hunched over, husking corn, and as my two little sisters and my girlfriend and I all hung out there on the patio, I would occasionally look out past my family's backyard at the acres of soybean fields, contentedly sitting there beneath the clear Indiana sky, content because the Indiana sky was all they needed.

Like those fields, I had everything I needed in Indiana. I had family, friends, Coach Briscoe, and my girlfriend. But my gypsy of a soul insisted that I leave. It insisted that I move to Charlotte, North Carolina, to take a job at a faith-based sports magazine—ten hours away from everything that I knew and everyone whom I loved.

And as I headed south, I envied the soybean fields.

———

I now understand that moment in the parking lot with Josh more clearly. Reality has indeed flooded my heart and mind. I'm out in the middle of the waters. But there seems to be no lifeboat near. And I cannot help but wonder if I've made some sort of mistake. I miss my family. I miss my friends. I miss her. I miss Indiana.

There is nothing that I need more than a piece of home. And it's for this reason that I'm excited to see Coach Briscoe in Roanoke, Virginia, three-and-a-half hours north of Charlotte. I guess Coach's family has been hosting a church softball tournament in Roanoke since the late 1970s, to raise money for missions in Paraguay or something like that, and the tournament is something I'm looking forward to witnessing up close. But the thing that makes me a little anxious is the fact that Coach thinks I ought to write a book about it all. I hardly feel qualified to write a book to begin with, not to mention somehow making a book about a church softball tournament compelling. But I'll give the story a shot nonetheless. Maybe it'll surprise me. There must be some sort of depth to it if Coach Briscoe is the one recommending it. It's actually surprising to me that he wants me to write a book about *anything* that he is associated with. After all, when Josh and I worked in the sports information department, he always used to cringe when we had to write stories about him for the numerous awards he received. There must be something here.

But all of this is beside the point right now.

I'm just excited to see Coach Briscoe.

Coach has always helped to affirm my direction: that I am following the path, that I am in the right place, that the present—the now, where I am mysteriously safe in the arms of God, no matter how uncomfortable or uncertain or fearful I am—is right where I need to be. Every protagonist in a story has a guide, and, though I do not feel worthy to be any sort of protagonist or to be a part of any story, I can certainly say that Coach Briscoe is my guide. I now need his wisdom more than ever.

I call Coach Briscoe "Coach" because that's exactly who he is—a mentor, a giver of wisdom, and a leader who cares deeply about those who are following him. His job as an athletic director is not just a job: It is a vocation, a calling from the divine. And people are not just people to him: They are God's children who have been placed in his path for him to love and encourage and inspire.

Coach lives an ordinary life. He is not a politician or a rock star or the CEO of a Fortune 500 Company. But he lives in the most intentional of ways; from his cheerful enthusiasm at work—how he strengthens those he works with, really making them feel like what they are doing has meaning and value; to his gentle care and intentionality in his household—how being a husband and a father is the best of things, a privilege, an opportunity and how there is no one in this world more important to him than his wife, Jamie, or their two children, Kate and Kinley. I know he is a man with flaws and struggles, for there is not one saint in history who has lived a perfect life, but it is as if he does everything with purpose and grace, even the mundane tasks and monotonous routines. And Josh and I, somehow, by some divine happenstance, were afforded an opportunity to see grace in action, through one man, each and every day.

Like any good guide, Coach Briscoe is actually the one who told me to go, to leave home. I think he knew it would be good for me. I think he knew it was time for me to wander from the nest, open my wings, and fly, or maybe fall, but learn nonetheless … and hopefully fly eventually. I hope I can apply all that he has taught me over the years.

I also think Coach understands what it means to feel as if you are being called into the wilderness, away from your comfortable ways. He recently left Grace College too. He and I had arrived in Winona Lake together four-and-a-half years before—when I was a freshman and he had just taken the athletic director position—and now it is as if we were leaving together. Though he and Jamie always saw themselves living in Winona Lake for the rest of their lives, something that he could not explain pulled him south to be an athletic director at a *high school* in Indianapolis. It didn't make sense to him. It didn't really make sense to anyone. But Coach Briscoe helps me to believe—through both his words and actions—that the path we take in our lives does not always have to make sense.

More than anything, Coach Briscoe has impacted my Christian faith. Outside of my father, no man has influenced my faith as much as Coach Briscoe. As I ventured through those formative years at Grace, a time when I was taking lots of weighty, theological courses for my Bible degree—which was good but also complex and sometimes confusing—and was also wrestling with some of the frustrations related to Christian culture—like how I felt so godawful about myself all the time, like I was never doing enough or always doing something wrong—it's fair to say that Coach Briscoe helped me believe in Jesus in the most practical of ways. I had some serious doubts about my faith, but every day I witnessed the selfless love and joy that flowed from Coach Briscoe's life as he loved his family, affirmed the worth and value of his employees, and brought intention, purpose, and joy into his vocation.

———

Since moving to Charlotte, however, my doubts seem to be resurfacing once more. I no longer have a daily model like Coach Briscoe to convince me of what I hope to be true. I no longer have my best friends to distract me from my doubts. My loneliness is forcing all kinds of questions about my faith to rise to the surface. All I seem to do anymore is think and overthink. Have I ever been lonelier in my life?

My apartment in Charlotte has ghost trails and creaks and a foreboding silence that sounds more like a scream. Don't get me wrong. It's not like I live in an abandoned asylum or something. It's a nice apartment on the second floor, spacious, with a balcony overlooking the pond out back. My boss set me up with it, and my rent is included as part of my salary, which isn't much, but the living situation is worth it, I guess. However, as elegant and graceful as my apartment might be in appearance, in all those external things that we make so important, it is a lonely place—and this is where the dissonance lies. And instead of falling asleep next to four of my best friends, like when I was a student living in the dormitories at Grace, now I fall asleep surrounded by four walls, and those walls are now my best friends, not by choice, but by default—because I spend most of my time with them. And they whisper all kinds of strange things to me as I stare at the ceiling in the evenings. All kinds of lies that make me question who I am, or where I am going in life, or whether I made the right decision to leave those Indiana fields and all my Indiana friends. And sometimes the television accompanies me and drowns the silence, humming to me its toxic lullaby, lighting up my room, pulsating throughout the duration of the night. But other times it's sin that accompanies me in the silence. And as it sweeps in, with all of its promises and fervor, it seems to momentarily rescue me from my isolation, and then, like a hurricane, it tumbles away, abandoning its destruction with no apologies or condolences, moving on to its next victim. And then the walls begin to whisper again, this time more horrifying things, until I am browbeaten, lying there unconscious, but guilty and ashamed; and somehow, I am supposed to call this "sleeping."

That's what is at the crux of my doubts about Christianity, I think: my shame and lack of self-worth. By shame, what I mean is that I am experiencing something of an identity crisis. I am desperately trying to get closer to God— reading, praying, trying to abstain from sin—but it feels as if I am really only on a treadmill, running as hard as I can but going nowhere at all; and no matter how long I am able to remain on my calloused feet, my legs eventually collapse, and I always fall flat on my face … sliding off that thing and onto the floor in a puddle of sweat … defeated … distraught … depressed that I'll never be who God wants me to be. And here's the most messed-up thing: It feels as if God Himself not only put the treadmill there but is also controlling the speed—often turning up the dial until I cannot possibly keep up—or the time of my run—never allowing me to rest and relax—and ultimately forcing me, over and over, to stare up at Him and beg for forgiveness as I lie on the floor of my exhaustion and shame.

This shame stems from my sense of identity, I think. Some people talk about the mistakes they made, but oftentimes I feel as if I *am* a mistake. Some people talk about the sins they are struggling with, but I feel as if I *am* a sinner, at the core of my being, incapable of doing anything good, of being fully accepted by God, unable to trust myself because of my "fallenness" and the "impurity of my flesh," and, overall, never good enough for this supposedly loving God who keeps torturing me through a manipulative game of hide-and-seek. Some talk about the areas of their lives in which they have failed, but I feel as if I *am* a failure: say, anytime I'm unmotivated to read my Bible or cave to lust or slug through an apathetic prayer or become angry or whatever it may be that doesn't seem to meet God's expectations of me. My inadequate performance and my inability to get close to God—which is all I've ever wanted—seem to dictate my worth. So what's the point of exhausting myself on this wretched treadmill? And what am I supposed to do with the fact that it was this seemingly psychopathic "God of the universe" that put me on the treadmill in the first place and tortures me on it?

The truth is, as the more I've delved into my faith over the last half decade, the more this shame has plagued me. I grew up Catholic, was confirmed Catholic, was baptized in an evangelical church two years later, and then began pursuing a Bible degree two years after that at Grace. But evangelicalism—or, perhaps more fair, the version of conservative evangelicalism that was handed to me combined with my ultra-critical personality—feels more works based than Catholicism ever was. I grew up in a loving family where my identity was one who belonged and one who was loved, but then God hijacked that identity. It feels that there is always more for me to do for God or something that I'm not doing! There is always something that is lacking, whether it be in my prayer life or my Bible-reading time or my church attendance. God feels so far away, so "out there," so uninvolved and apathetic. Some tell me I should read the Bible more or pray more, that this will help me feel "closer to God" and that this will solve all my problems, and I've tried that, and I suppose it helps a little … sometimes. But mostly I just end up feeling guilty for not reading the Bible and praying more (why does the idea of "more" always feel like a never-ending road?), which makes me feel even more guilty whenever I stumble and sin, because it was my fault for not being close to God in the first place!

That being said, I don't know what the phrase "close to God" even means. Whenever I hear that talk, I think about a nagging girlfriend saying, "I just don't feel *close* to you anymore." Solution: *Stop* doing the thing that is making you drift away or *start* doing something else that will pull you closer. God is generally displeased with me, I think. A "personal, growing relationship with God" seems to take so much work. And I'm a little tired of trying to crack the code that will make the genie emerge from the lamp. I'm tired of pitifully pulling my body back onto the treadmill.

I'm afraid that I might abandon the faith altogether if I am unable to attain some sense of self-worth. Should a "loving God" really make me feel this way? I fear that this whole Christianity thing is a sham.

Am I having a crisis of faith?

Maybe this place called Roanoke can be my lifeboat.

And maybe Coach Briscoe can help me to believe … just as he always has.

———

Alone but alive:
Is this drive the prelude to my life?
Paramount views. Joy in the journey.
An empty passenger seat beside me
reminding me of the route I chose,
hoping to God I'm not my own,
for such futility would leave me empty.

Whatever guilt I feel for leaving,
whatever song that Change might sing—
for my brother or for her,
for friendship or for love—
the blame is mine.
But if all runs dry, like Carolina in July,
I would not change a thing.

For if I'm free, I must wander;
to meander through meaning
and to make mistakes while dreaming
is living—a journey unpredictable,
the narrative of Change,
when I loved and left for life again,
searching for my name.

2

BORN TO LEAVE, LIVE TO RUN

I finally arrive in Roanoke—at a hotel near the Roanoke Regional Airport. This is where Coach Briscoe has asked me to meet him: There is a "coaches' meeting" being held for the tournament in one of the conference rooms. I have no idea what this meeting entails. All I know is that I get to see Coach. And this is all that matters. He is someone who embraces me for who I am, not as I should be, and it is a freeing thing to rest and exist in such an aura of love and acceptance.

Walking down a long, well-lit, burgundy-carpeted hallway outside a conference room, I see Coach Briscoe's thin, six-foot frame off in the distance. I cannot mistake his fair complexion and the short, grayish-blond hair atop his balding head. He is wearing khakis and a golf polo, his signature outfit, and is talking on his cell phone, his back to me. It is a strange thing to suddenly see a person whom you love and miss because you immediately realize how lonely and incomplete you feel without that person.

Coach's phone call apparently ends because he lowers his phone and places it in his pocket, then begins to walk back into the conference room.

"Coach!" I say.

He turns around.

"Cope!" he says, beaming. He begins walking toward me. We come together and embrace. "So happy that you're here! Thank you so much for coming!" he exclaims. His greenish-blue eyes are watering with joy. Never have I had a boss or mentor who cared about me so deeply.

I have not been with him for more than ten seconds, and he is already opening my eyes to see value in the present—in the moment—when ironically all I've been doing for the past four hours on my drive is questioning the past and attempting to micromanage my future, bombarding God with so many questions, all birthed in the chaos of my mind, that it is not at all possible for me to hear His gentle voice asking me to rest and to trust. In Coach Briscoe's voice, in the present that he is welcoming me into, it is as if I can feel my mind beginning to calm. To be utterly lost in the present is a freeing thing. In the present, you realize you are in the place you need to be, even in the littlest of moments—the daily routines we take for granted and the random conversations, the untimely phone calls and the traffic jams. And because you have escaped into the great, adventurous "now," it is as if you suddenly understand that all of life's consuming questions about the future and big regrets about the past only produce unnecessary angst and fear. You are where you are, and that is all that matters. Here I was, content in an instant, after spending the entirety of my drive yanking out my hair.

"Welcome to the Interstate Church of God Softball Tournament," he says to me as I follow him into a conference room. He begins introducing me to a number of people: Twila, his mother; Charlie, his father; Brooke, his sister; Tony, his brother-in-law; and all of his nieces and nephews. Though I understand very little about the tournament, it's obvious that the whole weekend is a family affair. Also, Brooke and Tony have about a thousand children. And by a thousand, I mean about four.

A hundred people or so arrive, and the meeting eventually begins, directed by Coach. I find myself sitting in the back of the room, marveling at how he freely and enthusiastically speaks to the crowd, setting the tone for the weekend and reminding the coaches what the weekend is all about: Paraguay. To say that I miss working for Coach would be an understatement, and I cannot help but reflect upon my four years under his leadership at Grace and all the wonderful memories we shared together. I guess it's easy to miss what once was. Comfort abounds in "what once was." But those who care for you the most, who are often a part of "what once was," know that the comfortable space is not where you belong. And it is for this reason I am in Charlotte. Because Coach Briscoe said that I should go to the place that is most uncomfortable, and his saying that is a sign of a deep and genuine love.

One thing I notice during the coaches' meeting, judging by the questions coaches were asking—about weather delays and different fields and one-pitch and two-pitch and all kinds of technicalities I do not understand—is everyone's passion for church softball. At least forty teams from churches all over the South and Midwest have come to Roanoke, Virginia, of all places, and I have a peculiar feeling that this is like the "Big Dance" of church softball. Some teams, I'm told, have been attending the tournament for decades.

I know all of this might sound strange to an outsider, perhaps borderline "cultish," and it is indeed a little strange to me, but it is also a reminder that meaning exists in collective joy—however odd, however niche that avenue of joy might seem; that collective joy can only exist in community; and that this type of meaning exists in its purest sense whenever it forms around a common cause, one that denies self and spreads love. In this case, spreading love to Paraguay. I pine for this type of community and collective joy in Charlotte. It's what I had with Coach Briscoe and Josh at Grace.

Another thing I begin to realize is Coach's vital role in the whole production. I honestly had no idea that Coach Briscoe was one of the main people in charge of the weekend—the linchpin behind everything that is about to happen—and, judging by his references to his parents as he spoke, I gather the tournament is something that Charlie and Twila started and is something that Coach is now running. I would later find out that his sister, Brooke, and her husband, Tony, are also key players in putting the tournament into motion each year. I look forward to learning more about this thread of the story, this "collective joy," in the next couple days.

———

Later in the evening, once the coaches have trickled out, I begin talking to Jamie Briscoe, Coach's wife, over in the corner of the room, next to some folded-up tables and stacked-up chairs, about their transition to Indianapolis and my transition to Charlotte.

"Everything was just so perfect in Winona Lake," she says to me, "from Chad's job, to the community, to our church. And it's kind of tough to see, at this point, why God called us to leave."

"Have you sold your house yet?" I ask, somewhat switching the subject. (It is best not to talk about God when you are not sure if you believe in Him.)

"No, we're renting an apartment right now," she laughs, being her typically bubbly, optimistic self. "There isn't much space for all four of us, but, you know, it'll all work out."

I nod my head.

"Enough about me," she says, "How are you?"

"I'm great," I say, hoping that I do not come across as too glib. "Charlotte has been awesome, and I really like my job."

I do not know why, but I cannot bring myself to tell her the truth about my existence. It all seems way too dramatic, too emotional.

One thought, however, does cross my mind as our conversation comes to an end: Maybe the book Coach wants me to write is a chance for me to talk about all the things I struggle to express—all the things I cannot understand. And maybe this book, if I am indeed inspired by the story, could be my friend, not my enemy; an opportunity, not a burden. After all, every journalist ought to keep a journal. And every journal ought to tell a story—one of progression, of evolution, of transformation, of change. If Coach Briscoe has taught me one thing, it's this: It is unnatural to remain in the same place. If we are human, then change is the only path to fullness.

———

I walk into Charlie and Twila's home—a cozy, one-story house on the north side of Roanoke. I'm told that they've lived there since the spring of 1981, and it has the kind of character and feeling that a lot of grandparents' houses have: walls that have seen generations' worth of memories, of fights and reconciliation, prayers and screams, love at its best and love at its worst, children born and raised and sent off to college, destined to find a job and move out but also destined to return from time to time to the place they miss the most … *home.*

It's pretty late by the time we arrive at their house, so we hang out for maybe ten minutes or so, just the Briscoe family and me, before we all retire to our beds. Twila directs me to a couch in their basement and, typically Southern and overly attentive to people's needs, asks me if I'll sleep OK on the couch, then apologizes that I have to sleep on the couch, then assures me that I won't have to sleep on the couch the next time I come to Roanoke. If only she knew that Josh and I bought a couch from a pawn shop in college that smelled like cat urine and cigarette smoke and wobbled like a broken chair and that I always slept on that just fine.

"Oh, Cope, I'm so sorry you have to do this," she says, as if sleeping on the couch means sacrificing a kidney. "You shouldn't have to sleep on this couch after driving such a long way."

I want to stop her from saying such nonsense, but it's kind of nice to feel like a saint every once in a while. "You sleep well, OK, darlin'?" she says, giving me a hug. "Good night now. See you in the morning."

"Good night," I say.

Seconds later I hear a click from the light switch in the stairwell, and darkness falls upon the basement. My mind swims in the black.

Maybe it's being there in the Briscoes' home, which has been around for decades, or my conversation with Jamie this evening, or all my racing thoughts about Indiana on the drive to Roanoke, but as I lie here, staring wide-eyed at the ceiling in this unfamiliar basement, I keep thinking about what a strange thing it is that we are all so prone to leave. Chad and Jamie and I all left the place we loved the most: Winona Lake, Indiana. And not only that, but what I find strange is the fact that society *expects* you to leave and applauds you if you leave, whether it's the pursuit of professional dreams or moving out of your parents' house or getting married and starting your own family. And yet, in the process of going all these places, we leave the ones we love. *Going somewhere* seems to mean *leaving someone.*

In my darkest moments, I wonder if it's all worth it. I might be pursuing a job that I love, but what if there's a death in the family? What if something happens to a friend? I might be able to get my creative fill as I tell stories in my career, which is why I left, but what if the story of my own life lacks love? I guess that's what worries me the most: love. Will my leaving ultimately lead to my being alone? The distance adds tension, and I added the distance, and therefore maybe I am inflicting the tension. And if the tension becomes too much to handle, will it all be worth it in the end?

I am not good at many things, but one thing I know I am good at is leaving. Why? I do not know. But it seems to be the very thing I do, time after time.

I made the best of friends in high school, and whereas three of them decided to attend the same college down in Tennessee, I went to a place—Grace—where I did not know a soul. I made the best of friends in college and fell in love for the first time and then accepted a job at Grace that was only a couple hours away from my family, but then I went to a place—Charlotte—far away from all of them.

Even spiritually, I was raised in the Catholic Church and confirmed as a Catholic, and then I left the church in high school and got baptized, the best day of my life, and started attending a nondenominational evangelical church. Then I went to a Protestant college and got a Bible degree, which was the most enlightening period of my life, but now I feel as if I am leaving conservative evangelicalism … exhausted from maintaining this "personal, growing relationship with God" as if it's a field plagued by drought … and taking care of this "Jesus that lives in my heart" as if he's one of those handheld digital Tamagotchi pets. I'm tired of all the things I have to do just for God to be happy with me. And I'm tired of all the pointless theological wars and the exclusivity in church.

I do not feel like I belong anywhere. And maybe that is why I keep leaving. But how many times must I leave before I find a home? How long will I wander? Well, here I am. I've wandered into this place—Roanoke—in search for a piece of home.

3

THE GRACE OF THE DAY

True to form, Coach Briscoe is up early, scrambling around in the kitchen, occasionally taking a bite from his breakfast plate while getting his belongings together for the day, never sitting.

"Good morning, good morning," he says, not a hint of grogginess in his voice. "You're up early."

"Mornin', Coach," I say wearily, stretching.

"I'm going to head out in about fifteen minutes," he says. "Do you want to come with me or come later with my parents?"

"I'll go with you," I say. "Let me get changed and brush my teeth."

"Oh! That reminds me!" he says, walking over to a box in the living room. "Here's a T-shirt," he says, removing a red shirt from the box and tossing it to me. "Here's another one too," he says, tossing me a navy blue one. "Do you want a gray one too?" he says, digging through another box.

"I'm fine," I laugh. "This is plenty. Thank you."

Coach Briscoe is obsessed with T-shirts. He says it's one of the best forms of marketing—and he's probably right. Still, I think he might need an intervention one of these days. He's out of control with his T-shirts.

"Never underestimate the power of a T-shirt," he laughs.

A few minutes later, we get on the road—in Coach's old, maroon Chevrolet Blazer. Coach says that he is going to take me to "see some of the fields." I have no idea what this means, but I am just happy to be with Coach—to sit there in the passenger seat next to someone who knows me inside and out, and, for the first time in a month, to feel understood, even without saying anything. In Charlotte I am afraid to be myself around people because I fear that they might not like what they see; it is for this same reason that I am afraid to be myself in romantic relationships. But around Coach, I can be exactly who I am.

It's probably seven o'clock or so, and there are patches of thin, early-morning fog hanging in the troughs of the billowing highway. We whip through each pocket of fog, then head uphill once more, around curves and bends, into the blinding beam of sunlight blasting over the mountainside into our windshield. Coach's windows are slightly lowered, and the crisp, Virginia mountain air cools my nostrils and purifies my lungs. The day has hardly begun, and yet I am reminded that the day is already perfect, even without me accomplishing a thing or checking a single task off my to-do list, but simply because grace is in it—in each molecule of the mountain air and each photon of the glaring sunbeam. The perfection of grace, which is everywhere, hangs in our midst each second of every day, yet we go around exhausting ourselves trying to accomplish things, as if grappling for vapor, thinking it will give us a steady handle on fulfillment! Why do I complicate that which is already perfect when all along I am surrounded by grace, which is fulfillment itself?

As we drive to the fields, I open up to Coach about the challenges of my transition to Charlotte, one of the first people I've *really* allowed to step into my struggles. Isn't this the great challenge in our superficial, affluent society—with all of its makeup that covers our blemishes, our houses and cars that make us appear whole, and our financial plans that blanket the lack of purpose we actually feel—to allow others to see our brokenness, our discontent? Were we made to *be* or to *hide*? Adam and Eve's fulfillment came from being with God; their sin caused them to hide.

Sensing that I might be questioning my move altogether, Coach Briscoe gives me the reassurance he knows I need to hear—telling me that my job in Charlotte is a great professional opportunity and, most importantly, a gateway to grow in my faith and to transform as a person. He reassures me that my relationship will work out with the Girl from Indiana if it is meant to be. And he tells me that he is proud of me.

All of this is advice I have heard before in some way or another, yet I think I could hear it one thousand times and still convince myself to believe something else! Maybe there is no such thing as hearing too much truth.

———

Coach and I arrive at a field called Whispering Pines—or, as Coach calls it, "The Closest Thing to Heaven." Out of all the softball fields in Roanoke that the tournament utilizes, Coach says, Whispering Pines is his favorite. I can understand why. Whispering Pines is seemingly out in the middle of nowhere, off a two-lane country road on the north side of Roanoke, and the main diamond seems to sit down in the valley of the Blue Ridge, as if cupped in God's palm. Hundreds of mature, towering pines fill the rustic space, and if you stand at home plate and look out into the outfield, all you would see are the layers of mountains beyond.

Standing here on the main diamond, in the silence of the early morning, just you and the field and God, brings with it the feeling that you have discovered some far-off, forgotten gem that you never expected to find, like the kingdom of heaven—treasure hidden in a field. Maybe that's why Coach calls this spot "The Closest Thing to Heaven." It does not feel as if it belongs in this world. It is far simpler, removed, void of all the world's constructs and ploys.

Players and coaches begin to arrive for their morning games, and after Coach introduces me to a few more people—and once the games eventually begin, thus officially putting the softball tournament into motion—we get on the road once more. Coach tells me that we are going to a place called Botetourt (pronounced *Bot-uh-tot*), a newly developed softball complex that he says is the best in the South.

Thirty minutes or so later, we arrive. Pulling into Botetourt feels as if you are entering the stately front gates of a mansion. From the road, you can hardly see anything of the complex, but as you enter the property and follow the road up the hill around a couple of curves, you get a feeling that the place you are going has the potential to be wondrous. It is.

At the top of the hill are four softball fields, all facing outward and overlooking the majestic Blue Ridge Mountains, with a brick, three-story press box in the center of them all. So basically you are on a suspended plateau, on quite possibly the flattest slab of land in Roanoke, with a 360-degree panoramic view of the Blue Ridge. The mountains here do not seem as close as the peaks at Whispering Pines, but the view is better, no matter which direction you turn your gaze.

By this point, the tournament is fully underway—forty-plus teams, all scattered throughout Roanoke County on different fields. Each field at Botetourt is occupied—four games, eight teams—and the sights and sounds are all reminiscent of when I used to play Little League baseball as a kid: families cheering from the stands, children wildly running around, the regular *ping* of the bat, and the infield and outfield chatter. The only difference, I guess, is that grown men—in their twenties, thirties, and forties—are occupying the fields, and there is a general feeling that we are walking into a hotbed of testosterone. And it smells like it too.

Gathered around outside the press box are Coach's parents and wife. Twila and Jamie are sitting at a fold-up table selling "Rally in The Valley" T-shirts to raise money for missions in Paraguay while Charlie is walking around seemingly shaking everyone's hand and laughing enthusiastically. I hardly know Charlie and Twila, but it seems that Coach gets his contagious enthusiasm from Charlie and his deep, genuine concern for others from Twila—and, I suppose, his Southern charm from both.

We hang out with all of them for a little, and then Coach says to Twila, "Mom, how about you and Cope go upstairs in the press box and you can tell him about how this whole tournament started?"

"Oh, I would find that just delightful," she says eloquently, rising from her seat. She then walks over to me and gently grabs me by the arm.

"This is an unbelievable story," she says to me. "How much time do we have?"

"I have all day," I laugh.

"Good, because we might need it."

And we walk up the three flights of stairs to the top floor of the press box.

4

THE GIRL FROM THE MOUNTAINS AND THE LADY FROM THE JUNGLE

As gorgeous as the mountain view is from the parking lot, the view from the top floor of the three-story press box is breathtaking. Gigantic windows take up each of the four walls of the press box, allowing you to watch any game on any field. It sort of feels like you are in an elevated glass box. What stands out most to me is the view of the mountains from this place. Now, not only are you on a plateau in the middle of the mountains, but you are atop a three-story building *on* that plateau. It is like being up in a lighthouse, looking out into something as wondrous and incomprehensible as the sea.

What is it about this range of mountains that seems to free me and terrify me, all at the same time? Never in my life have I spent much time in the mountains. All we had in Indiana were cornfields and basketball courts—all flat—and I've basically spent my entire life in Indiana. So maybe I'm captivated by mountains because such sights are new to me. But there is undeniably something haunting and mysterious about those peaks. I feel so small in their presence, a grain of rice in their shadow. It is as if they want to say something to me, as if they want to teach me something.

"Where would you like me to start?" Twila says, sitting down next to one of those large, wall-to-wall windows and removing her sunglasses.

Twila kind of resembles my Italian grandmother, her silvery hair contrasted with her dark-tan skin. Her eyes smile and sparkle when she talks to you.

"I guess start wherever you see the story starting," I say.

She thinks and then says, "Well, it starts with a girl named Tabita [pronounced Tabitha]. It was a beautiful, beautiful September afternoon. September 10, 1962, at Anderson College...."

———

Twila tells me that she felt called from a young age to attend Anderson College (now Anderson University), just north of Indianapolis, Indiana. It didn't matter that she grew up in Welch, West Virginia, nearly twelve hours away; that her father encouraged all three of her older sisters to attend schools close by; and that she would be leaving everything she ever knew—her family, her friends, and those beloved West Virginia Mountains. She knew she was called, by some magnetic pull in the cosmos, to leave.

The idea of attending Anderson College most likely went back to her deep Church of God roots. This is the denomination with which the tournament is affiliated. Twila's grandfather received a Church of God gospel tract while working on the railroad tracks in the early 1900s and went on to establish many of the Church of God mountain churches in southern West Virginia. And as Twila ventured through high school, she, too, felt a deep call within to the ministry, which meant only one thing to her: She ought to attend a Church of God college, Anderson College, a day trip's westward in Indiana.

"My father didn't want me to leave," Twila says. "He was adamant about my staying close, just like my three older sisters. And he was a strong disciplinarian—you did not challenge his thinking. I started praying for strength, that God would help me address my plans and goals with my father. I needed my father's blessing."

One Sunday evening, in the spring of her senior year, her father was in the living room watching *Bonanza* on television, and Twila mustered up the courage to talk to him.

"Dad, for many years I have felt the call to go to Anderson College," she told him. "I feel like this is where I need to go, but I need to know that I have your approval and that you will support me."

"There ain't no reason fer you to go," he grunted. "There's good colleges in this area, and you can go there like yer sisters."

"No, Father, I cannot do that," Twila boldly responded. "I have a calling to go to Anderson College, and if you choose not to allow me to go, I'll stay home and keep house for Mother and save your money."

Her father dismissed the conversation without offering any conclusion.

"Children didn't approach their parents like that in a disciplined family," Twila says. "I was trembling in my boots. I thought he might smash my mouth."

What I find most interesting is that there was no middle ground in Twila's mind-set, and maybe this is one of the truest attributes in a calling: the feeling that you cannot do anything else, that there is no other way. It also seems that a true calling is uncomfortable, stretching you to the very core—and not just challenging for the one who is called, but also for those in that person's circle. And maybe this is one reason how we know we are following a call: We are always vastly uncomfortable, challenged at the core of who we are, yet also carried by joy.

One month later, in late July, Twila's father dug up the subject once more and told her, "Now, ah've been prayin' about this. And if you rilly think this is ware God wants yuh, then you sure bett'r go."

She said she was sure.

So her father wrote her a $25 check for her Anderson College room deposit. And one month later, Twila, her parents, and her younger sister loaded up the car ("I reckon yer takin' everythin' but the kitchen sink," her father told her), and they stopped at a local Esso gas station to purchase a map before getting on the road, as this was only her father's second time leaving the confines of West Virginia. They drove through West Virginia, through Ohio, and into Indiana, where they slept at a motel near the college.

The next morning—September 10, 1962—Twila's family helped her move into the dorm.

Morrison Hall, Room 100.

They grabbed lunch at a sandwich shop that afternoon, and it seemed to dawn on Twila—and on all of them—that the time was coming that they would have to say goodbye. After lunch, that dreaded moment finally came.

Before they left, Twila's mother told her, "God be with you," and as they pulled away, Twila stood there in the lawn in front of Morrison Hall, watching the car scoot along until it was completely out of sight. Then, she says, she looked up into the clear, blue Indiana sky and, in a moment of surrender, prayed, "Oh, God, I am right where You want me to be, and I am ready for this journey!"

What she didn't know at the time was that one of the greatest journeys of her life would begin the second she walked into the dormitory.

As she made her way to her dorm room, her resident director, a North Carolinian named Mrs. Deese, said to her, "Your roommate will be a missionary's daughter from South America."

And no more than a few minutes later, the door to Twila's room slowly opened, and in came Mrs. Deese. "Twila," she said, "your roommate has arrived."

And this missionary's daughter stepped onto the scene.

"Hi, Twila," the missionary's daughter said, "I'm Tabita."

"Hi, Tabita," Twila said. "I'm Twila."

"From that moment it was as if a long-lost sister had come home," Twila says. "I remember the moment like it was yesterday. There is no person on this earth I treasure more than Tabita Mayer Kurrle."

They might not have realized it at the time, but that moment—when Tabita walked into Room 100 of Morrison Hall at Anderson College on September 10, 1962 and met Twila—sparked a friendship that would last a lifetime … and would forever connect two families, the Briscoes and the Kurrles … and would forever connect two places that were an entire world apart: Virginia and Paraguay.

————

What a strange, unexplainable thing it is to dwell in the wondrous plans of God—that He might call you twelve hours westward to experience a moment, a second, a person, who might change your life forever!

Twila goes on to tell me that she and Tabita became the best of friends at Anderson. Through all this, Twila saw firsthand Tabita's heart for missionary work. Whereas Tabita's three siblings had all come to the States and it looked as if they might stay in America, Tabita knew that she was being called far away from the comforts and luxuries of the United States. She knew that she would one day continue her parents' missionary work in South America. That was *her* calling. And Twila knew all too well the power of those winds that pull you away from comfort.

And so Twila and Tabita both graduated from Anderson College. Twila married Charlie, who had transferred from a junior college in Kansas to Anderson, and they both eventually picked up teaching jobs in Roanoke, Virginia. Tabita went on to get her master's degree at Ball State University in Muncie, Indiana, but never lost sight of becoming a missionary in South America. Once she got her master's from Ball State, the time came for her to leave. Twila and Charlie drove back up to Indiana to say goodbye.

I imagine it would be a weird thing to say goodbye to your best friend, who is moving a world away. You must also remember that this was the late 1960s, so there was no such thing as a cell phone or the Internet. Would they ever see each other again? Was this the last time they would ever hear one another's voice? Would Tabita ever be able to return to the States? Would Twila and Charlie ever be able to visit Tabita in South America? They did not know. Tabita's specific calling was yet to be determined. All she knew was that she was being pulled into the unknown.

They said their goodbyes on campus at Anderson College, there where they had first said hello, there where they had become best friends. The story ended where it began, but it had to end so that it could perhaps begin again.

Tabita hugged Twila and said to her, "Twila, my dear friend, you must know that whether I live or whether I die, I am the Lord's, I know," echoing the words of a famous hymn. And then they went their separate ways.

———

It is interesting to listen to Twila tell this story about her and Tabita in the context of everything transpiring around us. As I look out the windows of the press box, all I see, in every direction, are the ensuing softball games below— games that are taking place to raise money for Paraguay. All because of that fateful day in September of 1962 when a girl from the mountains of West Virginia met a lady from the jungle of Brazil.

The story of Twila leaving Welch, West Virginia, to go to Anderson, Indiana, and Tabita leaving Anderson to be a missionary in South America resonates with me because I, too, feel as if I am following a call, and I do not know where it might lead. However, in seeing the tournament fleshed out in front of me—all because of a friendship between roommates that began forty years before—the beautiful mystery of a call is reaffirmed within me.

The mystery of a call is something that we cannot see but turns out to be something far more than we could possibly imagine.

The unimaginable cannot come without uncertainty.

I think I am trying to convince myself of something I do not yet believe, hoping with everything within me that God's presence will be enough to satisfy me in my lonely, uncomfortable state, hoping with everything within me that maybe God is up to something unimaginable, and that I will have the courage to be bold and courageous like Twila and Tabita, and that I will allow the wind of the Holy Spirit to push me wherever it blows and maybe even enjoy its direction and maybe even smile as I feel its gentle wind blowing through my hair. And yet, as I mentioned earlier, it is difficult for me to believe in God's presence right now. In this new phase of my life, God feels so distant *to* me, so controlling *of* me, so disappointed *in* me.

However, receiving Coach Briscoe's encouragement this morning and hearing Twila's story this afternoon has, at the very least, comforted me that I am doing the right thing in moving to Charlotte and pursuing writing. And, though Charlotte has thrown me into a lonely state, maybe this has nothing to do with Charlotte and everything to do with me. Maybe Charlotte has only exposed what is already there. *Maybe I do not yet know who I am.*

I once heard a story about a rabbi who made a wrong turn while walking home and found himself standing outside the large gate of a Roman fortress. A Roman guard atop the wall peered down and yelled, "Who are you? What are you doing here?" When the rabbi did not answer the questions, the guard kept asking them, to which the rabbi eventually responded, "I'll pay you double if you stand outside my house and ask me those two questions every morning!"

My point is, I know that I'm in pursuit of *doing* the right thing, of answering the guard's second question—allowing these winds to blow me south. But I do not yet feel that I know who I am. I don't know how to answer the guard's first question.

How can I know *who* I am without knowing *whose* I am? And if I really belong to God, then why do I feel so miserable? And if this is indeed God, then do I want to belong to such misery? While one wind pushes me south to where I feel like I need to be, there is another wind—something like a hurricane—within me that seems to violently toss me around. Some might say that these winds within us that toss us around and make us reactive are our insecurities. And I think that at the crux of my insecurities, strangely enough, is a faith that is cloaked in shame.

Who am I at the core?

The first word that comes to my mind is *sinner.*

Always lacking. Never enough. Totally depraved.

5

PARAGUAY AND HEMINGWAY

After Twila and I talk for quite some time in the press box, we eventually head downstairs, rejoining the Briscoes at the T-shirt table. For the next few hours, I hang around the press box as Coach Briscoe introduces me to people I talk to about the tournament, which, interestingly, always ends up being about much more than the tournament itself. People share with me story after story after story about how this weekend in Virginia led to personal transformation and growth—to abandoning their addictions or saving their marriages or confronting the darkness within themselves or stepping further into love and selflessness, all of which they would attribute to following the ways of Jesus. This is a special weekend and a special place.

As evening approaches, it is time to return to Twila and Charlie's house to get showered and cleaned up before the annual church service, which I'm told is a staple of the weekend. Tournament participants set competition aside for a couple of hours and come together, united for one cause: Paraguay. Then the games continue once more on Sunday, sometimes stretching into the middle of the night or the wee hours of Monday morning.

Upon arriving at the outdoor amphitheater, where the church service is held, I can immediately see how such a place could bring everyone together. The amphitheater, though not far from the interstate, feels like it is buried in the Blue Ridge. As I sit down before the start of the service, there alone in the back row,

I keep looking to my right, toward all the layers of peaks behind the building, clothed with thick dark-green foliage.

The church service begins pretty typically: praise and worship led by a band. Though there are women, children, and families in attendance as well, it is a moving thing to be surrounded by so many rugged men—players and coaches. It is inspiring to hear all those low, off-key voices of tattooed athletes and blue-collar countrymen and others who might be considered a little rough around the edges, voices that are, yes, imperfect, but so full of heart. I actually find myself singing a little bit, comforted by the fact I am not surrounded by Sunday-morning perfection—the facades, the superficiality, and all those attempts to appear that we have it all together, which only seems to scare the guests away because, really, who can stand to be around someone who thinks he has it all together?

Next, we are asked to take a seat, and a video starts to play on the gigantic screen hanging centered above the stage.

It is an update from the Kurrle family in Paraguay.

As I watch the video, Paraguay—a country that is 4,500 miles away, nuzzled there in the southern hemisphere between Bolivia, Brazil, and Argentina—suddenly becomes real to me. Featured in the video are Tabita (whom Twila had told me about extensively) and her husband, Martin (whom Twila had mentioned to me in our conversation, though I have not written anything about him yet), but these are the only names I recognize. Apparently, Tabita and Martin have four children, who are also serving in Paraguay: Norberto, Marcos, Priscila, and Nila.

Marcos and Norberto, who I figure are both around Coach's age, share a few things in the video, and, for reasons I cannot explain, I feel myself strangely drawn to them, hoping that maybe one day I might be able to meet them. The enthusiastic Marcos seems to have passion running through his veins, and the soft-spoken Norberto seems marked by great gentleness and humility. Also, their families—Marcos's wife, Cristiane, and their children, Mateos and Alheli, and Norberto's wife, Julie, and their only son, Timothy—are such beautiful people! What an extraordinary thing it is to see a group of people who have abandoned everything for a call, especially when that call is rooted in service, and especially when that service is rooted in bringing hope to those on the margins of society—the impoverished, the abandoned, the broken. Could there be a profession more reflective of the call of Christ, the type of sacrifice we read about in the Bible, than that of a missionary? Maybe these people who have sacrificed everything can help me to believe.

What's interesting about Norberto is that, I'm told, he attended Anderson University at the same time Coach Briscoe did. Fittingly, Coach and Norberto went on to forge a deep relationship, just as their mothers, Twila and Tabita, had done decades before while attending Anderson. It is beginning to dawn on me that this weekend is about much more than a softball tournament. This is a story that flows from an unbreakable union between two families and two countries.

Later in the service, after a sermon and a few more songs, Coach Briscoe calls all the coaches to the stage and, one by one, each coach approaches the podium and shares with those in attendance how much money their team raised for Paraguay this year. This is by far the most moving part of the church service as each coach says anything from fifty dollars to five thousand dollars. There is no greater form of worship than giving, though it seems most, including myself, often attend church on Sunday to see what they can get. Once more I realize that this weekend is about much more than a softball tournament. It is about a movement rooted in social justice and generosity: Something so strange as a softball tournament has become the financial lifeline for a mission that is an entire world away.

After the service, Coach Briscoe introduces me to a number of coaches, some who have been attending the tournament ever since it was based in Johnson City, Tennessee, more than three decades before. They tell me stories about the great rainstorm that blew in one Sunday in the 1980s (which did not delay the tournament but only made it muddier), and about the dreaded teams from Hickory, North Carolina, that won the tournament more than any other team in the 1990s, and about the time in the early 2000s when they played through the night until six o'clock in the morning. At one point, a man named Eli, a hefty Alabaman countryman, tells me that whenever he comes to Roanoke for Labor Day weekend, he can hardly sleep because he is so excited, so he usually goes to the softball fields at four o'clock in the morning, or something ridiculous, and just sits there, as if to become one in spirit with the dirt and the bases. I am not sure what to say to him when he tells me this, but he is too excited for me to tell him that he probably does *not* become one in spirit with the dirt and the bases.

To the people here, Labor Day weekend is some sort of Christmas. And it is easy to see that it is the *relationships,* more than anything, that bring this tournament to life. Tonight, I've heard stories about players getting baptized in the hotel pool after the church service on Saturday evening ... or umpires asking coaches some of life's most fundamental questions because they noticed something distinctly loving about the people in this tournament ... or church vans pulling over on the side of the road on the way home because a player wanted to make a public proclamation to his teammates about following Christ.

It is in the arena of genuine, vulnerable relationships that lives are dramatically changed. And it is my genuine, vulnerable relationship with Coach Briscoe that has allowed me to step into this story.

Maybe this story, too, can change me. Actually, I think the change has begun.

————

Heading into this weekend, I was honestly prepared to tell Coach that I was not sure if this would make a good book, but I cannot do that now. I am seized by this story, as odd and obscure as it might be. I can see it meeting others where they are. I can feel it meeting me where I am. In a sense, I feel as if I am trapped in it. And there is no other way out of the labyrinth but to write my way out. I am reminded of this quote from Ernest Hemingway's 1954 Nobel Prize acceptance speech:

> *For a true writer each book should be a new beginning where he tries again for something that is beyond attainment. He should always try for something that has never been done or that others have tried and failed. Then sometimes, with great luck, he will succeed.*

Maybe this is a book where I try something that is beyond attainment, something that has never been done before.

I think I will go to bed this evening praying for luck.

6

THE HEART OF A MAN NAMED "SLEEPYHEAD"

Today is my last day in Roanoke.

The plan on this Sunday is for me to spend ample time with Charlie—Coach's father and the patriarch of this story—much like I did with Twila yesterday.

Upon getting ready for the day, Charlie insists we go get a breakfast burrito from McDonald's. I have never liked McDonald's, but Charlie is talking about their burritos so enthusiastically that I do not have the heart to tell him I'd rather not go. "And they are only a dollar, Cope!" he exclaims. And before I know it, we are walking into that smelly place. It ends up tasting all right, and it was indeed only a dollar, which is a fair price, I think.

"Well, whaddya say I take ya around southwest Virginia?" Charlie says, as I get in the passenger seat of his white minivan.

"Sounds great," I say.

"They don't have sights like this up in Indiana," he says with a wide smile.

As Charlie and I drive and talk, there is hardly a moment that passes without him laughing or making some sort of a joke. He is a boisterous, witty man who has all sorts of strange phrases that sometimes take me a moment or two to understand. For example, when talking to me about my girlfriend, he might say something like "So, it sounds pretty serious, Cope! But when is she gonna start warshin' your socks?" Then he'll wait for me to understand what he said, and I won't understand what he said because it's such an absurd thing to say, but I'll laugh anyway because it's such an absurd thing to say, and then he'll burst into laughter the moment he hears me let out the slightest confused giggle. Surely, Charlie must be the most cheerful old man I've ever met. He is like a beardless Santa Claus, a little plump and very jolly. He wears big, rectangular glasses, and whenever he smiles, which is all the time, his eyes get all squinty and look like penny slots.

At one point, while driving to Blacksburg, Virginia, Charlie respectfully asks me to turn off my voice recorder, and he opens up to me about some of his personal flaws and struggles in his life. This is a different side of Charlie. No more jokes, no more cheer, no more laughter. It catches me off guard. But it is a magnificent thing to witness a man of his age reflecting on his life with such humility and perhaps even a dose of regret, and yet it is in this brokenness that grace seems to shine all the brighter. Tears well up in his eyes, as they also do in mine, and I feel as if I've digested a teaspoon of Solomon's wisdom, all because Charlie is willing to pour himself out, for a moment, and give it to me.

———

Isn't this the great challenge of the spiritual life: being willing to pour ourselves out—the good and the bad—for the sake of someone else? The sharing of our flaws seems to be a lost conversation in our society, and yet, when we choose transparency and vulnerability, we usher in the healing power of grace, for only in brokenness can grace fill up the cracks.

My dad once told me a story about his own father, my grandfather, whom everyone used to call "Sleepyhead" (I suppose because he liked to sleep). My dad and all his siblings say that they had a wonderful, loving childhood, but it also sounds like Sleepyhead did some interesting, quirky things. For example, one time, Sleepyhead was in a drunken stupor and was trying to get my dad, who was ten or so, to call Mamaw or something. Dad refused, so Sleepyhead, quite logically, pulled a knife on his son and threatened him. Sleepyhead never laid a finger on my dad (only a knife!), but some of the things he did were shocking. Throughout Dad's childhood, Mamaw kicked Sleepyhead out of the house a number of times and even divorced him, though they would later remarry. Mamaw ultimately held the household together and made sure that it was a safe, loving place for each of her children.

However, what Dad also remembers about Sleepyhead was his generosity. For example, Sleepyhead convinced Mamaw that they should adopt two local boys whose parents were both in the hospital. So they did. And they welcomed my Uncle John and Uncle Phil into their tiny, three-bedroom, Elwood, Indiana, house, where they were already raising two children of their own.

Later in life, when Dad grew old enough to go to the bars with Sleepyhead, Dad noticed how Sleepyhead always seemed to be giving his hard-earned money to people who needed it, even when he was in the most sober of states. He might slip a twenty-dollar bill to a homeless person or give forty bucks to a friend.

I don't think my dad would deny that his father had some struggles—perhaps a real addiction to alcohol that affected lives in very real ways—but what had the deepest impact on my dad was Sleepyhead's heart. It was perhaps because of Sleepyhead, who was a "sinner" and an addict, that my uncles are who they are today: loving, selfless, joyful people who have a genuine concern for helping others. If it weren't for Charlie, a "sinner," would there be a softball tournament that funds the mission in Paraguay? Probably not.

Perhaps it is better to fall a thousand times and care for others than to be quarantined somewhere, avoiding sin but not caring for others. The best, of course, is righteousness and love.

The stories of Charlie and Sleepyhead resonate with me because their stories are my own. It is the story of Moses and of King David, of Peter and of Paul, of Augustine and of Luther—where brokenness is met by grace and where sinners become saints. Sleepyhead might have had an addiction, but he also had a heart. Charlie might have had a past, but in Christ he has a future.

This is a God that I can believe in, I think. One who meets us in our brokenness. One who accepts us for who we are. One who would take someone like Charlie, like Sleepyhead, like me … and fill the brokenness with grace. The fact that a tournament so beautiful as this exists because of broken people seems to demonstrate that maybe God is willing to see us as more than sinners. I want to believe that I'm more than a sinner.

7

SABBATH AND CITIES

Charlie and I arrive in Blacksburg, Virginia.

He takes me to Virginia Tech's campus and mentions that this place is especially beautiful in the autumn, as the maples and oaks shine with amber and gold and those gray, gothic castlelike buildings fade into the background as earth showcases her vibrancy. As we drive around, I can almost picture that mountainside mosaic—of the Allegheny Mountains to the north and the Blue Ridge Mountains to the south. Never have I witnessed a mountainous fall—I've only seen photographs—and part of me is tempted to drive back up to this splendid place come October. There is a hint of coolness in the air on this early afternoon, and I think that's why autumn is on our minds. It is as if I realize that Charlotte will undoubtedly change me just as autumn will inevitably change the colors of these dark green mountainsides. However, it is up to me whether I allow Charlotte to change me for the better or for the worse. I must allow autumn to have its way with me. I pray that there is life on the other side of this confusion and loneliness. I hope that I will shine.

That's one of the things that Coach Briscoe always stressed to his employees whenever I worked for him at Grace. No matter what we were going through in life—no matter what challenges we faced—he saw it all as an opportunity for growth, for change, for depending on something bigger than ourselves (which builds humility), for a better story that God was authoring in this mess of chapters that make up our lives.

One time, I remember Coach calling all of us student workers together before summer vacation. We sat around a small, round table in his office, and he looked at each one of us, a seriousness in his eyes, and said, "Don't return to Grace in the fall as the same person." He then pointed his finger at each one of us, almost sternly—uncharacteristic for him—and he said, "Come. Back. *Changed.*"

———

After Charlie gives me a tour of Blacksburg, we head back to Roanoke. It's about a forty-five-minute drive. Charlie tells me he is going to show me around downtown Roanoke before we head back to the fields. The entire morning we have been talking about anything and everything—the tournament, our struggles, and all the beautiful sights of Virginia.

"So you've been raising money for Paraguay for almost three decades, huh?" I ask him, trying to better understand the origins of the tournament.

"Well," he says, "we were just having fun at the start of it all."

Charlie tells me that he always had a passion for sports ministry because it was through a sports ministry in Wichita, Kansas, that he found his own faith. It was while playing baseball alongside his friends and teammates that deep relationships were formed, which naturally led to conversations about meaning, purpose, and spirituality.

So when he and Twila moved to Johnson City, Tennessee, in the 1970s, Charlie decided to arrange a church softball tournament on Labor Day weekend, hoping that maybe he could impact others the same way he was impacted in his youth. The tournament was birthed in 1978, but 1979 was the first time that it was technically a tournament. Four teams from the Tri-Cities area in Tennessee attended. They played all day Saturday and all day Sunday after church. It was a huge success.

The following year—1980—Charlie somewhat apprehensively said to Twila, "Do you think we should do the softball tournament again this year?"

"You *better* do that again," she told him directly. "Remember how much fun everyone had?"

In 1980, they had six teams. And in 1981, when Charlie and Twila moved to Roanoke, Virginia, and hosted the tournament there, they had twelve teams, many of which drove all the way from Johnson City. After all, what else were they supposed to do on Labor Day weekend besides play church softball?

Three years in, the tournament had become a staple in the Briscoes' lives and in the lives of others, but not a dime had been collected for Paraguay. Each team was asked to pay an entry fee, but this was only to cover renting the fields and umpiring. Twila and Charlie always hoped that perhaps one day the softball tournament might become a fundraiser for Paraguay, but the tournament was not bringing in any money. If anything, the tournament—as fun as it was—only caused more stress in Charlie and Twila's lives, especially as it grew. Not only was it a challenge for them not to *lose* money personally in hosting the tournament, but they also caught a lot of flak from surrounding churches, and, yes, even their own church, for planning a weekend-long church softball tournament that extended into Sunday, the Sabbath.

"There's nothing Christian about you guys," a pastor once told them.

"A ball is the devil's tool," someone else once said.

But Twila and Charlie would not be stopped. They would not fold to formulaic Christianity that believed in such a small god who was so controlling and so against enjoyment—and I use a lower-case *g* because there was nothing grandiose or wondrous about this version of a deity, and therefore it was only a projection of others' insecurities. What a sad, sobering thing it is to think that Christians—pastors, even—build their entire lives upon the foundation of a god that is hardly enjoyable, one that, for example, doesn't permit church softball on Sundays. It seems to me that these types of gods are often used in an attempt to manipulate or control others. And, even though I can denounce this type of god in my head and in my writing, I wonder if this type of god—the finger-pointing, guilt-tripping god that doesn't want you to enjoy anything that isn't related to prayer, the Bible, or church—has corrupted my heart. Maybe the gods we so readily denounce are often the gods we are most likely to follow.

Anyway, the fourth year of the tournament, twenty teams showed up. Word seemed to be spreading. In this particular year, after paying the umpires and renting the diamonds, the Briscoes had forty bucks left over, the first year that the tournament turned a profit.

The tournament continued to steadily grow, there in Roanoke, Virginia, and more and more money was sent to Paraguay each year.

By the tenth year, one of the coaches grabbed hold of the vision and challenged each team to raise $120 to support a Paraguayan child who was attending Alpha & Omega School, a school in the jungles of Raúl Peña, Paraguay, that provided a Christian education for Paraguayan children, a school that Tabita and Martin had started years before. And from that point forward, it became a tradition for each team to raise as much money as they could for Paraguay. They began to collectively play softball for a reason. Something that began with having fun has now raised over $250,000 for Paraguay.

———

Charlie and I are back in Roanoke and have crossed over its intricate railroad system and into the downtown area. It is a winsome downtown, with its brick, colonial, two- and three-story buildings and double-hung windows, giving it a simple and intimate Southern feel. We drive past an old soda fountain and drugstore on the corner of Market and Lee, then make a left down a street that is paved entirely in brick. It feels as if we have stepped back in time. I can hear a train humming a couple streets over, and we pass a big, red-and-cream-colored trolley with whimsical arched windows.

Comparing Roanoke to Charlotte's modern architecture and corporate feel, I find it a refreshing thing to be in a place like this on a quiet Sunday—to see the churchgoers walking along in the shadows of 1950s buildings, beneath faded Coca-Cola advertisements painted on the brick, on the way to Sunday brunch. Here, in the heart of this quaint city, it is as if everything that Charlie and I discussed on the car ride seems to make perfect sense....

I have always been drawn to cities and their downtowns, and Roanoke is no different. I guess my rural upbringing made room for an urban heart to emerge. In college, my friends and I would sometimes drive up to South Bend, Indiana, in the fall and board a train that would take us straight into Millennium Park in the heart of Chicago, my favorite city in the country. It was while escaping in that cold, windy city that I always seemed to learn something about myself, as if the city and I had been sitting in the intimacy of a quiet coffee shop and dialoguing with one another. Not one time have I visited Chicago and left without a sense of joy in my spirit.

What I found interesting about Chicago—and any big city, for that matter—are the locals. In Chicago, I remember walking past the businessmen and women on those windy streets, scuttling about during their lunch hour, whipping by me as if each one of them was in a hurry to save the world. They were talking on their cell phones, or not talking at all, always looking straight ahead, like robots, and I wondered if they had completely forgotten where they were. They were in the best city in the nation, and yet, by the way they were walking, you would have thought they were fleeing a burning building. They did not seem to be enjoying their city, a city that seemed so easy—for this outsider—to enjoy!

And yet this is my spirituality these days. As I mentioned earlier, I hardly enjoy it. In my past, I have claimed that I have found the secret to life and its meaning—God—and yet I metaphorically walk around hanging my head and hitting my leg over and over, as I did in so many golf tournaments in college. No, really, I remember walking up the fairway or the rough (mostly the rough!), hanging my head and punching myself in the thigh over and over when I was playing poorly in tournaments.

Unworthiness.

Unworthiness because of my performance.

Unworthiness because my performance did not meet personal expectations.

And it is similar in my spirituality. I am the pastor who condemned Charlie and Twila (except I am condemning myself!), robbing the spiritual life of enjoyment. I am the businessman in Chicago surrounded by spectacular views yet not knowing how to enjoy them because I am lost in the anxiety of the workday. I am back in college, golfing again, walking up the fairway and bruising my thigh with my fist like a freaking psychopath! And what's worse is that I try to convince others to follow Christ, telling them that it will free them and bring them joy, when deep down I know that it has only bounded me in a cage of my lacking performance!

But talking to Charlie has given me a glimpse of what I hope the Christian life can be: enjoyable. I admire Charlie and Twila for continuing to host the softball tournament even when others condemned them for doing so. Charlie and Twila recognized that these people's spirituality lacked pleasure, happiness, and, well, fun—and instead was based on legalism, control, and manipulation.

Perhaps I have made spirituality far too complicated all this time. My thoughts are so scattered on the subject of faith and how it pertains to my identity. I have no idea what it all means. But I think I must break everything down. I must further explore my shame. I must discover who I am. Am I more than flesh and bone? Is there a greater depth to my existence? This unfamiliar phase has made me unsure of everything these days.

I am, however, sure of one thing: This weekend in Virginia is a gift to me because grace is in it. I entered this weekend feeling alone. By the end, I feel alive. The *stories* I've encountered this weekend have brought me to life.

And I am thankful for how I am being changed through something as unassuming as a softball tournament. If God has dared to meet me here through these stories, that must stand for something, right? If I'm alive, can I be all that lost?

———

Why are we asked to leave
when we are wired for each other?
For Adam, You make Eve;
but You ask Abraham to murder
his only son as some expression
of devotion through violence, some lesson
for generations in salvation.

"For man to be alone is not good,"
yet You call men into the wilderness—
into forgotten neighborhoods
and the depths of lonely stresses,
to far-off countries without their families,
forlorn figures without friends,
all just to begin again.

You ask man to leave and the leaves to fall,
and in doing so, both leave life to die,
crackly and dry, wet and thin, prolonging
the soil's absorption, which brings life
again by spring—sweet tranquility in this mystery!
So how lonely were You, my Lord,
when You left heaven with Them for me?

YEAR II

8

THE SECOND DRIVE

The narrative of Change.
 When I loved and left for life again, searching for my name.

It has been a year since I moved to Charlotte, but I am still searching for my name, I think. I keep thinking about those two questions that the Roman guard in the parable yelled at the rabbi who was standing at the fortress gate: "Who are you? What are you doing?"

I still do not think I can answer the first question.

Who am I?

And I don't mean vocationally or relationally or romantically.

Who am I at the *core* of my being?

Who does God—if He exists—say that I am?

It is difficult to know who you are when you are in a spiritual no-man's-land. And it is even more of a no-man's-land than last year. More questions. More doubts. Fewer answers and absolutes. If we are spiritual beings—and I like to believe we are—then it is easy to feel rather lost and insecure while deconstructing our faith. And by now I am convinced that this is what this phase is for me: a deconstruction.

Two years ago I graduated from college, my Bible degree in hand, with all sorts of answers to life's biggest questions. I had been seized by the sin of certitude. I could tell you what I thought was right or wrong doctrinally speaking, who was living in Christ and who was living in sin, what the Bible says and what that means for our culture, and what the purpose of my life was—to glorify God, of course! My theology was so well packaged. My worldview was so dualistic. People were either Christians (saved), or they were lost (unsaved). If they were unsaved, then it was my responsibility to lead them to God, however forced and unnatural my rescue attempt might be. But now I have more questions than I have answers. More concerns than I have comforts.

In Charlotte, I've realized that I don't like the faith-lens that I am viewing reality through. For example, on a personal level, the shame is still taxing. Guilt and conviction are okay for a short time—it is your conscience speaking. But shame seems to be unhealthy. No one ought to have such a low view of him- or herself, to be so plagued by unworthiness. My shame is even worse this year, it seems. Probably because of the mistakes I've made in Charlotte—the innocence that has slipped away from me—in this new culture with new friends who live differently than my BCBs (Bible College Boys); and probably also because of the internal isolation that spiritual no-man's-land evokes. My overall sadness only complicates things and makes me feel that there is something deeply wrong with my faith as I wander through the darkness, as hope and light and truth and all those things that a good Christian claims to have seem displaced from my own reality.

Am I depressed? I've heard people say that dreaded word before but never in my wildest dreams believed that it would become a part of my existence. No, it can't be depression, and I won't treat it as such because then I'd have to talk about it. There's nothing worse than to be a man and be forced to talk about his emotions.

And so my solution to every internal problem, which I translate to be a spiritual problem, is to simply do more. I'm still running along on the proverbial treadmill, yet I seem to be wiping out more frequently, spending more of my time on the ground and the rest of it wondering why I'm even daring to run again. Like a child who keeps running back to his abusive father for no practical reason whatsoever other than the fact that he *needs* to be loved, I keep getting back on that darn treadmill, believing that this time I'll get close to God and never leave His embrace. Yet it never works. Then again, why should I be surprised? This is the same God, after all, who was apparently so *angry* with humanity that He could think of no other solution but to unload all of His wrath on His only Son. Even if Jesus *did* make a way for us to get back to the Father (as I've heard it said a thousand times), why would I *want* to get back to the Father if He is so wrathful at His core? How can I trust a God like that? A crucifixion seems awfully abusive.

Generally speaking, I still go about my life feeling that there is something I must do to improve my relationship with God, that there is some spiritual discipline out there I could adopt, and that there is always some sin in my life I could shed. I still think that God is perpetually shaking His finger at me in cosmic condemnation—probably because of my lack of a prayer life or my failure to do my daily devotionals or my frequent skipping of church or my puking all over my friend Nathan's backyard fence a couple weeks ago from drinking too much cider and rum and beer, which was really kind of embarrassing. Anyway, my relationship with God is like any other romantic relationship I've ever had: There's always something that I *could* be doing or *shouldn't* be doing that would make the relationship better. Relationships are so freaking difficult!

Speaking of relationships, I don't like what my faith-lens reveals about them either. I don't like entering conversations with an agenda (how can I witness to this person?) as if I'm selling insurance. I don't like my mentality when I hang out with people who might have a different sexual orientation or religion than I do. And I don't like the fact that deep down I think that they need to change their lifestyle or belief-system since, you know, that's what it means to "stand up for the Bible in a secular culture" instead of meeting them where they are, as a genuine friend. How are you supposed to fully love someone if, somewhere in your mind, you are judging them?

By the way, I think it's interesting that so many Christians wage war against culture, and yet it was Jesus who became man and entered into *our* culture. Nonetheless, this idea has become ingrained in my head over the years. On this same note, I don't like how, whenever someone shares with me his or her faith or worldview—whatever that faith or perspective may be—I automatically start tearing apart their theology and ideas in the back of my head, as if I have all the answers, instead of genuinely listening *to* them and learning *from* them.

Now, I might not say any of these things, but I am indeed thinking them—still living out of a mental construct where I am arrogant enough to be so certain about life and its design, even though it seems to be saturated with something so incomprehensible as the divine. I know that this arrogance isn't a healthy mental construct because of how it affects my treatment of others and, if I'm being honest, my treatment of myself—and that's why I am trying to deconstruct it! But what bothers me is that it still exists. I guess you could say that my theological arrogance has birthed a certain ignorance—where I think that I have little to learn from those who are most different from me. It's just easier to elevate doctrine, and it's quite an ego boost to think that I've got it all figured out and can tell people what to do.

My Christian faith is so Jekyll/Hyde right now. I go back and forth between some form of conservative evangelicalism (which is deeply ingrained in me because of my past) and skepticism (which scares me because I've been told that doubt is dangerous and indicates a lack of belief). I often find myself doubling down on the beliefs that were handed to me and reading the works of apologists, which I suppose is a good intellectual pursuit, but deep down it's a way for me to hold on to certainty in my uncertainty. It's as if I'm clinging to the edge of my previous faith paradigm. Clinging because I'm afraid of what comes after the fall. An edge because there's nothing stable about what I believe right now. But in this clinging and in this fear—this arrogance and ignorance—I think that I've been hurting a lot of people. Maybe it's time to let go of the edge.

Even in this no-man's-land, I still find myself captivated by Jesus and who he is, and I believe, and I hope, that I forever will be. I guess maybe I am still searching for a version of Christianity that resonates with me. Is there one? I feel like I am some sort of nomad wandering through the desert: I do not know where I belong, but I know I belong somewhere; I do not know where I am going, but, with each step, I know I am nearing a destination; I do not know exactly what I am looking for, but I have some vague idea. I suppose I am looking for myself, and maybe it is there where I will encounter the divine. Still, the desert is lonely.

I have, however, experienced something of an underlying spiritual hope in all of this. The interesting thing about deconstruction is that as I've begun to challenge my formulas for experiencing God—notably, prayer, Bible reading, and church, since these are, in fact, the primary avenues where enjoyment has been robbed from my spiritual life—other avenues are opening up.

All kinds of avenues.

For example, I feel God in nature and in relationships, when, say, my roommate Adam and I get that restless look in our eyes on a Friday night, throw a couple of articles of clothing in a plastic bag, and decide to take an impromptu trip to the beach, driving three-and-a-half hours down that long, dark highway to Wilmington, North Carolina, blasting all kinds of songs from all kinds of genres, and with each mile it is as if we are mentally removing ourselves from all of Charlotte's hustle and bustle, with its cluttered city streets and all the bankers scrambling along them in suits and ties, chasing after their retirement plans. It is usually around midnight when we drive across that big, white bridge into Wilmington and enter that charming college town—with its Southern colonial buildings on the banks of Cape Fear and all the patchy marshland growing out of the river—and we'll put the windows down and breathe in the thick, salty air coming off the Carolina shore, and we will mute the music and smile and not say a thing, perfectly content to take our last breath, simply because we will die with salt in our lungs.

Then we'll park at a beach entrance and maybe walk around for a little, feeling the cool midnight sand in our toes, sipping our malty lagers, or maybe sit on the hood of the car and look up at the stars as our cares and fears and anxieties rise from our chests like a balloon toward the heavens, and I will thank God in my mind for my beer and my new best friend and for the grace that abounds in the simplicity and silence of creation. Then we will retire to the car and sleep uncomfortably in those sticky leather seats and sweat through the night and wake up in the morning and suddenly realize that we never checked the weather before leaving. And we will either get lucky with a hot, summer day, as all the beautiful college-age belles lie out in a line like a pod of seals, or we will be forced to drink beer in the rain. Anyway, I feel God in nature and in relationships when I encounter the beautiful depth of everything that is my present reality, finding that reality to be cloaked in love and grace.

I feel God on the margins and in authentic spaces, when, say, I leave behind the corporate feel of southeast Charlotte, where I live, and drive thirty minutes north to a neighborhood just outside uptown to write at a 24/7 French bakery called Amélie's that is crawling with all the beautiful rejects of this white-collar banking town—the minorities and the gays and all the tattooed, pierced-up hipsters in tight jeans and unbuttoned flannels and all the artists who care only about expression and ideas, not hair gel or 401ks or showering. There, I feel as if I can be unashamedly myself—more at home and more understood than church has ever made me feel—creating *real* things, talking about *real* issues, in the *real* world. Anyway, I feel God on the margins, when I encounter the depth of different human experiences and all that I have to learn from people who I have never dared to see; and in these authentic spaces, where I consider where I might belong—creatively and socially—if I were to let go of the edge.

I even feel God in spaces where I'm told that I should not feel God, like the other night when my friend Nathan (also a BCB) and I continued to allow Charlotte to have her way with us, which she is good at, shedding us of our innocence; when the two of us had a number of high-gravity beers, then for some reason decided to try chewing tobacco for the first time, which left the two of us lying on a putting green in the middle of a corporate park, the starry sky spinning above us as if we had been flung off a merry-go-round, and the two of us talked honestly about our struggle with the theological formula that was handed to us and our overall hatred of ourselves, perhaps stemming from that formula, and our biggest doubts and fears and anxieties in this new stage of our lives, as the chewing tobacco—having numbed our egos—and the alcohol—having drowned our pride—propelled us into a vulnerable space, bringing us to a place where we confronted ourselves together and wrestled God together and cursed life together, and I must admit it was as if heaven were in our very midst even though we had plunged into unknowing. Anyway, I feel God in spaces where I was told that I should not feel God, there in the depths of doubt and darkness.

Why do I feel alive in all these spaces that seemingly have nothing to do with God, yet prayer, Bible reading, and church feel so empty?

Is it possible that all of life has the potential to be as sacred as a prayer?

Last, there are the stories: I feel God in stories, particularly *this* story.

I often find myself thinking about those Paraguayan missionaries in this strange phase of my faith. Them and the apostles. Their sacrifice astounds me. I know that it would be illogical to conclude that an idea or religion is truth just because someone died for a cause like the apostles (after all, terrorists do the same thing) or gave up their comfortable lives to serve others like the missionaries (after all, there are worse jobs out there), but their unreserved commitment to a cause at the cost of comfort is profound nonetheless. Backward. Rebellious. Countercultural, while at the same time diving into a culture fully so that they can serve it. I want to believe like they believe. I want to be so convinced that something is true, or perhaps so captivated by the pursuit of truth, that I would give my life or sacrifice my comfort for that thing. For Christ. For faith. For love.

There must be another way of belief.

I must give like they give, see how they see.

Anyway, I feel God in stories.

———

Though I can't tell you who I am, I *can* tell you what I am doing. As I've said, I can answer the Roman guard's second question in the parable. I was brought to Charlotte to write—to do the one thing that has always been in my blood, that has always brought me meaning and life, ever since my youth when I would stand at that big, boxy 1994 Macintosh and type stories into the night, stories about flying dogs or about Old Testament Jedi warriors or about an unassuming squirrel named Zipper who did something heroic, I'm sure, though I do not remember what exactly it was he did. All I remember is that I turned that one-hundred-page story about a *squirrel* into my seventh-grade English teacher for extra credit—and boy, do I owe her an apology if that poor woman took the time to read the whole thing! I felt quite sheepish carrying that "manuscript" into my classroom and handing it to my teacher. Never did I want my classmates to think I was an overachiever; I just liked to write. If my peers only knew that Zipper was the most badass squirrel to ever grace the pages of junior high literature, I'm sure they never would have judged me. Anyway, Charlotte has been filled with writing—and not about fictional squirrels, thank goodness. I began writing a monthly column for the sports magazine, and because of connections that came through the magazine, I lucked into a couple opportunities to collaborate on projects in book publishing.

Though my move to Charlotte has brought with it all kinds of questions and emotions and an internal loneliness spawning from my spiritual unknowing and my insecurity in my identity, my transition here seems to make more and more sense when it comes to answering the Roman guard's second question in the parable. Tabita knew not why she was being pulled from a Brazilian jungle to a small college in central Indiana, of all places. Twila knew not why she felt so convicted to leave the mountains of West Virginia, so much so that she told her father that she would not attend college anywhere else if he didn't allow her to go to Anderson. But I've a feeling that each Labor Day weekend, when Twila sees each coach take the stage and announce how much money the church or team has raised for Paraguay, and when Tabita opens up her mail and sees that check in the coming weeks, they know why they were each pulled to that seemingly random place in Indiana. For relationship. For justice. For purpose.

Maybe my answer to the Roman guard's second question can help lead me to an answer to his first question. Maybe this "doing"—writing—can lead to being—to knowing who I am. Maybe writing *this* story can usher in the truth of my identity. Then again, maybe this will involve abandoning God altogether.

———

Writing (doing), in a sense, forces me into a state of being because I must sit in my unknowing and dare to evaluate it. And this spiritual no-man's-land undoubtedly has the same effect, as it forces me to make my home in the desert. With nothing around for me to cling to, I am forced to delve into my very self. I hope that it's in this exterior discomfort that perhaps I'll find an inner truth: my core identity. In the desert, I look out over the horizon, and it feels that there is no end in sight. All looks the same. But I think I am beginning to realize that maybe this is the point. Without something in the distance for me to focus my gaze upon, I can only find hope and joy and security and energy from within, from my interior life.

What's in there?

What's within my very self?

Based on my spiritual experiences this past year—the sense of aliveness I have felt in ordinary things that are hardly sacred to the secular eye—something tells me that this core identity is much deeper than "sinner" or "mistake" or "failure" that transactional, relationship-based, atonement-focused theology has told me I am. Spiritually, I'm more determined than ever to find whatever it is at the core of my existence—my true self. Do I believe like the apostles and those Paraguayan missionaries? No. But I *choose* to believe because I find strength and hope in *their* belief. Here in the desert, sometimes I want to turn around and return to where I came from, perhaps to my previous paradigm where my theology was so well packaged, and doubt was extinguished at all costs, but I know that there is no going back, for I no longer have any idea what is north or south or east or west. All I can do is keep walking, through the hundreds of miles of discomfort … and see where it is that I arrive.

Even romantically speaking, Charlotte has propelled the Girl from Indiana and me into a similar no-man's-land where I am, once again, forced to venture into a deeper place within myself. I sometimes find myself clinging to that relationship, as if it is where I find my sense of worth, which is deeply unfair to her. Sometimes she'll send me a text out of the blue and remind me of her love, and for a moment, it will feel as if my inner agony is all worth it—the distance, the conflict, the daily battles unfolding on the front lines of my mind—and I will find myself rooting my very identity into her words, looking at the text each morning for a month as if it is oxygen for my lungs, hoping that one of these days I will truly believe her words, refrain from questioning her devotion, and know without a doubt that I am lovable. And yet I know that this clinging can only last so long. I must *choose* to believe in love, not because of the reciprocity of love, not because of her, but because of love itself. And so I've made a commitment in my mind: to fight off the lies that taunt me, to combat my pessimism that has always seemed to sneak up on me when it comes to love and romance, and to press forward. To keep walking in the assurance of my belief. To dare to believe in love itself. Even amidst the inner chaos that the Narrative of Change has caused.

When I think about change, and this season of life that I am in, I always think about Coach and Jamie Briscoe. They are both adaptable and open to what God might be doing in each of their lives. And that is why they left Winona Lake and are in Indianapolis, as uncomfortable as it might be. I talked to Coach the other day, and they *still* have not sold their house in Winona Lake. Nor does Coach understand why he was called to move. They, too, are in no-man's-land. They have no idea why they are in Indianapolis, but they have chosen to give all of themselves, and live in the moment, while they are where they are. Perhaps they struggle to find an answer to the man's second question in the parable, and yet their answer to the first sustains them: They are rooted in God, in one another, in something of Benevolence. They are not trying to control the course of the river; they simply enter into its flow.

Is there such a thing as an inner river of love, grace, and peace that is always accessible, something that sustains me in my unknowing? Others seem to have found it. How can I find it if God says that sin and darkness are at the core of who I am?

With all of these doubts I am carrying, I couldn't be more excited for another weekend in Roanoke. I mentioned earlier that I've been thinking a lot about those Paraguayan missionaries, and this year presents itself with the opportunity for me to think about them even more. Coach Briscoe told me the other day that missionary Marcos Kurrle—one of Tabita and Martin's four children—will be in attendance at the tournament this year.

Speaking of the Kurrles, I received kind of a strange email the other day from Coach Briscoe, sometime in late April or early May, asking me to keep Marcos's brother Norberto in my prayers. Apparently, he got into a car accident or something like that. That's honestly all I know right now, and at the time I received the email, I admit I was quite distracted with something I was working on and had completely forgotten who Norberto was exactly. It wasn't until I re-read some of my writings from last year that I remembered he was the one who went to Anderson with Coach Briscoe, just as Twila had done with Tabita.

Anyway, I hope everything is going okay with that.

Jerusalem, here's your cloak again,
absolutes and jewels in its pockets.
Go ahead, throw it over your skin,
quickly, before the Lamb locks it
up with the curtain he split in two—
all this cloth you adopt as truth,
all this cloth for the righteous Jew!

The Protestants are quoting scripture again,
convinced they know the truth,
magically breaking divine inspiration down to absolutes,
shouting "amens" and shaking their fists,
like punching the air will cure our nation,
while a gay kid sits in the back of the church,
wondering why God hates him.
The conservatives think Jesus is white again,
American through and through,
and theologians are critiquing The Shack *again,*
because they have nothing better to do,
and because the God of the universe
can't possibly be a large, Southern, black woman, right?
Wait, why couldn't He? Or She?

If they are my brothers and sisters,
then why do I feel so alone
in this room of five thousand?
Aren't we all just broken cisterns?
Pilgrims, in transit, not yet home?
Hungry for a love to be found in?

Let me roam through the barren, desert nights,
so I can find mystery by morning,
or stumble beneath the strip of lights,
philosophizing about joy and meaning
with someone who needs it.

America, open your closet of cloaks,
your god is far too small.
You cannot define the unfathomable
because Love wins after all.

9

THE TREE BY THE LAKE

I arrive at the hotel once more for the annual coaches' meeting in Roanoke, and Coach Briscoe is expectedly giddy when he sees me. As we embrace before the start of the meeting, it is interesting to consider how infrequent our gatherings have become. The year before, when I saw him at this tournament, I was coming off of a year where I had seen him nearly every day at work. Now I have lived in Charlotte for a year, and I think the last time I saw him was for a couple hours over the holidays—and that's only because we both happened to be in Indianapolis. How difficult it has become just for me to see those who I love the most!

Our joyful greeting there in the hotel hallway—as we pat one another on backs that have carried around burdens and pains that unfortunately neither of us knows about in detail—seems to be a perfect reflection of how things are now. Not just between Coach and me. But how it is with all my close relationships in Indiana. I'm confident that my "closeness" with all my Indiana friends will always remain because of what we've been through together in the past; however, we are unable to venture through life together, day by day, as we once did.

And yet, this is also what makes the reuniting of two people all the more joyful. They can physically be journeying through life from two separate places, but their souls have the potential to connect throughout all of life because of a moment in time, in their pasts, when their souls were intertwined.

This is how it feels to be with Coach once more.

Last year at this tournament, I was adjusting to the fact that I had moved away. Now I am adjusting to the fact that my moving changed the relationships I care about the most and seems to be changing my spirituality. But if I am the pilot of the sailboat and the wind is the Holy Spirit, then I must choose to believe that, though things might change, the new land is where I must go. I have chosen to leave shore, and therefore I am at the mercy of the wind.

Coach Briscoe and I only have time to exchange small talk before the meeting begins, as I have barely arrived on time, which is probably no surprise to him. We enter the conference room, and as Coach makes his way to the front and gathers everyone's attention, I quietly take a seat next to Coach's wife, Jamie, and his parents, Charlie and Twila. We whisper our hellos as the meeting starts.

The coaches' meeting is much like the one the year before, filled with all kinds of Paraguay-obsessed, softball nerds. The only difference in the tournament this year, Coach explains, is that the entire tournament will be played on Saturday, as a massive storm is expected to blow into Roanoke on Sunday; this means that the annual church service will be held on Sunday morning instead of Saturday evening. Some seem a little disgruntled about going from a two-day tournament to a one-day tournament at first—since this year's tournament would have to become more of a rushed, one-pitch format to fast-track the games—but they soon understood. It was only church softball, after all. Then again, in Roanoke on Labor Day weekend, it's never *only* church softball.

In less than an hour, the meeting approaches its end, and Coach concludes by calling Marcos Kurrle—the missionary whom I mentioned earlier—up to the front of the room.

This is my first time ever seeing Marcos outside of pictures and videos. He is average height, somewhat thick in a muscular sort of way, and is sporting a wide, radiant smile as Coach introduces him to all in attendance. Coach then asks him to pray, and Marcos prays a beautiful prayer in broken English. Marcos prays as if God is there in the room, sitting among the coaches. He prays as if the success of the tournament is entirely dependent on God. Marcos, perhaps more than anyone here, understands the importance of this tournament as the mission's financial lifeline. His prayer is eloquent, concise, pure, and bold, his voice rising and falling with each praise or request. It is easy to see he is a passionate man. I have yet to meet a Church of God member who lacks passion, which I love about their denomination. There is nothing so contagious as passion.

As he prays, I cannot help but hope that I will have the opportunity to interview Marcos this weekend. Journalistically, I've never interviewed a missionary before and am curious to have a better understanding of his life; and I also know that it's vital for the sake of the story that I talk to any Kurrle who attends the tournament, as they are rarely able to attend. Marcos provides vital insight into that world that the mission is for. Personally speaking, I also hope that talking to a missionary, who has given his life to a cause, fueled by his faith, might help me to better process my spiritual doubts and my direction in the world.

Maybe I need someone who lives an entirely different lifestyle to critique my own life.

Maybe someone from a developing country can evangelize me.

Maybe the experiences of someone who lives 4,500 miles away can help me to find myself.

Upon the conclusion of his prayer, everyone in the coaches' fraternity starts to scramble around, and Coach Briscoe shouts a few more last-minute announcements over all their movement.

Charlie, Coach's father, immediately approaches me and begins talking to me.

"How ya doing there, Cope?" he says, with an eager tone and smiling eyes.

"I'm great, Charlie," I say. "It's so good to see you!"

It is refreshing to be reunited with Charlie once more, in a grandfatherly sort of way. We connected last year. He allowed me to step into his life. I allowed him to step into mine. Though it is only my second time in Roanoke, the place is already beginning to feel like a piece of home. I guess this is natural when surrounded by people who are as congenial and welcoming and loving as the Briscoes.

"You know who that is, right?" Charlie says, directing my attention toward Marcos who is nearby talking to a group of people.

"Marcos, right?" I say.

"Yes, that's right," he says. "And that's his wife Cristiane and their children Mateo (pronounced Muh-tay-oh) and Alheli (pronounced Ah-luh-lee)."

Mateo is a lanky boy who is probably ten or so, and Alheli appears slightly younger. They are both standing there quietly next to Cristiane. I make a mental note that Paraguayan children are better behaved than American children.

"You heard about Marcos's brother, Norberto, right?" Charlie asks, switching the subject.

"Uhhh, I got an email a month or so ago," I say ignorantly, "but I was a little confused about what happened."

"Yeah, it didn't happen very long ago," he says, losing his bubbliness, his face beginning to straighten. "Just keep him in your prayers," he says, lowering his voice. "Norb and his family were in a car accident. His wife, Julie, and their only son, Timmy, both died there on the spot. The only ones who survived were Norberto and the daughter who they had just adopted, Anahi."

"Oh, OK," I say dumbfounded.

I was not expecting to hear such a thing and am afraid to ask for any more details. I feel kind of sick to my stomach.

"I will definitely be praying," I say stupidly.

———

One morning my senior year at Grace, Josh got an early-morning call from Coach.

There was nothing surprising about Coach calling us in the morning. He was usually calling to wake us up for a meeting. Why Coach put up with us for so long, I have no idea. I guess the administration found us to be pretty cheap labor, since we were students handling the responsibilities of a sports information director, which is typically a full-time position with benefits. It was indeed cheap labor, and we were indeed students, which Josh and I believed gave us the right to do all kinds of stupid "student" things—like climb on buildings and break into the tunneling system and shoot water balloons at kissing couples and sneak around campus like fugitives and miss important meetings with Coach Briscoe. Anyway, he usually called us to wake us up and was somehow always cheerful about it.

But *this* morning-call from Coach was different.

I remember waking up in a haze to the sound of Josh talking on the phone to Coach. Josh kept saying, "No, no, no, no," over and over, in the strangest of tones, as if he were whining or something. I had never heard Josh, an overwhelmingly positive person, sound like this before, and I immediately knew something was wrong.

I'll remember those lonely moments for the rest of my life—lying in bed, staring wide-eyed at the metallic springs on the bottom of Josh's bed, who was bunking above me, and trying to decipher what in the world he and Coach could possibly be discussing.

When the phone call ended, silence filled the room. Josh might have still believed I was asleep as he lay there trying to process whatever it was Coach had just told him.

I eventually couldn't handle it any longer.

"What was that about?" I eventually asked, nearly choking on my words.

Josh let out an exasperated sigh, as if he'd hoped the silence would protect me forever. He then told me that a volleyball player at Grace had died and that a friend of ours—a volleyball statistician who lived upstairs in our dormitory—was in the hospital.

"What happened?" I asked.

"I'm not sure," Josh said, sitting up, his feet dangling above my bed. "Coach said that he'll give us the details when we head over to his office."

Both were part of the athletic program, and Coach Briscoe, who oversaw the athletic program, often talked about how he felt each student-athlete was like his own child: He felt responsible for them.

So we walked to Coach's office on that wet and gloomy autumn day, unusually silent, shocked and confused, dodging puddles on the way there. It was obvious it had stormed the night before, and we knew the rest of the campus would soon be awakening to the news of a much larger storm—a tragedy that would shake the faith and the soul of this tiny, northern Indiana Christian college.

When we arrived at Coach's office, Coach gave us the details with puffy, watery eyes and gentle tears. We had never seen Coach like this before.

He explained to us that a tree by the lake had collapsed on the two of them while they had been relaxing in a popular hammock on the water's edge, just as many students have done over the years. Apparently, the tree's roots had deteriorated over time, sitting there on the bank of the lake. The tree killed her and ended up paralyzing him. They were simply in the wrong place at the wrong time.

What were the chances? *A tree.* A tree that happened to collapse at *that* particular moment in time when two *people* were under it.

Throughout the rest of the day, the Grace College campus was in a state of shock and disarray. Residents of our dormitory, where our friend lived, and the volleyball team in particular had sunk into a consuming despair. Theories abounded. Questions about faith and doubts about God moved to the forefront of students' minds. Few felt like praying.

But that evening I found myself sitting in a three-hour prayer class, a requirement for my Bible degree. I can't say I felt like going, but I couldn't afford to skip any more classes. I walked into the classroom that night like everyone else, grappling for answers, hoping for some sort of explanation.

The class was taught by sort of the grandfather figure of Grace College: an older, snowy-haired man named Dr. Peugh, who had wisdom in his wrinkles, glasses that rested on the tip of his nose, and a wedding ring that represented fifty-some years of love flowing from his commitment to his wife. He was a beacon of knowledge and wisdom on our campus. Week after week, we (well, those who weren't skipping) attended his class just hoping to perhaps absorb a single ray of his insight.

When Dr. Peugh walked into his classroom that evening, a vulnerable space filled with despondent students, it was as if he stepped into a place that was covered in the shattered glass of our broken faiths. Sticking with the metaphor, he decided to remove his shoes, walk toward us anyway, and bloody up his feet.

He began the class by telling us that we were not going to cover any material on this day. His tone was soft and solemn. It was easy to see he was shocked like the rest of us.

He then opened class by telling us a story that I will never forget—about a student he once knew who died way too young.

"At the funeral, a hundred people or so accepted Christ," Dr. Peugh explained. "The pastor then stood up in front of everyone and concluded, 'This is why so-and-so had to die, so that these people could be saved.'"

"I was sitting in the back," Dr. Peugh continued. "And I thought to myself, 'Who are *you* to try to explain the ways of the Lord?' The entire world could have accepted Christ, and the pastor *still* would have no right to say why so-and-so had to die. No one knows why tragedies unfold in this life."

Dr. Peugh's story did not answer a single person's question in that naked, silent classroom, and yet it was exactly what we needed to hear. In fact, it was one of the first theological ideas that really ever made any sense to me—that nothing is explainable.

"And that God," he continued, "wants to meet you here ... tonight ... because He cares about you and loves you and grieves alongside you."

The idea of suffering is still extremely confusing to me theologically, especially during this phase of my life when I seem to be deconstructing my faith and no longer know what I believe. Dr. Peugh's words were enough for me to cling to at the time but hearing about Norberto's car accident once again brings to the surface some of my questions about suffering.

I've heard some well-respected theologians say that God plans some things and allows other things. Does He really? Does God plan things? Does He allow things? And if God is sovereign in that way—orchestrating certain events and permitting others—does that make Him a psychopath? Judging by the tree that fell in Winona Lake and by Norberto's car accident, it seems so.

———

I threw a brick from the bridge when my friend was driving by.
He asked me why from his bedside,
and I revealed the intricacies of my plan,
how the pain would bring us closer,
how the suffering would make us stronger,
how I loved him beyond all measure,
enough to bring him to surrender.
And now I'm in the psych ward
surrounded by walls of bricks.

I took my child to the candy store and watched the man walk in.
He said he needed a companion

then took my child by the hand.
Authorities found the tapes peculiar,
how I consciously turned my back,
how I allowed this sick transaction,
how I enabled the attack.
And now I'm his companion in the courtyard, wearing matching clothes.

Do You really have a plan, some road map, some knowing?
Do You really allow the terror, as if blind to the suffering?
If the plan is to prosper, not to harm, then what about the slave?
If You allowed the Holocaust, do they curse You from their graves?
Am I supposed to believe
that You'd shape my life
but neglect the refugee,
that You'd hear my cry
but turn a deaf ear to missionaries?

10

A HOME IN THE JUNGLE

It's Saturday afternoon at Botetourt. The tournament is approaching its fifth hour, and the song of the unfolding games reminds me of the stories that flow through this sacred place on Labor Day weekend—how community is opening its arms to all, offering freedom through the lost art of open, vulnerable relationships.

The air is thick and muggy this afternoon, and it is apparent that summer has won its daily wrestling match with autumn, here in the ring of the valley. Something seems to be brewing on the other side of the mountains, and a thin, grayish haze will sometimes climb over the Blue Ridge and hang there in the distance for all the people at Botetourt to see—a foreshadowing, a warning, as if the haze is a messenger informing those at the fortress of the approaching enemy.

For now, however, it is dry.

Once more, I feel as if the mountains are teaching me things about myself. All morning, as Coach Briscoe and I have paid close attention to the weather radar on our phones, we have noticed how the storm systems dissipate as they approach the valley. All because of the mountains. I am no meteorologist, but it's interesting that something sprouting from the earth can fight off something so mysterious as a storm in the sky.

I wish I could be more like these mountains—standing firm, unchanging, despite the chaos of an approaching storm, fighting off the darkness with strength and boldness. If the Valley could speak, I imagine she would sound very confident, resting in the bulwark of the surrounding peaks. It has dawned on me today that I can be just as confident in my own life when storms or temptations come my way; I do not need to cower upon seeing the hanging haze. I must realize where I am—in the presence of God—and not worry so much about what is coming. How easy it is to see the foreboding clouds of darkness or temptation and submit myself to their will, when all along God is simply asking me to rest in His valley, in the comforts of His defenses! I must rest more and worry less.

———

Marcos eventually arrives at Botetourt in the early afternoon. I've been anticipating being able to spend some time with him. I think he has been riding around Roanoke with Charlie all morning (Lord, help him!) who has probably been telling Marcos nonsensical things like "My wife is blind in one eye and can't see out of the other—that's why she married me!"

At Botetourt, Coach introduces me to Marcos for the first time, right outside the press box. Marcos firmly shakes my hand with a big grin.

Marcos has a square, sort of intense face with a big nose and a bold jaw. He has short, brownish-blond hair and low, definitive eyebrows. If he were not smiling from ear to ear, if his eyes were not so welcoming, he would definitely appear more intimidating. As Coach explains to him the details of the book, Marcos keeps repeating a fluctuating, "Okayyyy."

Marcos sounds a lot like Borat, I think to myself, recalling that stupid, fictional film character from Kazakhstan played by Sacha Baron Cohen.

"Well," Coach says, smiling, placing his hands on both of our shoulders, "I'll let you guys hang out for a bit."

And then he walks away.

"Where would you like to go?" I ask Marcos awkwardly. "We can either go up in the press box, or, you know, we can walk around."

"Let's walk," he says definitively.

"Sounds good," I reply.

"My English is so-so," he says as a preface, "but I think we can understand each other."

"I don't think that will be a problem," I grin.

Marcos goes on to tell me that this is his third time attending the softball tournament and his first time in seventeen years. He went once in 1987, the year of the infamous "mud games," and again in 1995.

"It's so different to see it first-eye," he says, pointing to a nearby field where a game is unfolding, then pausing and thinking. "How do you say that?" He pauses again. "To see it with your own eyes!" he exclaims. "That's what I mean."

We share a laugh together, and then I dive right into the interview, afraid that my time with him is limited. "How important is this tournament for you guys financially?" I ask, right out of the gate. "Like, how dependent are you guys on this tournament annually?"

"Hmmmm," he says, thinking, "I can say that 40 percent of finances, of all the ministries in Paraguay, are being helped by this tournament."

I know that Coach Briscoe always calls the tournament a financial lifeline for Paraguay, but 40 percent is far more than I ever imagined. I cannot fathom living a life where my livelihood is dependent on one weekend—and, on top of that, a weekend that I have little control over. Here we were today, for example, closely following the weather. If the entire tournament were canceled, would the coaches and players want their money back? If they didn't get their money back, would they still show up next year?

"Friday, before Labor Day weekend, is a fasting day in Paraguay," Marcos says. "Most of the pastors in churches pray and get together. Maybe close to a thousand people are praying … It is a special prayer time. It's all prayer. You cannot do nothing without prayer."

"What's it like for you to be so dependent on this tournament for your finances?" I ask.

Marcos laughs, as if realizing the absurdity of it all in the context of my materialist American mind-set.

"My wife and I started a new church in Asunción, the capital of Paraguay, a year and a half ago," Marcos says, answering my question with a story. "As a father, it's hard for me to say, 'Let's go to the capital and start something.' We had $180 from somebody and $200 from someone else. That's all we had when we moved to Asunción. I said, 'I have this, and we can eat with this. So let's go.'"

Living in such a way is completely foreign to my American-infused mind. This is the kind of belief that I desire. My mind has been corrupted by the stresses of planning, the lust for comfort, and comparisons that lead me to believe I am poor.

"I have so many stories," he continues. "Can I just tell them to you from the beginning?"

"Of course," I say. "Take me to Paraguay."

———

Marcos is who he is today because of a friendship, a brotherhood.

Whether work or play, Marcos and his older brother, Norberto (the one who was recently in the car accident), were always by one another's side.

They were born in Argentina where their parents, Tabita and Martin, were missionaries at the time. Then, when Marcos was three years old and Norberto was almost five, sometime around 1976, Martin, the son of a farmer, sold the profitable land he had inherited, replete with shrubs and herbs for tea, and bought a truck so that he and Tabita could serve as missionaries in Paraguay, where they felt called.

Martin then purchased ten times the amount of land he had owned in Argentina in a small town called Obligado in the southeastern part of Paraguay. It was there that Martin and Tabita planted the first Church of God assembly in all of the country.

"Norberto and I could not sleep through services because our house was connected to the church," Marcos laughs.

Five years later or so, Martin sold that piece of land in Obligado and bought six times the amount of land two hours north in a jungly town called Raúl Peña. Martin's decision to move to a place that was seemingly in the middle of nowhere seemed nonsensical to most, but Marcos says that Martin felt a strange pull in his soul that he should establish his family's roots in the jungle.

"Really, the *jungle*," Marcos emphasizes. "There were seven to eight houses and a little market and that's all. Jungle. Jungle. Jungle. One street coming in. Market, three blocks down."

As they were transitioning from Obligado to Raúl Peña, Marcos remembers the journey sometimes taking them two or three days (though it was typically only two hours away) because of the flooding. They would travel with camping gear in case the road was underwater.

Upon completing their move, Marcos remembers chopping through the tangled jungle with his machete, at eight years old, alongside Martin and Norberto, trying to clear out space to build a church.

"We were a little scared of the jungle because Dad said, 'You'll see snakes all around,'" Marcos reflects. "I killed maybe fifteen to twenty snakes. Grab a piece of wood and kill it … but those next five years in the jungle were fun."

It was in Raúl Peña where Marcos made some of his fondest childhood memories—whether it was bike racing with Norberto on a trail that their father had carved through the jungle (the loser had to give the winner a marble) or competing against one another in "rustic bowling," which was basically bowling with a wooden ball down a wooden board into wooden pins.

Marcos and Norberto's day-to-day schedule, however, involved more work than play. There was no electricity. They lived off the land. Their water came from a well. Lots to do. Lots of chores. Whatever the case, they were always together. When their sisters Priscila and Nila were born, there in Raúl Peña, Marcos and Norberto shared a room together in their family's eight by nine-meter house.

Though Martin's decision to move his family to Raúl Peña was strange and seemingly illogical, they ended up bringing hope to an off-the-grid, abandoned community. This is true religion, it seems: gravitating toward the forgotten and the marginalized. This is the way of the Christ.

But Martin and Tabita didn't stop there. They were not ones who believed that they could solve people's problems just by planting a church and giving people Jesus. They longed to, yes, meet people where they were at in their spiritual needs, but also—and perhaps more important—meet people in their day-to-day practical needs. One of these was education. The public schooling in the area of Raúl Peña was severely lacking, as was the case in much of Paraguay at that time.

"Sometimes we kids would get to the school, and the teacher was not there," Marcos says. "We knew where he lived, so we would get on our bikes and go to his house and say, 'Teacher, Teacher! C'mon!'"

It's interesting to consider how much of a burden school seems to be in America. I always dreaded school. Yet here are these kids in Paraguay so anxious to learn something that they would wake up their teacher from his sleep! How spoiled are we in America to view blessings as curses?

"In Paraguay, public schools are not good schools," Marcos says. "The teacher just wants their money. Not everybody. But many. That was the main reason Mom and Dad said, 'We need to do something for the kids.'"

So they started a Christian grade school called Alpha & Omega to complement the church they planted, where children in the community would be given an opportunity to receive a top-notch education from qualified, passionate teachers. Tabita would oversee the school while Martin continued to pastor the church.

This space in the jungle has since developed into a massive campus with buildings and courtyards and playgrounds and all kinds of opportunities to provide the best experience for Paraguayan students in attendance. There's even a college there today.

———

I hope I can go to Paraguay one day. I would love to visit Raúl Peña and see what has become of that dark, wet space that used to be nothing but a tangled mess of roots and weeds. Why the Kurrles ended up in that abandoned place, I have no idea. No one knows, really. Not even Martin. He was merely following a call—something outside of him that pulled him and the voice within him that moved him. But Raúl Peña is a reminder to me that there is *nothing* that God cannot use to help others. He can step into the jungly, tangled mess of my heart, in whatever lonely state it may be, and cut through my roots of pride, eliminate the festering weeds of sin, and light up the darkness once more. I am quite all right with God taking His machete and hacking away within me.

I must further explore the jungle within myself. It is scary: entering into that foreboding wilderness of my insecurities and wounds. It is lonely: finding my home off-the-grid while others live their exterior-obsessed lives with their social media facades and professional successes. It is hard work: sifting through the tangled weeds of hurt and pain and unhealthy tendencies. But at the bottom of the pain is joy. Maybe it's in the jungle where we discover our inmost potential. It is where we become who we are. And that is why I must further explore my jungle: to finally know and become who I am. It will be difficult, but I must enter into it with the determination of Martin as he moved his family to Raúl Peña.

No, Martin's decision to plant his family's roots in Raúl Peña was not a flashy or sexy move by the world's standards. It was illogical and even ridiculed. But it was there in the jungle, after putting in the painful work of ripping up the festering weeds and killing snakes and hacking away at tangled vines, that he built a home for his family and a church for the community and a school for the families in that community. It was in the darkest, most complicated place that he found potential, in the loneliest place that he impacted others, and in that strangest, most uncomfortable place that became a sacred space.

11

PARTIES & PAHM

The storms have retreated now, leaving the summer air in the valley thick and stagnant and sticky. Marcos and I are walking laps around the perimeter of Botetourt, occasionally sitting in the bleachers at one of the four fields, then arising and walking once more. It is humid, but it is not unbearable. The sheltering clouds are protecting us from the summer sun. The overcast sky, for now, is unthreatening.

Marcos shares with me that he and Norberto were only around Alpha & Omega, the school in the jungles of Raúl Peña, at its genesis. Once Norberto turned thirteen and could no longer attend the school, Martin and Tabita sent him off to trade school in Argentina, a day's trip away that entailed eight different bus rides and a ferry ride. The following year, Marcos joined Norberto at the same school. The trade school, Martin and Tabita believed, would better position their children for success considering Paraguay's broken education system.

For Marcos, however, Argentina turned out to be a crossroads of sorts. No one else at school was as far from home as the Kurrle brothers. No one else at the school believed what they believed. And Marcos says that it was not uncommon for some of the older kids to haze some of the newcomers.

Marcos felt like he was on an island. Geographically. Relationally. Spiritually. All he had was Norberto.

"I just know I cried because I was homesick," Marcos says. "Some other kids would be mean to me and bad because it was my first year. I went to my room and cried. I don't remember how my brother found out, but I remember he came and prayed with me."

Marcos says that a lot of kids would tease him because of his faith because they had seen him carrying his Bible around his dormitory or around campus. They'd often mockingly say to him, "Hello, Pastor!"

"I hid my Bible for some time," Marcos admits. "But Norb said, 'No, we can't do that, buddy. We cannot hide who we are.'"

Norberto was Marcos's rock while they were at trade school. From the jungles of Raúl Peña—where they moved to a new home out in the middle of nowhere—to the trade school in Argentina—where Norberto would comfort Marcos in his loneliness and encourage him in his faith—no person seemed to be more present and have more of an impact on Marcos in his formative years than his older brother, Norberto. In Argentina, they were the only piece of family that the other had. And their bond was all they needed.

"Going out, being by ourselves, we grew even more close," Marcos says. "Since I had my brother there already, it was a little easier. We would play soccer and Ping-Pong all the time. No one wanted to play the Kurrle brothers two against two in Ping-Pong! I thank God that I had him. You never can say what would happen, but if I didn't have him, maybe I would fall from my faith."

Their time together, however, was limited. It was only a three-year school—catering to students who were thirteen, fourteen, and fifteen—so after two years with Marcos, Norberto moved on to a different school that was two hours away, leaving Marcos on his own. Suddenly, Marcos felt like he did not have a single friend there at school who believed what he believed or lived with the same values.

"Here the boys are doing whatever they want," Marcos reflects. "They bring pornos in, and I'm fighting by myself there. I could call Norberto sometimes, but we didn't have cell phones at that time, and Norb did not have a phone in his apartment."

The pressures of Marcos's environment became overbearing, and Marcos remembers once going to a raging dance party with a friend, experimenting with the scene that his peers had been raving about. His friend got pretty drunk, and

Marcos realized that the scene wasn't really for him, but he could still feel the pleasure-focused environment at school shaping him, as his Bible went back into hiding and as he began to speak vulgarly like the rest of his peers.

"There was a struggle," Marcos says. "I was by myself that year, and many, many times I asked myself, 'Is it really real that God exists?' Because my friends would come in and tell me all they did on the weekend—how they drink, have sex, everything."

It was at school, in isolation, away from his family and his older brother, that Marcos found himself at the great crossroads of faith, where the world begins to glitter and glow in a much more tangible way than heaven ever had, where the pleasures in this life seem more obtainable than eternity ever was. I am at the great crossroads, I think.

One weekend while at school, sometime in the early summer, Marcos remembers his parents asking him to return to Raúl Peña for an evangelistic campaign. A Brazilian pastor was coming to preach at Martin's church. Marcos says that he truthfully did not feel like going, but he is glad he did.

"That weekend, I remember until today," Marcos reflects. "It's unbelievable how God talked to me. The pastor said, 'God is calling you; God has a place for you.' That's when I decided I was going to serve God. The next time I came home, I was baptized.... I came back to school with my power back, and I picked up my Bible again."

As for Marcos, he never looked back.

————

The first time I ever partied was in high school at PAHM. This stood for "Party At Hamza's Momza's," obviously.

Hamza was the coolest kid in our high school. He was a brilliant, soft-spoken Islamic kid who was well respected by everyone, by his teachers and his peers. He also had a thick head of hair and could grow the sweetest Afro in the school, which I suppose isn't saying much since Plainfield High School, in the suburbs of Indianapolis, surrounded by cornfield-laden towns, was predominantly white. Still, Hamza was really cool. And his Momza was pretty cool, too, because we hosted parties in the basement of her house, which was located behind the local

Kroger, which was the perfect place to host a party because everyone could park at the local Kroger.

My first PAHM was the day before Christmas Eve my junior year. My best friend and I had just been dumped by our girlfriends. They had hardly been relationships at all, but we were emotional time bombs nonetheless, living our lives absorbed in two-and-a-half-minute punk rock songs, ready to rage in our bitterness and juvenile victimization. And that night, we did. I remember dancing into the night in that crowded basement, breaking open glow sticks and painting one another with neon, and—honestly—it all felt very magical. I can still feel that night, that basement, that intoxicating liberation I experienced in doing whatever the hell I wanted.

I never did party much after that. I might have attended one more PAHM, but then an organization called MIT, which obviously stands for "Moms In Touch," discovered the party photographs on MySpace and shut us down immediately. Truthfully there was nothing all that bad about PAHM—drugs and alcohol weren't allowed there—but I don't think MIT liked the idea of a bunch of horny teenagers in togas, and perhaps with good reason. MIT was not a fan of Hamza or his Momza. Plus, I got really involved in a new church soon after that, got baptized, and ended up getting a Bible degree. There was nothing even comparable to PAHM at Grace, since we were only allowed to have girls in our dormitory for a few hours every other Saturday … and still had to keep the door cracked open … and still could expect the RA to come in every fifteen minutes just to make sure that an orgy hadn't broken out.

In some ways, here in Charlotte, I feel like I am back at PAHM, compelled and curious, mesmerized by the streaks of neon in the darkness. This new place presents me an opportunity to go wherever I want and do whatever I want without a single soul knowing my name, without being packaged in a social box. And if I'm already miserable while trying to live the "Christian life"—always shackled in guilt and shame—then maybe I just ought to let go of my spiritual paradigm and live as I please. I hate feeling so innocent, so inexperienced, so stupid. Then again, if I knew who I was, I'd feel much more comfortable being unashamedly myself; instead I am shamefully me.

I want something to click into place within me as it did for Marcos when he was at his own crossroads—when he returned home from school to attend the evangelistic campaign and the Brazilian pastor touched his soul, convincing him once and for all that he was following the right path and living by design. Maybe these stories that I gather here can continue to help me. Maybe Marcos can help me.

———

Who made you feel small for your innocence?
Who mocked you for your lack of experience?
Now you are following the crowd,
the opposite idea of art in its rebel essence,
doing the one thing you hate: conforming,
sharing stories of wild nights,
existing like a snake,
shedding skin with each season,
the remains of your innocence in flakes.
How I loathe this creature
that tempts then transforms its victims,
turning meaning into wandering,
humans into reptiles,
growing into shedding,
as our skin sinks into the soil,
impossible to reattach.
From the start,
he has tempted us to follow,
and therefore fall like him,
from that mansion and into the weeds,
from home into the balance
of life and sin and death,
of scooting amongst the dirt.
Won't You help me run freely again
on these legs that You gave,
on these feet for moving?

Won't You help me reclaim
all I lost in my mistakes,
this forsaken innocence
I chose to throw away?

12

SOLITUDE & LONELINESS

Once Marcos said no to the world and its temporary pleasures, there at that evangelistic campaign in Raúl Peña, and decided to commit his life to something bigger than himself once and for all, he was pulled deeper into the unknown, into the depths of the dark blue waters.

At age seventeen, for example, Marcos felt an urge within him to pursue ministry as his career. He knew that ministry would not be a comfortable life. Having grown up with two parents as missionaries, he knew the challenges and the torments of ministry all too well. But ministry was where he was feeling called. It was the path.

There is nothing comfortable about following God, it seems. So why do it? Because maybe that is where we become fully alive as the spiritual beings who I hope we are. I want to believe that what Christ said was true—that "life to the full" is possible. I want to believe that there is something else at play in this world. A spiritual realm. A magical realm. An energy that holds everything together.

As Marcos shares with me more about his decision to pursue ministry, we take a seat at a picnic table on the third-base line at one of the fields. The wind has steadily been picking up for the last ten minutes as the sky has darkened in the distance beyond the mountains. Once more, it feels like the peaks surrounding the valley are trying to fight off whatever is forming on the other side.

"One weekend, I went home (to Raúl Peña), and I lay down in my bed," Marcos says. "I was praying, and suddenly a strong light, very strong light, shined on my window. It was ten at night. There were no cars. No streetlights outside. I'm in the jungle. Nothing but jungle and stars. I feel something … I don't know what I feel, but I start crying. And I feel something come upon my life."

Marcos says that it was an odd thing for him to cry so violently. He hardly ever cried, especially at this stage of his life. He *hated* to cry. Tabita and Martin rushed into his room because they heard him crying, and Marcos could not stop—not even around his father, a man's man and strong disciplinarian whom Marcos hated to look weak around. It was as if Marcos were truly overcome by a liberating fear, as if he had experienced the supernatural. He had been touched by the mystical, the Mysterious Other.

"I told them, 'I don't know what's happening. I feel like I really need to serve the Lord,'" Marcos recalls. "I couldn't stop crying. I could not explain it. I'm not going to do that just in front of my dad, cry there. It was really something. I said, 'Dad, I really feel like I must prepare myself. I want to serve God.'"

In the remainder of Marcos's third year of high school, the nagging feeling that he was called to so much more—to full-time ministry—never went away. It wasn't the fact that he felt he would rather be a minister than an electrician, which was the career he was pursuing academically. It was the fact that he felt like he didn't have a choice. There was no other way.

Marcos challenges me to believe that when we say no to the unhealthy temporary pleasures of the world and say yes, in faith, to a transcendent enjoyment; when we stop living like this earth is all there is and, in faith, claim our heavenly citizenship; and when we begin to see our own plans as futile and accept God's imagination and hope for us, in faith—as seemingly impractical and mysterious as it might feel—as reality, that God takes us deeper into His strange, wondrous ways. Going deeper is not always easy, but it is always good. Going deeper sometimes involves terrifying risk and lonely expeditions, but it is always freeing. All of this might seem backward, but it makes perfect sense, for eternity cannot possibly fit into an explainable world, and a divinity cannot possibly fit into logic, and God cannot fit into things like words.

This was undoubtedly true for Marcos.

He was being summoned.

Pulled into the intangible, the unknown.

———

Marcos left behind his electrical dreams—a profession that would have likely led to a lifestyle of stability and comfort—and decided to attend Bible college.

The summer heading into his first year at Bible college, however, he seemed to catch a glimpse of the nature of the call he was following.

"That summer, I got really sick," Marcos says.

"Sick?" I say.

"Yes," he continues. "I almost died."

Marcos tells me that over a period of days, his temperature climbed higher and higher and higher. He and his family had no idea what was going on. Martin and Tabita took Marcos to a hospital in Argentina, and the doctors gave Marcos some medication. He spent eight days in the hospital, and the medication seemed to help. He was eventually released, and Marcos had only a couple days to get packed in preparation for Bible school.

That's when he got sick again.

And this time it was worse.

"One day I was lying down, and I was shaking," he says. "I could not walk. Mom and Dad put me in the car. I said, 'Lord, I want to prepare myself (for ministry); what are You doing?' I do not want to die. But something is not right."

A local pastor advised Martin and Tabita: "I think your son might have malaria. You need to go to Brazil. They will give you medicine."

After a three-hour drive to Brazil, Marcos says, doctors there discovered he had malaria within ten minutes of doing his bloodwork. They believed Marcos had contracted malaria thirty days before (many of malaria's victims don't even last thirty days), perhaps when he went fishing with Martin and Norberto at a nearby river. The doctors also said that, in the three-step process of malaria and "3" meaning death's bitter end, Marcos was at 2.5.

Thankfully the medicine kicked in and did its job. Marcos recovered, and he finally went to Bible school … three weeks late. To say the least, flirting with death didn't make for the greatest start to the semester or, most importantly, to pursuing his call to ministry. But perhaps it was a warning for what was to come in the life he was choosing. Following Christ and entering into the ministry would bring him supreme meaning and ultimate joy, for it was the path that had chosen him, but it would be hard. It would be uncomfortable. It might take him to the cusp of death. It might bring martyrdom. It would certainly be painful.

But in a sense, contracting malaria had only solidified his call, adding coal to the burning flame of desire within. Strangely, he could hear his call clearer than ever. When he went off to Bible school, it was as if he had been born again and was beginning the first day of his life, on a new and exciting journey.

––––––––

It is time to take a break.

We have been talking for an hour and a half and, though I know Marcos is kind enough to answer my questions for however long I need him to, it seems like a good place to stop for now.

As he walks back toward the press box, where there always seems to be a gathering of people, I consider following him, but then I decide to go on a walk by myself instead. I need to take time to reflect on what Marcos has shared with me and how the stories he has shared might apply to my life.

As I walk, I find myself drifting farther and farther away from the softball diamonds. I stumble upon a gravel path on the complex that weaves its way downhill, past some buildings, and spits you out in an open field. If anyone were to look out and see me, I'm sure it would be a strange sight: me walking around alone in a field. But I do not really care because it feels right, and I feel closer to the mountains, and I think I am getting in touch with myself, and perhaps I am therefore also getting in touch with God, whoever God is, whatever God is, wherever God is.

For whatever reason, Roanoke has become a place in the last two years where I can step out of my loneliness and enter into solitude—and believe me, there is a real difference between loneliness and solitude. The former feels oppressive, like there is something wrong with you; the latter, freeing, like everything is okay. This is becoming a retreat of sorts as God breathes life into me *through* these stories that I gather.

I am inspired by Marcos's relentless pursuit of what felt truest to him in the midst of the unknown. The moment those blinding lights shined mysteriously through his window and touched him with something of the divine, he knew there was no going back. He returned to school for a year to pursue electricity, tempted each day by the comforts of what that lifestyle would entail, but he knew that path did not belong to him. He went home for the summer and nearly died of malaria, forcing him to miss the first three weeks of Bible school, but he went to Bible school anyway, only more determined. Surely nothing but death would stop him.

Sometimes it is tempting for me to want to return to what is simple and comfortable. To move back to Indiana. To be with those whom I love once more. To reclaim the faith paradigm I'm losing. But there will be no moving back to Indiana anytime soon; I'm confident of this. And there will also be no returning to my previous spiritual paradigm anytime soon; I'm also confident of this. I've always been told that doubt, when it comes to faith, should be extinguished at all costs, but doubt, I'm finding, is actually a gateway to transformation, wisdom, and knowledge. Healthy deconstruction is how true growth takes place. Always questioning. Always reforming. Always further exploring truths. Never arriving. No, this path is not for everyone. But it is the path for me.

Like Marcos, I cannot go back to what once was, and I cannot fight what is propelling me forward. How can the captain of a sailboat make any headway toward the northern coast when gale-force winds keep blowing him south, day after day, year after year? The only solution is to *use* the wind to empower the sails and to hold onto the hope that life will begin anew in a beautiful, unfamiliar place. It is the only way of going anywhere at all: to *partner* with the wind. Or else the captain will spend his whole life fighting to get to where he wants to go and sailing nowhere. I am not interested in being stuck. I don't want to fight anymore.

13

RUSHING INTO THE RIVER

After an hour or so of personal reflection, I return to the softball fields to seek out Marcos once more. He agrees to a second round of interviews, and we once again start walking together around the perimeter of Botetourt.

"Where were we?" he asks.

"You had just finished telling me about how you got malaria right before going to Bible school," I say to him.

"Ahhhh, yes," he responds. He then begins to tell me about his and Norberto's educational journeys over the next several years and his entry into ministry, which I will briefly summarize:

Marcos completed his first year of Bible school in Posadas, Argentina, and roomed with Norberto who was continuing with his next level of trade school. Norberto then followed in his mother's footsteps and attended Anderson University in Indiana. Marcos, on the other hand, attended Bible school for two more years in Posadas, and then followed in his father's footsteps by attending Bible college in Germany, Martin's native country, because of an overseas scholarship he received. After finishing school in Germany, Marcos went to Anderson University for three months, where Norberto was still attending school, to take classes and learn some more English.

Three continents.

Two years.

It was there, at Anderson, that Marcos met Coach Briscoe for a second time. He had first met Coach back in 1987; but now, in the mid-nineties, they were far removed from their childhoods and were on the brink of finishing their schooling and entering into the real world. Over the years, Norberto, Coach, and Marcos would become the best of friends.

Marcos then returned to Raúl Peña to be a youth pastor there at the church in the jungle, where his father was still the head pastor, and he officially began his professional life in Christian ministry.

"I was excited to come back to Paraguay," Marcos says. "I really had three invitations to stay in Germany—three churches—but I don't know what it was. I could not stay there. I need to go back to Paraguay. There is so much to do there."

Marcos was so in touch with who he was and what he knew he was called to do that not even ministry opportunities in a thriving first-world country like Germany could woo him from serving in the developing country of Paraguay. You know that someone's faith is real to him or her when it has nothing to do with personal gain or advancement in the world.

The following year, after Norberto completed his bachelor's degree, he also returned to Paraguay to serve. After going on their own educational journeys, Marcos and Norberto, once more, were reunited. Norberto happened to be in a dating relationship at the time—with, yes, Julie, whom he had met at Anderson—and was trying to decide whether or not he should return to Anderson, where Julie was still in school, to begin his master's degree.

Norberto would eventually end up returning to Anderson, but his year in Paraguay was perfect timing. That's because Martin and Tabita were fulfilling a need that year within the Church of God, pastoring a church that was thirty minutes away, an assignment that allowed Norberto to fill in for his father as the head pastor in Raúl Peña, while Marcos continued pastoring youth.

"When my parents left, that was seventeen years they were in Raúl Peña," Marcos says. "But Norb and I were both together again. It was great. Unbelievable. Though we are different, we love working together. He was the boss. I followed him."

After serving together in Raúl Peña, things speed up once more.

Norberto returned to Anderson for his master's degree. Marcos was offered a youth pastor position at the Church of God in Santa Rita, an hour or so away. Norberto continued dating Julie. Marcos met Cristiane. Norberto married Julie. Marcos married Cristiane.

While Marcos was serving as a youth pastor in Santa Rita, an opportunity arose for him to be the head pastor at a church in Naranjal, which is in between Raúl Peña and Santa Rita.

At Naranjal, however, there was a caveat.

The church there was severely scarred.

"It was difficult a little bit because the pastor two before, at a Mennonite church, had problems with adultery," Marcos explains. "So the Church of God came in, and the *next* pastor's wife had a problem with adultery. The wife of that pastor stayed in town, married this other man, and lived three blocks from the church. It was a little town, and no one believed anymore."

As Marcos tells me all of this, I sense that this was his first real ministerial challenge since graduating from Bible college. And it is perhaps one of the most challenging things in ministry in general: repairing the wounds in the deep recesses of people's souls.

"How tough was that?" I ask. "I feel like repairing is sometimes more difficult that introducing something."

Marcos goes on to tell me a story about a man in Naranjal who lived near the church and would walk by the church each morning on his way to work. The man later told Marcos that when he and Cristiane first came to Naranjal, he would often think to himself while walking by the church, "That poor little pastor. What does he want to do here? Nothing will work here."

The man had seen two pastors come through Naranjal and fall from ministry because of adultery. He lived in a community surrounded by people whose faith had been shattered because they had been let down by leadership, because the leaders' actions did not back up their words.

Several months passed, and people slowly began coming to the church once more as Marcos and Cristiane regained the people's trust and strengthened their confidence in the gospel through their actions. One of the people who began attending the church was the man's wife.

One Sunday, Marcos decided to gather the congregation down by the river for a number of baptisms, which would be followed by a celebratory picnic. Marcos knew that a handful of people in the congregation wanted to be baptized. So fifty or sixty people gathered on the bank of the river as Marcos stood in the water, baptizing anyone who wanted to make a public proclamation to follow Christ. After five or six baptisms, Marcos asked, "Is there anyone else who would like to be baptized?"

The cynical man, who'd had so many doubts about Christianity and so many scars and wounds from the church, suddenly emerged from the crowd. Tears were streaming down his face. He frantically removed his shoes and sprinted into the water, eventually falling into Marcos's loving arms.

"Until today," Marcos says, "he is the strongest leader there. He plays bass at the church, and his whole family is serving God. I have this image right now of him running into the water. That gives me so much strength and power to continue! The Holy Spirit touched him that day."

———

My family once had a strange-looking, black-and-white sheepdog with an underbite and a mischievous personality. I named her Blackspot, naturally, because her tail protruded from a gigantic, black spot on her ass. Clever, I know. I was seven or something.

Anyway, Blackspot's biggest fear in life was thunderstorms. Most dogs don't like storms, but it seemed that Blackspot had a borderline panic attack each time a storm rolled through. Whenever there was even a hint of thunderous grumbling in the distant sky, Blackspot would shake uncontrollably, cowering in a corner of our house.

We believed the origin of her fear might have stemmed from a time when we left her at home for our neighbors to dog-sit while we were on vacation. While we were gone, a massive thunderstorm, bringing with it clunks of glassy hail, swept through central Indiana. I can only imagine how terrifying that had to have been for Blackspot: to be alone in that house surrounded by all those noises—the deep rumble of thunder, the tirade of hail on our rooftop, and the sharp crackling of age-old trees being split by lightning nearby.

Aren't we all just trembling dogs, cowering in the corner of our houses during those storms of life that open up our wounds? Don't we all have mental or emotional or spiritual scars that reveal themselves in the dark skies and howling winds?

I am convinced that some of the deepest wounds that exist in this life are the spiritual ones, much like the community in Naranjal experienced as it witnessed religion's ironic marriage to infidelity for so many years. As Marcos says, "It was a little town, and no one believed anymore." It is a tragedy indeed for faith and religion to bring hurt rather than hope, to open wounds instead of inspiring wonder and awe, to portray a small god rather than the God of the universe.

Most of the people I know have spiritual wounds. And I believe these wounds from religion's sword cut deep because they are somehow associated with the deepest parts of our selves. When this foundation is tampered with, the very structure of our lives can feel shaky or unstable. It often leads us into the desert, where we begin to question what we believe and why we believe it.

This is where I am right now.

Marcos's story resonates with me because my own spiritual wounds have propelled me into this lonely, desert phase of deconstruction. I am the man in Marcos's story staring at the church building in Naranjal and shaking my head in disbelief because of all the flaws it represents.

Today, I believe I am ultrasensitive to the narrow-minded thinking of some Christians, not so much because this type of Christian scarred me, but more so because I used to be one of them—and I despise who I became. For example, when I was delving into Christianity, I remember a couple of my peers, who were really into their faith and seemed smart, asking me if it was difficult for me to have a family who wasn't "saved"—a generalization they made because they knew my family was Catholic. I don't remember what my answer was, but at the time, as impressionable as I was, their question terrified me. So I naturally began praying profusely for my family's salvation. And whenever I was around my family, I would sometimes pick fights with them about all kinds of nit-picky doctrinal things. And I would justify my actions with the lofty nature of salvation. But I didn't just do this with them. I did it with anyone whose beliefs were different than mine. In some senses, I'm sure that I am *still* that narrow-minded person who emerged from college with my Bible degree thinking that I held all of the answers to life and spirituality in my palm ... and perhaps I will continue to be that person until I effectively shed the remainder of my skin from my previous paradigm.

Am I saying that what I learned and acquired from my previous paradigm was bad? Not at all. Stepping into that paradigm was the most transformative time of my life. It taught me to think, to evaluate, to journey. But it's no longer a journey if you think you've arrived. Even the deep and profound *truths* that this version of Christianity helped me to awaken to must be deconstructed and constantly unpacked—because the second we believe that we have attained the Absolute is the second that we have made an idol out of our own idea of who we think God is.

The real question is whether our thinking and spirituality reflect a small, boxed-in God or an incomprehensible deity who inspires the Christian imagination. And that is why I am struggling to belong in a faith community today. It seems that the ideas I have heard preached from most pulpits reflect a god that is far too small. The more controlling the god that is being projected, the more inaccurate that picture of God is. The more manipulative the god that is being explained, the more that God is like a devil. The more that someone assures us that he or she can explain God, the more that god is an idol of man.

I am tired of being told what to believe; I want to explore *how* to believe. I am tired of being told what to do in order to become someone who is worthy; I want to discover how to *be* worthy. I am tired of the shame and the exhaustion; I want to live out of a place of rest and peace.

Maybe then I will—like the cynical man in Naranjal—rush toward Marcos into the river to be baptized.

Maybe we'll stand there in the river together.

14

THE MIRACLE OF THE 666

A meaningful journey almost always begins with a question.

In the parable about the rabbi who stumbled upon the Roman fortress, the rabbi was willing to pay the Roman guard double to ask him those two questions—"Who are you?" and "What are you doing?"—each day because he understood that the guard's questions would ground him in the purpose and meaning of the day, flowing out of his own identity. It seems that meaning can only be attained if we are willing to either pose a question to ourselves or truly listen to a question posed by others or perhaps by God. Our willingness to engage in the scary, meaningful questions of life often serves as a portal into a different realm where we discover life in its fullness through the grueling processes that fullness entails.

All this to say, the next phase of Marcos's journey began with a question—one that propelled him and Cristiane into the very heart of their ministerial calling.

As Marcos and I continue to walk around the fields, Marcos shares with me that after six years of rebuilding the broken church in Naranjal and slowly reigniting the coals of faith in the community, he and Cristiane felt a call to move to Asunción, the capital of Paraguay. And this move was spurred by a question.

The question came one evening while Marcos was helping out at a Game Night that his church was hosting for the youth in the community. One of the purposes behind Game Night was to give kids a healthy and safe place to have fun—away from the temptations to party or drink or do drugs, like many of their peers were doing.

As Game Night was coming to an end late that evening, a seventeen-year-old girl approached Marcos and asked him, "What can we do now? Where can we go?"

"I looked at the time, and it was almost eleven," Marcos laughs. "I said, 'I am going to bed.'"

Marcos's entire day had been spent at church: preparing for church service, preaching, planning Game Night, and eventually helping at Game Night. He was tired. Exhausted. Ready to sleep.

However, as Marcos went home, his mind became restless as he pondered those two questions: *What can we do now? Where can we go?*

"What did she mean by that?" Marcos reflects. "I went to bed. Cristiane was sleeping, but I woke her up, and I said, 'This girl asked me these two things.' And I could not sleep for one hour more. I keep wondering, *What are the young people doing now? Where are they going now?* That very night, I decided: We need to do something for the young people in Paraguay."

As months passed, the girl's questions continued to weigh on Marcos's subconscious. He wanted to give the youth something to do. He wanted to give the youth a place to go. Not just for an hourlong Game Night once a week. Beyond that. He could not shake the Idea from his mind. Such seems to be the nature of the purest ideas and dreams: not only do they knock on our doors, but we also welcome them into our homes and allow them to stay there for as long as they choose to stay.

The longer the Idea made its home in Marcos's mind, the more he began to partner with it and explore what it might entail. What if he took the Idea six hours away to Asunción, the capital of Paraguay, where there was an even bigger need to provide a safe hangout for teens because of the city's growing population and its concentration of bars and clubs? The thought seemed random at first, but the more he dove into it, the more it made sense. Not only for ministry but also for personal reasons. Moving to Asunción would give Marcos and Cristiane the opportunity to continue their education at a university in the city, which was something they had wanted to do for a long time. In their six years in Naranjal,

Marcos, along with finding his passion for youth ministry, had also developed an interest in radio broadcasting, and Cristiane had developed a passion for teaching.

The capital's call, however, was also the most uncomfortable voice that the Kurrles could have heard at the time. That's because Marcos and Cristiane also had a baby boy, Mateo, their first child, who was only two years old at the time. Relocating with a child seemed inconvenient and scary and risky. Plus, the Kurrles liked it in Naranjal. It felt like home. The church was flourishing. The work was meaningful. They loved the people, and the people loved them.

"God really worked through a dream in my dad," Marcos continues. "One day, I drive there (to Raúl Peña), and I start (talking to my parents) by saying, 'Mom and Dad, do you have an idea of what I want to do?' Dad starts to cry, and he says, 'Last night I had a dream that you went to another city.' For me, it was a big sign from God. We usually do not talk about dreams or the emotions of things. I almost started to cry, and I said, 'God, thank You.' I know my dad, and he does not make decisions without praying and fasting, without making sure that this is God."

Over the course of the next year, everything about the Kurrle family's potential move to Asunción continued to miraculously fall into place. A pastor whom the Naranjal community trusted expressed interest in leading the church. And a woman at the church *also* had a dream about the Kurrles leaving before anyone even knew they were considering the idea. Why was everyone having dreams about them moving from Naranjal? It got to the point where, as sad as the church would be to lose the Kurrles, it was also as if they had heard the call too. To stay would have meant to ignore the many signs of the divine.

So Marcos and Cristiane left.

With only $380 to their name, a baby boy in their arms, and without knowing a single soul in the capital.

"Did you know how long your money would last? Did you know how many meals you could cover before you ran out of money?" I ask, realizing once more how American I must sound.

"We didn't make such calculations," he laughs. "For us to eat—would be enough. We were sure that God was sending us. Why wait?"

As Marcos shares with me the nature of his mind-set in moving to Asunción, I cannot help but wonder if our precise calculations in America sometimes hold us back from ever doing what we are meant to do. The reality is that taking a risk will never be convenient or entirely logical, or else it would not be called a risk in the first place! And a call, if such a thing exists, will almost always be lacking convenience and logic because convenience and logic are of this world, but a call, of course, comes from a deeper level of reality.

Luckily for Marcos and his family, Norberto was able to set them up with a temporary place to stay because of his connections through a radio ministry at Anderson University. Three months later Marcos found an apartment to rent. Next, Marcos and Cristiane enrolled in school—Cristiane in education and Marcos in broadcasting. And, finally, they began laying the groundwork for their ministry—that they planned to call "Youth Planet"—a safe space for the youth in Asunción to have fun and socialize throughout the week. They figured that it might take a year or two to get connected in the community and find a strategic location for their ministry, so Marcos and Cristiane began looking for odds-and-ends jobs to support their family in the meantime.

Four months after their move, however, on June 6, 2006, Marcos received a call on his cell phone from a number he didn't recognize. Marcos answered.

"Are you Marcos Kurrle?" asked the man on the phone.

"Yes," Marcos replied.

"I want to talk to you about kingdom business," the man said.

"OK," Marcos said hesitantly, no idea who in the world was on the line.

"I know a little bit about you," the man continued. "I want to come pick you up and show you something."

"OK," Marcos replied again, pausing. "Do I know you?" he eventually said.

"No, you don't know me," the man replied. "Where do you live? Explain, and I'll come pick you up."

For whatever reason—perhaps by some stroke of Providence or perhaps in a moment of sheer stupidity—Marcos proceeded to give the stranger his address.

"He comes, probably fifty-five years old, very gentle man," Marcos remembers. "I see him in his truck, and he says, 'Come in.' I say, 'OK.'"

When Marcos and Mateo got into the truck, the man handed Marcos a picture. The picture was a family photo of Marcos, Cristiane, and Mateo. Turns out, Marcos had printed off one hundred of those photos before they left Naranjal so that they could give them to people as a reminder to pray for them as they moved to Asunción. On the photo, it read, in Spanish: "Pray for our youth project in Asunción."

Marcos was baffled. Here they were, over six hours away from Naranjal, on the opposite side of the country, in a city where Marcos did not know a soul, and *this* man had a photo of his entire family.

"How did you get this picture?" Marcos asked the man.

"I'll explain to you later," he replied.

A few minutes later, they arrived at a four-story downtown building, located one block from one of the main streets in Asunción. The man explained that he owned a brake-fixing business that he operated out of the building.

The man then led Marcos through his workshop on the first floor, then up to the second floor where there were more work-related belongings, then up to the third floor where there were a hundred chairs or so, as if a church congregation had been meeting there, then up to the fourth floor, a large room, where there was a bathroom, kitchen, and a couple of sofas.

"Tell me about your project," the man suddenly said.

"Well," Marcos said to him, "I don't have a project right now. But I want to do something for the young people. I feel like the churches do not do much."

On that cue, the man—who was named Antonio—*finally* shared his story with Marcos and explained exactly who the heck he was.

"I have *one* relative in Naranjal," the man said. "I hardly ever visit him, but this Easter the Lord touched me, and I felt that I needed to visit my relative in Naranjal. I went. On Sunday morning, I picked up my relative's Bible, and your picture fell out. God touched me, and I said to myself, *I need to pray for this man.* I asked my relative, 'Who is this person?' He said, 'Oh, he is somebody that went to Asunción, and he wants to do something for the young people.'"

Marcos found out that Antonio's relative was a Christian man who worked at a gas station in Naranjal. When Marcos was filling up his truck the day of his family's departure, Marcos gave the man a picture of his family and said, "Pray for me. We are moving to Asunción."

The gas station attendant was the last person in Naranjal whom Marcos gave a photograph to.

And now this photograph was six hours away in the hands of a man named Antonio who owned a brake-repair business in the heart of the capital.

"I have been praying for you," Antonio said, "and God gave me peace that I should give this room to you, for free, to use for your ministry."

Marcos was shocked. There had to be a catch, some agenda, something, that would cause this man to do such a generous thing.

"My mind was like, 'Is this true?'" Marcos tells me. "I'm not ready. I have nobody. I have nothing. Is this God? Or is this old man a little crazy?'"

Then Antonio said to Marcos, "Come back tomorrow with your wife, and I want to pray for you and give you this place … for free."

When Marcos got back to his house, he turned on the radio and began listening to a local Christian station. He sat there, thinking, trying to get his mind around the happenings of the day. He and Cristiane had thought that it might take a couple years for them to officially launch their youth ministry. And this man was offering them a place *tomorrow* for them to begin. Free of charge.

When Marcos turned on the radio, a song caught his attention.

Ten fe, creer, y el milagro ocurrira.

Have faith, believe, and the miracle will happen.

The chorus continued to repeat itself, as if a point was trying to be made.

Ten fe, creer, y el milagro ocurrira.

Ten fe, creer, y el milagro ocurrira.

When the song ended, Marcos, moved to tears, knelt down on the kitchen floor and desperately gripped the radio, hanging on the edge of what might happen next. Marcos says that it was as if God were speaking to him—through the speakers of his radio!

The host of the radio show began to speak, quoting a passage of scripture, that, in Spanish, said something along the lines of, "I encourage you to go, do the work, and I will be with you until you finish the work of the church."

The timing of this passage was the final confirmation for Marcos. For the next ten to fifteen minutes, Marcos says that he bawled uncontrollably.

"To me," Marcos says, "that was God saying, 'I am *with* you, Marcos. I am here. I am giving you a place. I want you to work with the youth.'"

As Marcos reflects on what he calls the Miracle of the 666—because it took place on June 6, 2006—he lets out a strained, passionate whisper: "God, You are too great. You are too much, Lord. Thank You, Lord."

———

For Marcos, all is grace. He seems to trace every positive thing he experiences back to God's favor on his life. Marcos's reality is marked by an awareness of God's love and grace that are continually entering *into* his life, which naturally leads to gratitude and humility flowing *from* his life.

Marcos reminds me of a solar blanket that stretches over a swimming pool. He is entirely dependent on the sun, the Source, in order to be the slightest bit useful. And when the sun emerges from behind the clouds, allowing the solar blanket to warm the water below, it is ultimately not the solar blanket warming the water—it is the sun. Marcos has not forgotten that he needs the power of the sun if he wants to be useful. And when he fulfills his purpose, he knows that it is not he who does the work but the power of Christ in him.

It would have been easy for Marcos to have made his ministerial successes about himself. After all, it was he who took the risk of moving his family six hours away to Asunción with only $380 in his pocket—but Marcos would say that it was an expression of God's grace that there was a call to begin with. I feel that it would have been just as easy for Marcos to pat himself on the back for printing the photo cards, to write it off as a good marketing strategy—but there was no doubt in Marcos's mind that—photo card or not—God would have connected him with Antonio or a place for Youth Planet. For Marcos, whether it was a big moment, like receiving a free room for his youth ministry, or a small moment, like hearing a song and passage of scripture on the radio that was *directly* related to the miraculous day he had just experienced, everything that happened all went back to God's hand in his life and therefore to the perpetual flow of God's love and grace.

If I were like Marcos and was a missionary or something, then maybe I would be able to trace everything back to God and believe in grace because I would be dedicated to serving God with my life. I've always been told that "God is in control" and that "God has a plan" and that He is sovereign and omniscient, but why would God care to guide or direct the events in my life when there are far more dire concerns in this world than that of a middle-class, white American male? We live in a world of war and slavery and rape and oppression—a place where children have cancer and bodies of refugees wash up onto shorelines and 35 percent of the world does not even have clean water. It actually ticks me off that God might answer my prayer about wanting to find a career in creative writing but would turn a deaf ear to the cry of a refugee.

Can grace—God's constant involvement in our lives—exist for a person like me whose problems are petty compared to the needs in the rest of the world?

Maybe if I were as dedicated a Christian as Marcos. But I, on the other hand, am always messing things up. I feel like I am always trying to work my way back into God's favor. It's been so ingrained in my mind that I'm fallen and wicked that I have begun to realize what a challenging thing it is to believe that I am actually loved. Following Christ always seems to come with a price. To work harder. To strive more. To read and pray more diligently. To repeat another Sinner's Prayer. To walk up to the altar and surrender once more. To accept Christ again and again and again because he must have left. And he must have left because of my lack of discipline, because God does not think I am devoted enough. If I am going to get kicked in and out of heaven again and again, then maybe I don't belong there.

Can grace exist without working harder to receive it?

What will it take for me to be enough? For others? For myself? For God?

It is ironic, I know, that I went to a school called Grace College and now write about spirituality at a faith-based sports magazine, yet still come across as if I do not believe in grace. I *want* to believe in grace. I *want* to, like Marcos, be aware of God's love and grace entering into my life so that gratitude and humility can flow from my life. But what kind of God would dare to enter into this broken soul?

No, I do not think I have even scratched the surface of grace.

Thank you, Marcos, for pulling me deeper into this incomprehensible mystery that—I hope—one day frees me.

15

"ONE IN ONE MILLION"

Marcos and I are once again sitting at a picnic table on the third-base line of one of the softball diamonds. It is midafternoon by now, and the weather is changing. The sky is growing dark, and the wind is rolling around with the dirt on the diamonds. It is not yet raining, but there is a feeling that the coming storm is making headway, that the darkness has managed to fight its way past the front lines of the mountains. And now the storm is on the verge of invading the valley.

Our conversation turns to the subject of Norberto. I know that my time with Marcos at the diamonds is now limited because of the dark clouds hovering above, and I have been longing all day to ask Marcos about his dear brother, who lost his wife, Julie, and their only son, Timothy, in a horrifying car accident four months ago. I cannot imagine the depth of the pain Marcos must feel as he watches his brother—his best friend—endure such a tragedy. Though the car wreck happened thousands of miles away, it is as if I can begin to place a finger on the scope of the trauma just by talking to Marcos today and therefore feeling closer to his brother.

"Tell me about Julie," I say to Marcos.

Marcos smiles and looks down at the ground reflectively, as if sifting through a sea of compliments that he could say about her, but also consumed in the grief.

Oddly, the wind picks up significantly as Marcos starts talking about his late and beloved sister-in-law. It is as if even the heavens are bothered by what happened to her.

"One in one million," he reflects. "One in one million. I don't know if many Americans would go down to Paraguay as a missionary like she did. Very few, I think."

Marcos shares with me that Norberto and Julie met and dated at Anderson University before getting married and moving down to Obligado, Paraguay, where Martin and Tabita had begun their mission many decades before. For the next twelve years, Norberto and Julie poured their hearts into the Church of God in Obligado and also helped start a Christian radio station, which has grown to become one of the largest faith-based stations in Paraguay.

"After I met Julie, I really see what a spirit she has to help people," Marcos reflects. "She always said, 'No worries, no problem.' Always content. I never saw her complain."

The sky is growing even darker. The wind is whirling. We eventually hear Coach Briscoe's voice over the press box intercom, announcing to all at Botetourt that the current games need to stop immediately and that the tournament has been delayed.

Marcos continues: "At Julie's memorial service, 3,000 people showed up. Just wanting to say, 'Thank you.' The service was two-and-a-half hours because people kept standing up and saying things about Julie. Julie did more in ten years than most do in their lives."

Cristiane walks toward our picnic table and says to Marcos in Spanish something along the lines of "We need to get going. It's about to storm." All I hear is *vamos* and see her pointing at the sky.

––––––––

This is the first thunderstorm I have witnessed in the valley, and it is a splendid sight—the dark billows climbing over the Blue Ridge and tumbling down those peaks like an avalanche, the rain filling the valley like a pail beneath a spigot.

As everyone flees the invasion, I stand out in the rain for a minute or so, alone, allowing the deluge to drench my face and heaven's grace to wash my eyes. No, this darkness is not the enemy we had all feared. It is much more mysterious, more beautiful, than a binary label like "enemy" or "friend." We think the storm is an enemy because of its magnitude and the fear in us that it evokes, but in this moment, I am finding that the storm is in fact a Love that bends down to embrace us and kiss us in our humanity. Though it comes disguised as an enemy, the darkness is an invitation into intimacy. Into the light.

It is fitting for the day to end like this—with rain—because talking to Marcos for the last four hours and getting lost in his story has been cleansing. Oh, if I could just be lost in a story every hour of every day, all my petty problems—all the chaos in my mind—would dissolve in the wake of these transcending mysteries! And I would always feel clean because I would never feel inclined to leave the place where I feel most free, where I feel most alive, where I am being cleansed and rescued and redeemed, abiding in joy through God's gift of story.

———

We eventually leave the softball diamonds and agree to convene at Charlie and Twila's house. The storm only worsens on the drive there, and many cars are forced to pull over to the side of the road because of the violent rain. I turn into the campus of Hollins University in Roanoke and follow a road up a hill to the right, parking my car so that I am overlooking an open field. I decide that I will wait here until the rain dies down.

As I sit in my car and watch the rain, I am overcome by a sudden urge to run out into the field. I picture myself sprinting across that space and extending my arms, as if about to fly, and catching the rain in my palms. I picture myself sliding into the dirt and gliding across the mud. I picture myself tumbling down a nearby hill, laughing wildly, then regaining my balance at the bottom and sprinting back up the hill and into the open field. It's as if I want to unite myself with the magnificence of this storm in the valley and celebrate its arrival through a reckless display of freedom. It's as if I want my joy back.

But I do not leave my car and sprint out into the storm and slide across the field. Fifteen minutes later, the rain softens to a drizzle; about fifteen minutes after that, I leave.

I am not angry with myself for not running out into the storm. It really would have been quite embarrassing to show up at Charlie and Twila's soaking wet and covered in mud. But as I drive away, I conclude that I am still afraid of entering into the storm and that perhaps I am still far too attached to the idea that the storm is an enemy and that I ought to find more grace in those ominous clouds, for they contain nothing but kisses that fall by the thousands.

———

This road through barren fields—
the golden openness I used to run.
We were Jedis, we were astronauts
from dawn to the setting sun.
I long to run through those fields again.

Now they're painted red
and I cannot put down my phone
to breathe or rest my head
as I drive through these fields alone.
This drive is my life's metaphor—
moving seventy-five through peace, calm
that should transcend the shore
of my chaotic mind.
But most of the time
these fields watch me sail alone.
I want to drive slowly through these fields again, windows down,
Tom Petty on the radio,
sitting seven in a Chevy
and no place to go—
Just me and my best friends
exploring a dirt road
through one of these open fields.
I want to feel free with my friends in these fields again.

But I never will,
so I'll paint it white with stripes
and throw my heart into a script that has no plot, no scene
that belongs to me—
How ironic
for someone consumed in stories
to have no scene,
just an existence

in cities separated by fields
that might bleed meaning
but now lack joy and simplicity.
My deepest fear: losing my creativity.
Sweet dissonance
between who I am and all my memories.
How fickle happiness can be.
How practical we become.
My innocence—
I buried it in that field.
It is a graveyard for us all.
I wish I could dig it up again.

Bones, hidden—
and by no fault but my own.
Is there a choice or is it imminent
that we grow and leave our home?
Jedi, astronaut, child—
Six feet under in that field.
I miss them. Can I have them?
Or is my fate concealed
as I grow older?
I want to sit on His lap again
and rest my head on His chest again,
to sit in Mass and smell the incense
as I sleep on my father's shoulder.
Is this life's meaning?
To venture into the field and regain ourselves?
To find the child we have left?
To discover the gold that once was ours
that the years forced us to neglect?
I want to have gold in my pockets again.
So I'll run into the open.

16

FOG

Today is a new day. I am trying to tell that to myself after last night.

I am wearing a number 9, red-and-white striped Paraguayan soccer jersey to the annual church service this morning. Marcos gave it to me at dinner yesterday evening. I am wearing it, yes, because it looks cool, but also as if to remind myself that yesterday was a good day, a blessing from above—because I was able to spend it with Marcos, one of the humblest and most sacrificial and inspiring men I've ever met. I say that I am trying to remind myself that yesterday was a good day because I had a horrible night last night.

After experiencing such a meaningful and inspiring day with Marcos and a joyous evening in camaraderie with the Briscoes, I retired to my hotel room, lay down in my creaky bed, and felt the oppression of negativity take my heart and mind captive. I don't know what this negativity is or where it comes from or how it strikes so suddenly.

Anyway, I felt the waves crash into me, and I tried to keep my head above the water. I attempted to distract myself by reading a book, but it did not help my situation. I fiddled around on my computer, but it did not help. I thought about looking at pornography, desperate for a temporary escape, but, by the grace of God, resisted the urge, and, praise God, for I would have felt even worse had I followed my longings into such a shameful cave of selfish simplicity. So I tried to go to sleep but could not. Then I tried to read some more but could not. I thought about going on a run, but the workout room was already closed. And, though I tried to resist, the strength of the tide seemed to pull me deeper into the dark, looming waters ... until eventually I went under, and I was suddenly overcome with fear.

Fears about this book. Fears about my finances. Fears about my job at the magazine. Fears about my relationship with the Girl from Indiana. Irrational fears. How easy it is for me to fall from fulfillment to fear, from contentment to loneliness, from divine freedom to earthly bondage. Nights have this effect on me for some reason. I have no idea why. But my soul seems to mirror the hour, as dusk turns to dark and as dark turns to black.

I feel embarrassed this morning. I do not know why I have nights like last night, why I feel the things that I feel, but I cannot help but wonder if I am still adjusting to this new life alone in Charlotte. It has only been a year, after all. Whatever the case, the Girl from Indiana gets the worst of it. Until I deal with my insecurities, whatever they are, I'm probably going to keep projecting them. I am becoming convinced that I am an emotional time bomb—a paranoid and neurotic monster!

Anyway, I guess that, in wearing this Paraguayan soccer jersey to the church service this morning, I am making my inner self aware that I forgive him, no matter what confusing things he felt last night.

I might have nights where my insides are tangled in a knot, but it will not stop me from telling stories during the day.

No, it will not stop me from telling stories during the day.

———

Rain is pounding the roof of the amphitheater in the mountains like a thousand horses' hooves.

The church service is about to start, but before taking a seat, I begin talking to an older gentleman named Rudy, as both of us are standing in the back of the amphitheater.

I met Rudy last year. He is probably in his sixties or seventies, and he is one of those guys whom you feel like you have always known, like a long-lost grandfather or something. His son, Drew, who lives in Florida, plays in the tournament each year, and Rudy used to play alongside him. Rudy can no longer play because his bones can't take the beating they once could, but Rudy and Drew still convene every Labor Day weekend in Roanoke. It's a touching father-and-son story. Like so many stories in Roanoke, theirs is born from the beauty of relationships.

Rudy is a skinny man, about six feet tall or so, and has thick, white hair combed to the side. He wears thin, oval glasses, and he always seems to be sporting sort of a wry smile. Joy seems to radiate from his face, especially whenever he's talking about Drew.

For the last two years, I have felt like I could talk to Rudy all day and never grow bored. He quotes the Bible like it is second nature and seems to know the book better than he knows himself. I've noticed that he still holds hands with his wife in public even after decades of marriage.

As we are talking casually over the battering rain, a picture of the entire Kurrle family appears on the gigantic drop-down screens at the front of the sanctuary.

"Do you know what happened that morning?" Rudy asks me, pointing at the picture.

"No," I say, confused as to what he is referring to. "What do you mean?"

"With Norberto," Rudy replies.

"Oh, no. I have no idea," I say. "I just know that Julie and Timothy died."

Rudy gives me a nervous look, as if to say, "Are you sure you want to know?"

I look into Rudy's eyes, as if to say, "Yes, I do."

He sits down on a plastic fold-out table and crosses his legs.

"Well," he hesitates, "I heard it was really foggy that morning...."

Rudy goes on to tell me that Norberto and Julie were on their way to the capital of Asunción to finalize the papers for their newly-adopted daughter, Anahi. Timothy was sitting in the back seat behind Julie. Anahi was in a car seat behind Norberto. They were on a lonely road in Paraguay, going in and out of a consuming fog, when a truck, recklessly parked halfway in their lane, emerged from the blanketing haze.

Norberto tried to swerve but couldn't in time.

Rudy then tells me that he had heard that Norberto was alone in that foggy desolate place for three whole hours—Anahi alive, but the love of his life dead in the passenger seat. Rudy says that Timothy died in Norberto's arms.

I rub my eyes, pondering this tragedy … as incomprehensible as God.

It feels as if someone has ripped my heart out.

———

It is the beginning of the service, and I am sitting in the back row of the amphitheater alone. A video appears on the screen featuring two people: Norberto—a middle-aged man, handsome, and fit with brownish-blond hair—and a precious blonde little girl who is sitting on his knee. This, I figure, is Anahi. She cannot be more than two years old.

I cannot stop looking at her.

I wonder if she knows.

I wonder if she understands, even vaguely, the tragedy she survived that morning.

I feel warm streaks on my cheeks as I gaze at the innocent, fortunate girl sitting on the knee of her scarred, unfortunate father. As up-and-down as my emotions might be from day to day, I do not know the last time I cried. Anger and angst, I am familiar with; crying, I am not. But in this moment, I am crying. Crushed. Despondent. Heartbroken for this poor man whom I love, though I have never even met him.

But then my mood changes.

My sadness turns to anger.

A righteous wrath consumes me, not in the name of God, but *against* God.

I was taught that God is sovereign—always in control—that He knows the number of days in each of our lives; that He has a plan, not to forsake us, but to give us a hope and a future. Believing that God has a plan has been a comforting thing for me in my own life when it involves a breakup with a girl or deciding what I should do with my life or encountering any type of resistance while writing a book. And oftentimes it seems to be true that God works all things for the good of those who love Him. But, no, I do not think this theology works here. No, I do not think it works when a tree falls on two students by Winona Lake.

As I look into Norberto's empty eyes on the screen, as he gives an update from the Kurrle family in Paraguay to those in attendance at the softball tournament, it is as if whatever remains of a faith I had left is pulled out from under me like a rug. It is as if I discover that all of my doubts about Christianity are no longer doubts: they are revelations of truth. I am forced to reckon with the fact that *if* Norberto's car wreck was indeed ordained—or even allowed—by God, then that God I worship is a psychopath! If I had a daughter and saw a grown man approach her in a store, and if I sat back and watched and I *allowed* him to take her away, then, yes, that would make me a psychopath. If I *planned* for this man to take my daughter, that's even worse.

I recently heard a conservative evangelical clergyman explain away the sudden death of a child in his congregation by suggesting that perhaps God knew that there would be greater pain later on in the child's life, that perhaps the child would have had a long, torturous bout with cancer or something like that, and that, in this sense, a painless death in a car accident is a *gift* from God.

You know what I have to say about that?

I say screw that. And if this book were not being published in the Christian market, I'd use an even stronger word.

That theology is not only total crap but also abusive. If that were the case, if God were *this* involved in our lives, then God could just as easily take away the cancer. It's cruel. Unjust. How can I continue to be a part of religion that worships a psychopath who would destroy the life of this man? A man who committed his life to serving God? Norberto is a missionary, for Christ's sake!

As I watch the video, I have never been more convinced that this whole Christianity thing is a sham. Could it be that Christianity is just a way for insecure people to bring comfort to themselves and meaning to their lives? Could it be that Christianity is just a way for people to explain away their fears and their problems and convince themselves that there's a heaven so that they don't have to deal with anything on earth? When religion is a crutch, you never have to deal with anything.

As Norberto speaks in the video, everyone's eyes are glued to the screen.

I keep thinking about Julie.

I keep thinking about Timothy.

I keep looking at that beautiful little girl on Norberto's lap.

I keep staring deep into Norberto's empty eyes.

My God, no one should have to endure what he is going through.

Now, half of his family is gone.

And today, it is just the two of them.

Norberto and Anahi.

In a way, the little soul on his knee is all he has left.

"I wonder why God took Julie and Timmy when they were doing His work," Norberto says, looking away from the camera, with a pain in his eyes that makes you feel—for a moment—that you, too, have lost your dearest loved ones. "But," he continues, looking up, "I also know there's still work to do."

I keep repeating the words in my head.

There's still work to do. There's still work to do.

How can he claim such a thing?

How does he refuse to give up?

How does he have any semblance of a faith?

When you see someone give everything, the cause he or she believes in becomes extraordinarily real, as if you can touch it or something. And for a second, though I cannot explain it, I feel as if God is sitting right next to me. And I feel as if Norberto's empty eyes are also the hopeless, empty, grieving eyes of Jesus.

YEAR III

17

THE THIRD DRIVE

The year began with such promise, professionally and relationally.

Professionally, I was coming off a year where I had the privilege of coauthoring two books, as I mentioned in the previous section, which was mostly lucky, but good for my career moving forward nonetheless. My writing career, I felt, was on the brink of really beginning.

Relationally, things were also on the upswing. Don't get me wrong: my relationship with the Girl From Indiana was rocky in the fall. I would often push her to the edge in an effort to manufacture honesty, for I was desperate for honesty. I would shove our relationship to the edge, as if experimenting to see if it would fall. It was all pretty manipulative, I admit. But manipulation is the most natural thing to do when personal insecurities are suppressed.

Everything, however, seemed to change in Las Vegas, where I flew to be with her, her mother, and her stepfather to celebrate Christmas. One night she and I walked up and down the streets of that splendid city, that neon glow in the barren desert, and we eventually found ourselves standing outside the Bellagio, awed by the fountains on the pond that danced in glowing beams beneath the hotel's luminescent crown. Then we walked into that baroque castle, with its marble floors and cream-colored archways and Greek-style pillars, past domed ceilings and bronze sculptures, talking and window-shopping at those high-end stores, carrying our shopping bags and feeling like royalty. And that's when she led me into a store that radiated with fluorescent blue, painting patterns on the marble hall. *A jewelry store.*

She guided me into a corner and then pointed out a ring, and I could hardly believe what was happening. One month before, our relationship was on the fringes; now our eyes sparkled with silver. Suddenly our future seemed to be as clear as the glass cases beneath our fingertips and as promising as the diamond display inside. Finally, we were on the same page. We were pressing forward, through it all.

I entered the New Year with nothing to fear. But maybe this is when one should in fact be most afraid—when one is dependent on circumstance to eradicate fear.

———

Mamaw died on January 16. It was unexpected. She was eighty-seven.

Has there ever been a woman more selfless than my Mamaw, my father's mother, who welcomed my two uncles, John and Phil, into her home when they were in high school and eventually adopted them, providing them with a family and, more than that, with the love and support that helped them to become the kind, generous people they are today? It didn't matter how small their home was. It didn't matter how unforeseen the adoption of two more teenage boys might have been. She and Sleepyhead, her husband, understood that human life defies human logic. Mamaw taught us all that life is, simply, about loving others through our actions.

I think I will always remember standing in the halls of St. Joseph's Catholic Church in Elwood, Indiana—where Mamaw had been a faithful member for over eight decades—and holding her ebony casket with my uncles and noticing tears on both of their cheeks before carrying her into that cathedral.

Few know this, but Mamaw is one reason why I write. Each morning she would methodically sit in her living room, gripping her red ink pen, and circle errors in the *Elwood Call-Leader* and *Indianapolis Star* as she read every article. She always found several. In my youth, I would print off my work for her, those stupid books about flying dogs, and, though she would circle my typos, she would also tell me, each time, that my stories were good and that she enjoyed them. I always called her "my editor"—I think it made me feel like a journalist or something.

I miss her. And I miss her stupid red pen that made me better because that's what she did: make those who she loved better.

————

I returned to Indianapolis one month later to celebrate my two-year anniversary with the Girl from Indiana, and, though we had a lot of fun, I could also tell that something had drastically changed. I say "changed"—and that's how it felt—but the truth is that, for so long, we had both just been in denial of the reality that we were not supposed to be together. After all, I did not know who I was. I was giving all that I possibly could and trying to love the best that I could, but how in the world was I supposed to legitimately consider marrying someone when I had no idea who I was at the core of my being and was therefore so needy for the love and affirmation of another in order to fill the void? It was a recipe for disaster.

Thankfully, she had the courage to confront our denial. On my final day, I remember trying to kiss her, but she did not kiss me back. Never had she felt so distant. I tried to kiss her again, and it was like kissing a corpse. Her lips were cold with apathy. I walked away, leaned against her bedroom wall, and, though she lovingly pursued me and comforted me in my teary-eyed confusion, I somehow knew that we were done, that, as wonderful as Las Vegas was, all that we had long suppressed was now rising to the surface. I would, at last, be forced to confront myself.

I would never see her again, that blonde Midwestern girl who taught me to love once more, who taught me that relationships can be fun, whom I will forever be thankful for. She and I took a weeklong break, and my roommate slept next to me on an adjacent couch in the living room each night, meeting me in my shock and anxiety, as I was forced to fathom a future without her, blindsided by rejection. Then we officially broke up at the end of February, and as I heard her voice for the last time, while wandering around the parking lot at work and talking to her on my cell phone, I pleaded my final case, entirely exhausted from the steady rising of all my fears that only seemed to reaffirm my deepest insecurities—most notably that I was unlovable, too different, too this, too that, that my love wasn't enough and therefore I wasn't enough. And when she told me her decision—which freed me from my deceiving optimism—I bluntly told her that I hoped she was certain, for if this was what she wanted, then I would surely leave and disappear forever, dissolving into her history.

She told me she was certain.

I told her I loved her.

Then I told her goodbye.

This time I, too, was cold like her lips, numb to the core, emotionless.

I immediately left work and went to my apartment. There I saw my roommate and told him I was going to go play golf in the rain. As he stared into the eyes of shame personified—I had given my whole heart and still failed—he told me that I looked sick and pale and that I shouldn't be alone.

I decided not to golf in the rain.

————

In the midst of such confusion—my first time experiencing the death of a loved one and my first experience with heartbreak—I found myself thinking often about Norberto.

Ever since I saw that tournament video last year—Norberto sitting in front of the camera, just months after the tragic car accident that robbed him of his wife and son, his adopted one-year-old daughter Anahi sitting innocently on his lap, blissfully ignorant of her family's tragic story—his words have been tattooed on the very fabric of my soul. How he looked into the camera, broken and confused, and somehow said, "I wonder why God took Julie and Timmy when they were doing His work, but I also know there's still work to do."

No, I would not dare to compare my own struggles to something as unexplainable as what Norberto has endured. Romantic heartbreak and the death of a loved one are natural losses that almost everyone goes through. They just happened to be hitting all at once for me. But those five words—*there's still work to do*—have strengthened me nonetheless this past year. Somehow, in the wake of unfathomable tragedy and unknowing, Norberto had found the strength to utter those words. He had found a way to gravitate toward meaning and something redemptive.

Where did his strength come from? What did he have that I did not have? What were the truths and treasures deep within him that allowed him to claim and cling to such profundities? Could he say such a thing because he knew who he was?

———

But at first, in my heartbreak and its fallout, I did not have the strength to say those words "There's still work to do." In fact, I got bitter instead of better and started living out of a reactive state. Whenever I was emotionally triggered, I would be so confused by what I was feeling that I would often react in an unhealthy way—which was oftentimes lust or, even worse, lustful vengeance, as if making out with a stranger could prove my manhood, as if getting drunk at a party would help me to forget about my problems. I was running from my brokenness. I was running from myself. Antipathy seemed to be the most accessible thing. My heartbreak turned to anger—not even so much against her, but more against God. It sometimes felt as if He was teasing me. Though I had felt God's guidance in other aspects of my life, when it came to dating, it felt as if I were a mule and God had tied a carrot to my head, laughing at me as I chased it around the barnyard, as I gave my all yet was unable to grab hold of what I so deeply desired. A humiliating thing it is to be the dumbass that is always chasing the carrot, thinking all along that he is making headway.

This combination of doing things I had never done in my personal life and making personal accusations against God that I had never made led to an even more amplified sense of guilt and shame—that I was indeed a mistake and a failure and a sinner. My pain had brought to the surface the crisis that was already there. And because of all the things I had done—the innocence that I had shed—now I felt like there was even more that I had to do to repair my broken relationship with God. More to prove. More of a penance to be paid. But why would I even want to repair something with Someone who tortured me with carrots? Why would I get back onto the treadmill?

But it was there, in the doubt and unknowing, in the pain and despair, in the brokenness and vulnerability, that God found me.

———

One day I was at a Starbucks in Southend (a neighborhood just south of uptown Charlotte), walking back to my table after using the restroom, when I made eye contact with a bearded man in the corner. Looking back, it didn't even make sense that I was in that Southend Starbucks because I lived thirty minutes away and drove by a handful of Starbucks shops on the way to Southend. But the next thing I knew, the bearded man and I were shaking hands and talking, then sitting down at a table and continuing our conversation.

He told me that his name was Dave Hickman and that he was writing a book but needed help compiling some of the content. When I told him that I helped people tell stories for a living, it was as if we both realized that perhaps there was something mysterious happening between us.

Dave told me that his book was going to be titled *Union > Relationship* or something like that. He wanted to write the book because the pressures of carrying on a "growing and intimate relationship with God"—as the church had told him for most of his life—had only led him to exhaustion, depression, and a performance-based spirituality, which ultimately revealed itself in a crippling panic attack in the middle of the night. For Dave, pursuing Christ was not only tiring but was also, in practical terms, not at all healthy. Atheism, I was also realizing at this point in my life, was perhaps a healthier option than following my treadmill God.

After a period of allowing the fog to clear, Dave said, he got a prescription for Prozac, went to counseling, and met regularly with a theologian and author named Fil Anderson, a dear friend of the late writer Brennan Manning. Fil began to guide Dave through a reading of the scriptures that involved a different lens— one of union, not one of relationship. *Relationship*, Dave told me, can carry with it such a negative connotation. We've all had relationships that required lots of hard work and maintenance. Most people have had relationships in this life that have failed. We bring all kinds of baggage to the word *relationship*. Yes, relationships can be beautiful things, too, but Dave seemed to be explaining to me that the word *relationship*, when it came to God, was a good start, but did not take things far enough. God was *closer than close* (this would end up being the title of his book) to us. Closer than we could possibly imagine.

As you might expect, it did not take long for me to feel drawn to Dave Hickman's story. Never had I heard a gospel like this before. Though I was yet to have a panic attack, I, too, felt exhausted from my treadmill spirituality and was yet to encounter the right church or theology to free me from the ideas that had become ingrained in my mind over the years. God always felt so distant. And whenever I approached Him, it usually had something to do with guilt or shame, and it always ended with a prayer that went something like "I'll do better next time, God. Please forgive me."

Maybe Dave Hickman could be the conduit for truth in my life as Fil Anderson had been for him. I don't think Dave realized it that day, but I needed him more in my life than he needed me for his book.

———

Dave Hickman and I continued meeting throughout the summer.

I provided him with some thoughts about the structure and direction of his book, and, in telling me more about his story and the theology behind the mystery of union, he provided me with structure and direction for my life.

Finally, after two years of deconstructing my faith, a magnificent reconstruction began to take place. And for the first time—and I really mean the first time—I began to awaken to who I was at the very core of my being, in my spirit. The fullness of Love was at my core; not sinfulness. Oneness was at my core; not incompleteness. I began to *rest in God* rather than *exhausting myself trying* to please Him. I began to become more aware of what was already true of me *in Christ* rather than guiltily thinking I must check all kinds of items off my spiritual checklist for my relationship with God to be healthy and vibrant. I began to look less at my performance and rest more in what God had already done and was currently doing. I began to live out of a place of original blessing rather than original sin—for at the very core of my being was the power and wholeness and sufficiency of *Spirit*. I began to live out of a place of fullness rather than a place of lack or incompleteness. I began to *abide* instead of *strive*. I began to be changed *by* grace, which was far more effective than attempting to change from a place of guilt or shame, as if to somehow attain grace. I actually began to sin less because I recognized that I was carrying God into that sin, and why would I want to do something like that when God risked indwelling me? I began to discover God as I delved deeper into myself, for this was where God resided—within—through the mystery of the Holy Spirit. Inside of me was a universe that I had not yet dared to explore, and now I was exploring it!

All of a sudden, strange mystical passages like John 17:20-26, Christ's prayer before he was arrested, began to make more sense:

*"My prayer is not for them alone. I pray also for those who will believe in me through their message, that all of them may be **one**, Father, just as you are **in** me and I am **in** you. May they also be **in us** so that the world may believe that you have sent me. I have given them the glory that you gave me, that they may be **one** as we are **one**—I **in** them and you **in** me—so that they may be brought to **complete unity**. Then the world will know that you sent me and have loved them even as you have loved me.*

"Father, I want those you have given me to be with me where I am, and to see my glory, the glory you have given me because you loved me before the creation of the world.

*"Righteous Father, though the world does not know you, I know you, and they know that you have sent me. I have made you known to them and will continue to make you known in order that the love you have for me may be **in** them and that I myself may be **in** them." [emphasis mine]*

Never had I tasted the beauty of such love and grace. Not before exploring the theology of union, the mystery of oneness with God, which, though impossible to put fully into words, is, to me, allowing myself to engage in John 17 experientially— trusting that I am being animated, in and through, by something that is bigger than myself, the Author of love, the Creator of life; that there is a mysterious depth to reality and to my very being; that perhaps there is an interconnectedness of all things that reflects this boundless love and grace. I've heard it said that no mystic would ever claim to be one with God, and neither do I, but that is because I have tasted of something that I must endlessly explore. No matter, my starting place is one of Indwelling Love, union; and therefore to hate myself is to hate God; to give in to shame is to arrogantly say that God's love and grace isn't big enough. There wasn't a single part of my being that was inherently bad, not with Spirit at my core. Did my body—my flesh—have unhealthy cravings? Yes, of course; but my body also allowed me to dance and to hug a hurting friend and to sprint into the ocean. Did my soul—my heart and mind, my emotions and intellect—have blind spots? Yes, of course; but my soul also allowed me to cry with someone who was suffering and to get lost in a good book and to examine my life. My Spirit wanted to gently infiltrate every aspect of my being.

Christianity, of all things, which often times felt to be the cause of my shame, was suddenly inviting me to leave my rigid biblical code behind, along with all my idolatrous formulas, and simply *experience* the mystery and wonder and beauty of God's love, which is Life. God went from being "way out there" to living within me and through me, every second of every day, for this is the message of Emmanuel—Christ *with* us—and of the Advocate—Christ *in* us, our oneness—a gift that Christ said was, somehow, even more valuable to his disciples than his bodily presence.

How had I missed all of this in my theology?

God had always been there, within me, but I had never been aware of what was already true! Now this seems to be the great spiritual journey for me: not exhausting myself arriving at some place, but instead opening my eyes to *what already is*. It was as if, in my theological foundation of total depravity and corruption, I could not possibly comprehend that the God of the universe would *want* to live within me, for I was just a sinner in the hands of an angry God, an insect dangling on a slender thread over a fire, as Jonathan Edwards, a minister in the 1700s, once said. I had always told myself that I was worthless, prone to sin, incapable of doing any good. But the mystery of union gave me worth because, by God's indwelling, there was a spring of unfathomable grace, an inner river! When you stare into the gentle eyes of an infant child, is it like looking into the eyes of a sinner or into the eyes of God? It was God's breath in the Genesis poem that made Adam a *living* being, and the same was true with me. Spirit, the breath of the divine, was at my core, which meant that, even though the world might be broken, Love was the truest thing about me. "Who am I?" wrote the late monk and Author Thomas Merton. "I am one loved by Christ."

This is who I am: I am deeply loved.

My spiritual journey is no longer one of attaining something that is "out there" but is instead a steady awakening to what is already true "in here," in the depths of my being.

I am who I am, and I am loved.

Just as Grace College up in Indiana sent me on an intellectual journey, Dave Hickman sent me on a journey of internal awakening down in North Carolina. Such is the nature of the spiritual life: there is always someone or something that can inspire us to move to the next level of faith and consciousness. Though the sadness and grief in my life remained, my anger was replaced by joyous God-discovery. I began reading more than ever before, particularly the works of Brennan Manning, author of *Ragamuffin Gospel,* whose words overall challenged me to accept my own acceptance, to simply awaken to what was already true and accept what I was seeing—that I was united with God, that I was loved—and to abandon the performance treadmill once and for all. Though my loneliness remained and was perhaps heightened because of the feelings of rejection and betrayal I had experienced that year, these complexities also served to be gateways for my inner monk and artist to emerge. Solitude became more accessible.

Do I still have doubts about my faith? Of course I have doubts about my faith. I think I always will. But as Anne Lamott says, "The opposite of faith is not doubt, but certainty." I have yet to find an answer, nor do I think I will find an answer, to explain the mystery of suffering. Why would Norberto, who had committed his life to serving God in the mission field, lose his wife and only son? I do not know. But now I think I *do* understand how Norberto could even dare to say something like "There's still work to do." Maybe Norberto has a profound understanding of his union with God as one who is deeply loved.

One evening during one of my brainstorming sessions with Dave Hickman, he shared with me a quote from the great Protestant missionary Hudson Taylor. I cannot think of a better summary of my spiritual journey thus far this year:

To **let** my loving Savior work in me **His will**, my sanctification, is what I would live for by His grace. Abiding, not striving nor struggling; looking off unto Him; trusting Him for present power; resting in the love of an almighty Savior ... —this is not new, and yet 'tis **new to me**. I feel as though the first dawning of a glorious day had risen upon me. I hail it with trembling, yet with trust. I seem to have got to the edge only, but of a sea which is boundless; to have sipped only, but of that which fully satisfies. Christ literally **all** seems to me now the power, the **only** power for service; the only ground for unchanging

joy. May He lead us into the realization of His unfathomable fullness.
(Dr. and Mrs. Howard Taylor, Hudson Taylor and the China Inland
Mission: The Growth of a Work of God (Littleton, CO: OMF International,
1996), 169.)

As I continued to learn from Dave Hickman, I could feel God leading me into the realization of unfathomable fullness. This concept itself was not new, but it was new to me. And it was this unfathomable fullness, this divine union, this steady awakening to "Christ in me, the hope of glory"—all that was already true about me at the core of my existence—that slowly began to eradicate my shame and restore my self-worth. If I were—if I am—one and full and whole and loved in the deepest parts of my being, not empty and broken and sinful, then that changed everything. It freed me from the exhaustion of running on the treadmill trying to get close to God because, through the mystery of the Holy Spirit, I was already as close to God as I could possibly be.

Not only have I abandoned the treadmill, but I've also concluded that it wasn't God who put it there: It was my *perception* of God, my conceptual idol of God, that put it there. And maybe God isn't wrathful at the core. Maybe God is loving. Maybe Jesus didn't have to be crucified to absorb the wrath of God. Maybe it wasn't so transactional, so substitutionary. Maybe Jesus, instead, revealed what was truest about the nature of God—that God *loves* us beyond all measure and will go impossible lengths to be *with* us, even if it means becoming human, even if it means death on a cross.

Maybe I don't need to run after all.

Maybe God is running toward me.

Maybe growing spiritually is about allowing this loving image of God running toward me to permeate every aspect of my being.

Maybe this is something of what it meant to awaken to this unfathomable fullness, this loving indwelling.

Maybe John 17:22 is true: maybe I am glorious; maybe I am mysteriously animated by the breath of Life.

———

Papaw, my mother's father, died at the beginning of August, the day before my birthday.

Had he lasted three more weeks, he would have celebrated his fifty-fourth wedding anniversary with Grandma. *Fifty-four years.* His love for Grandma did not hinge upon a feeling or a circumstance; it flowed from his unwavering commitment to her, and hers to him. In a chaotic world where things are constantly changing, going to Grandma and Grandpa's house for holidays and special occasions was a form of consistency for all of us. It was always a reminder of what love could be, what life could be, and what God was: consistent, always present.

Papaw and I rarely had serious conversations when we were together, but we always had fun. We spent our time together mostly relaxing in his basement—Papaw in his cloth navy recliner and me in a beige leather recliner—watching college basketball games for hours, falling in and out of sleep, then waking up and having playful arguments about sports. Papaw loved basketball—especially local basketball—that is, unless it had to do with the Indiana Hoosiers, whom he vowed to forever despise when they fired his idol Bobby Knight in 2000. And, though Papaw and I rarely had serious conversations, our last conversation was the most serious one we have ever had.

I remember my mother calling me one August afternoon, while I was in Charlotte working in the offices of the sports magazine and telling me that Papaw wasn't doing well. I didn't know what that meant exactly, but she gave it to me very bluntly: "We're worried that he doesn't have much longer."

When my mother told me all of this on the phone, I thought she might be overreacting. But when I called him on my cell phone in our office parking lot—while taking cover beneath an overhang as a routine Southern afternoon shower fell upon Charlotte—and heard his faint, broken voice on the other end of the line, I immediately knew that something was not right. He was not the same. He was weak, the weakest I had ever heard him. Suddenly I felt scared. This was the very reason why I had always feared being in Charlotte, ten hours away, because of moments like this. First Mamaw. Now him. Was it worth it, being this removed from the people I loved the most? Just to pursue a dream that would inevitably fade when I dissolved into the soil?

I did not know what to say to him, so I started telling him about a new book project that I was going to coauthor with a family in Indiana, the Zellers, whose last name was like royalty in Indiana basketball circles. I knew Papaw would enjoy hearing about the project because, one, he loved hearing about what I was writing, and, two, he loved Indiana basketball and was a fan of the Zellers. The book was going to be written from their parents' perspective as they shared stories about raising three sons—boys who were just as successful off the hardwood as they were on the hardwood because of their character and integrity.

"I just want you to know that I am going to work on it for you," I told him. "Anyone who gave me someone like my mom had to have been an amazing parent. And you're an amazing grandpa."

In that moment, I do not recall hearing much on the other end of the telephone. Maybe it was because he was quiet and weak, or maybe it was the soft pattering of rain on the metal roof above, but I'll never forget the words I heard him faintly say: "You're a special grandson."

You are special.

Three words that God says to us each and every day.

In Papaw's weakest moment, he was sharing the gospel with me.

He died the next day.

I was hurting inside, but I also remember feeling mysteriously comforted by something that was bigger than myself, something divine, as if I were not alone, as if I could feel God running toward my suffering. As Dave Hickman once said to me, "God is big enough to be that small," for if God was willing to be dwindled from "infinity to infancy," then surely God can also meet us where we're at in our losses and our struggles and our angst. My soul was broken, but because of this "with-ness," it was as if my spirit were an infinite well of hope.

A few days later, I delivered the eulogy at Papaw's funeral, and, though I do not remember much about what I said, I do remember telling everyone there that I wanted to write that book for him. It is sobering to write something for someone knowing he will never read it. And yet I am led to believe that my God of unfathomable grace will let him read it, someway, somehow; and maybe Papaw can give a rough draft of the manuscript to Mamaw, there in heaven, and she can circle all my typos and convince the saints to intercede on my behalf throughout the editing process in order to preserve the sanity of their perfectionist grandson.

I miss my Papaw and my Mamaw.

———

Uncle John's wife, my Aunt Becky, died a month later. It was a suicide. Sometimes I wonder if she, in attending Papaw's funeral, realized where she wanted to be: not here. Though I did not know this until after her death, I guess she had wrestled with depression for much of her adult life. It did not matter that she worked full-time as a church secretary or was married to one of the most jovial, sacrificial men I know, my Uncle John. She had an illness.

I know that whatever Aunt Becky was going through was beyond my comprehension, but I cannot help but feel flooded with anger at this stage in my grieving. My Uncle John has gone through too much this year. In a seven-month span, he lost the mother who adopted him and his wife of sixteen years. No one should have to experience what he saw that horrific day when he walked into his house.

I do not know how much more my family can handle this year.

There is hardly any time to process anything at all.

In Norberto's words and in Dave Hickman's teachings—that help me to awaken to the all-accessible spring within and enter into its infinite depth—I will continue to find my strength.

———

I was broken from the year's wave of losses.

But this time I was "broken" in a different aspect of my being.

No longer in my spirit, the source of my identity crisis.

This time I was broken in my soul.

See, as transformative and freeing as my spiritual discovery had been at the core of my being—my spirit—the year's wave of losses had left my *soul* in a complicated, chaotic state: vulnerable, fragile, wounded. I suppose what I'm saying is that theology—a healthy understanding of who one is at a core level— can perhaps free us from ourselves and help us to cope with the world, but it in no way frees us from the hardships of the world. There will always be a tension. There will always be complexities in our hearts and our minds. There will always be voids within our souls, an abyss. Love can perhaps saturate the pain but cannot possibly eradicate it. It's the world we live in.

This pain and confusion, stemming from all the loss, left my soul in a suspended state of ambivalence. I had left shame behind, but my soul was unpredictable. My mind would be at rest—content with all that is—one second, then react out of desperation the next; my emotions would be at ease one second, then overwhelming the next. Internally, there was a peace in my spirit but a steady conflict in my soul. Union seemed to breathe life into my identity crisis but did not fix the depth of my hurting. Externally, I had no mental or emotional construct to adequately handle the losses of the year, so I kept running to different material things, whether it be a new project or a new romantic pursuit, believing that it could be my soul's salvation.

A couple weeks ago, for example, I had the feeling—for perhaps the first time this year—that a sliver of positivity might unfold in my personal life. For the last several months, I have been talking to a girl, a special girl, another one of those mysterious creatures called blondes. We became close friends and helped one another through the grief of our previous relationships. Also, she's a counselor (she doesn't charge me either), which is probably good for me, since many have told me that I ought to go to therapy. But I don't want to go to therapy. I don't want to be viewed as weak.

Anyway, we decided to start dating. It didn't take us long, however, to realize that it felt as if we were throwing our hearts into a blender—being in another long-distance relationship—and that we were both too hurt from our previous relationships to do that again. So, two days ago, we decided to call it quits.

It was a fling, at best, but as I drive up to this holy ground in the mountains, old wounds feel fresh once more, as if the sword went in yesterday. I obviously have not dealt with the pain from this year. I am still far too needy, I think, for the love and affection of another. I am far too insecure—perhaps no longer so much in my spirit, in my identity, but in my soul, the complexities of my heart and mind. I must allow this newfound spirituality to permeate every aspect of my being.

I know that this involves somehow confronting all the inner turmoil swirling around in my soul, all the loss and the heartbreak from this year, yet I have no idea how to effectively dissect each painful element of loss. How does one begin again? Where does one begin? I am desperate to begin again. Is therapy the key? It all sounds way too dramatic. It's not like I'm depressed or anything. Or am I?

At least now I have a starting place for knowing who I am. I will try to cling to the reality that God is in me and with me—that I am one with the divine and can therefore begin to confront my pains and wounds with the power and fullness of my inherent identity. I will try to choose to believe what Norberto said in the video: that there is still work to do. And that pain is never the loss of a plot. Rather, it is the beginning of a beautiful story.

———

Where do you go,
sweet self, sweet love,
sailing adrift into the night,
dissolving soft into the black?

Why so silent,
small self, small love,
as I'm left here on the shoreline
fighting your apathy's attack?

Will you return,
lost self, lost love,
or is this your farewell flight,
your great escape from all I lack?

Do you align,
true self, true love,
when morning colors drown the night
and Love stabs me in the back?

18

VOICES IN THE VALLEY

I nstead of driving up to Roanoke on Friday as I usually do, I arrive at Botetourt at a quarter past ten on Saturday morning.

Not only am I in need of a retreat because of all the loss this year, but I also need a retreat because I am far too absorbed in work. Since Papaw's passing, I have decided to say yes to any project that comes my way, as if one hundred yeses will somehow heal the complexities in my soul, though I must admit the work does distract me, which, for now, is what I need to press forward through the heaviness. Working, I suppose, is my bandage, though I am sure that I will eventually have to deal with what is underneath. For now, however, these mountains are what my soul needs; these stories, the antidote for my heart and mind.

After exchanging our typical joyous hellos and how-do-you-dos with Coach and some of his family outside the press box at Botetourt, I tell Coach that I am going to retire to the top floor of the press box for most of the day, where I will write and interview anyone he sends my way.

———

As I walk up the stairs to the press box, step into that silent, sacred space on the third floor, and gaze out at the mountains in the distance, my mind becomes flooded with memories from the year before. I think of the storm that slid down the mountains and sent players scurrying for the parking lot and into their cars … and how I stood in the rain for a bit, not wanting to move, soaked, watching the lightning, mesmerized as if it were a fireworks show. I look at the mountains now, over at the spot where the storm conquered them a year before. Now the sun is beaming over them; the sky, a naked blue.

"*Welcome home, old friend,*" the mountains say to me.

"I'm a different person this year," I tell them.

"*We know,*" they say. "*But can't you see that we are the same? Our appearance may change with the seasons: we are lush in the spring, as flowers sprinkle our feet; a darker green in the summer; a speckled mosaic of burning orange and amber in the fall; and dressed in the bride gown of winter. But can't you see that these are the colors of my love, in every phase and every season? Though we reveal ourselves to the valley in hues and shades, can't you see that our silhouettes, stenciled today into this open Virginia sky, will always be the same?*"

"What does all this mean?" I ask.

"*Life is nothing more than the valley in which you live. Yes, there are joys— plenty of joys if you wish to see all in the valley through the lens of our colors, for all is gray without the colors of our love. But there is also inevitable pain in the valley, and this is what makes where you live the valley. You were not made for the valley, Beloved. Yet beauty will be revealed in these peaks. And it is all for you.*

"*At the start, we did not have to display our splendor, but we chose to do so anyway, not to pound our chests or flaunt our glory, but rather to comfort you, so that you can see us, and even be with us, while you journey through the valley. Your wonder for the unchanging stencil of our peaks, and the varying displays of our love, will help you to persevere in the valley. One day you will hike up these slopes—and it will be an enjoyable hike, not an exhausting hike! —and rest on these ledges, and you will look down and reflect on your journey through the valley. Mountains and canyons, hills and valleys—none would exist in a two-dimensional world. But would you rather breathe—love and cry, live and die—or live as a cartoon on a screen?*"

"I do not want to be a cartoon," I say. "So when will I be able to rest on your ledges? When I die?"

"*No, nothing of this world is your home. Not even the mountains. After you rest on these ledges, I will then ask you to return to the valley, just as I asked Moses to do when I held him on Mount Sinai. Our peaks are not your home, yet they are a reflection of your home. The mountaintop is a thin place, where heaven seems to meet earth, but our peaks rise from the same ground where the valley caves. Your ground is our ground. Our ground is your ground. I am the ground of your very being. We are here with you. When you grow weary, do not forget to look at the unchanging outline in the sky and experience all the colors of our love. Most importantly, remember the ground. This space between heaven and earth is thinner than you might think."*

19

STORIES FROM
THE THIRD-STORY

Coach has been sending person after person up to the top floor of the press box for the last hour and a half. After two years of meeting and talking to lots of people here at the tournament, you'd think that I would have talked to everyone by now. Not the case. Today, I have been interviewing people I have never even seen before. If it weren't for my computer crashing two years back, when I lost all my interviews from my first year in attendance, I'm convinced I would have over thirty hours of audio files on my computer. I lost some good stories when my computer crashed. Also, I cried when I lost them. I really did. And then I thought about how I would never amount to a respectable journalist because I lose my interviews before publication. So I cried again. And then I pictured myself, sometime in the future, on the brink of breaking a big investigative piece for *The New York Times*, having just conducted a breakthrough interview or something, only to accidentally drop my voice recorder down a sewage drain before I could back it up to my computer, and losing all my data once more, because of water damage and poop damage. I did not cry when I thought of this, but I did consider never writing again. Because of the possibility of poop damage.

Anyway, some of the people who have talked with me today have shared some pretty gripping stories. Others have simply gushed over how much the tournament means to them, which is fine, but I don't want this book to be a public relations piece for an obscure softball tournament. I write about this weekend in Virginia simply because this sacred space moves me in a way that helps me, and many others, to get in touch with their true selves.

This press box is my monastery this weekend.

————

Coach walks through the press box doors once more, this time with a physically-fit bald man wearing eyeblack; he looks like he is probably in his low forties. Coach introduces us. His name is Bobby Roe Jr., which is a cool name with a neat sound. He confidently shakes my hand, grinning widely. Coach leaves us alone, and after some small talk, we take a seat and look out the press box windows at one of the fields below.

"That's my family down there," he says, pointing to a woman sitting behind the chained backstop at home plate. She is holding a baby in her arms.

I have no idea how to react whenever someone shows me a baby, so I give him an "Awwww" hoping that this might suffice. I think it did.

"Where is your family from?" I ask.

"Alaska," he laughs.

"Seriously?" I say.

"Yep," he tells me. "I bring a team from Alaska every year. We wouldn't miss this tournament for the world. I'd write a $10,000 check today to be here, no question."

I shake my head in disbelief.

"Why is this place so special to you?" I ask.

At this point, a couple of Coach Briscoe's nieces and nephews burst through the press box doors and start running around like playful dogs. Bobby kind of shoos them away, as if indicating that he is about to talk about something personal with me—about to voyage into something that is dark and messy—and they, thankfully, run back down the stairs as if chasing a bone. I am tempted to yell, "No kids in the monastery!" but I myself don't feel like yelling in the monastery.

"Last year," Bobby says, looking down at his wife and baby once more, "I would say I was an alcoholic." He pauses. "I would associate playing softball with drinking beer, and I'd drink a lot, you know. I'd drink so much, and get in a groove, and I got to the point where I thought that I had to have five or six in me before I even took the mound and played."

But his drinking didn't only take place in the realm of softball. Bobby explains to me his unique lifestyle—how his job consists of spending two weeks at a time laboring in the oil fields in the Alaska North Slope before having the next two weeks off at home in Anchorage. When he returned home, his idle time often resulted in him drinking excessively with his friends.

"Drinking was causing problems in my life," Bobby says.

Before last year's softball tournament in Roanoke, Bobby told his wife that he was going to quit drinking. She didn't believe him.

"Telling my wife 'I'm sorry' wasn't cutting it anymore," he says. "I would apologize but then still drink. 'I'm sorry' didn't mean anything."

Their marriage was on the cusp of ending.

"You go to Roanoke, get your head straight, and figure out what you want," she told him before he left.

They didn't talk for a week.

At the church service last year, Bobby admitted to his powerlessness in front of his teammates and vulnerably knelt at the altar. Bobby hasn't had a sip of alcohol since. Empowered by God and supported by his dear friends and teammates, he quit. Cold turkey. This weekend, he is one year sober.

Bobby points at his wife below once more, who is fumbling with a bag while holding their baby.

"Our baby daughter was born on Easter Sunday this year," he says. "We adopted her the next day."

His willingness to leave behind an old life led to new life.

His resurrected life led to fullness.

"I woke up this morning," Bobby says softly, "and I had my beautiful baby to look at, my wife, and I have not had one argument with her since I decided to stop drinking.… My life has opened up so much. It's the best feeling I've ever had."

Bobby eventually stands up to leave. I shake his hand and thank him for opening up to me. I don't think I would be so transparent if I were Bobby.

And yet this is the culture at this tournament: brokenness and transparency; humanity at its core.

————

A couple of months ago, I was walking through SouthPark Mall, an upscale shopping mall in Charlotte, lurking around in the shadows of the upper class. I remember walking by a department store and seeing a couple of stone-faced mannequins in the windowsill; they were dressed in long-sleeved plaid shirts, leg-tight chinos, and leather boots. If I owned that particular outfit, I am convinced that I would talk to girls with such confidence that I might actually get a date with one. And then, over dinner or drinks, she would find out that I was a writer and feel embarrassingly deceived. And then I would cast all of my insecurities upon her just to make her squirm and teach her to never again trust a man wearing a $200 outfit … because he is probably hiding something.

Anyway, something about looking at those mannequins in the department store window made me consider how horrible an existence those poor hunks of plastic had. How tragic it would be to be a mannequin! They try to appear human, but beneath their seemingly flawless image and desirable accessories is nothing but hollowed-out plastic. Mannequins must be the worst of all inanimate objects. They are fakes of things. They look flashy and attractive on the exterior, but they have no internal significance. They appear human but are empty within.

And yet what makes them especially tragic is that these mannequins are more like us than we realize. They are our mirrors. We are so afraid of vulnerability that we'd rather sit in a department store, alone, gathering dust, exhausting ourselves trying to look good. Through our careers. Through our pictures on social media. Through the proud showcasing of the American Dream we've attained. A tragedy, it is, to live like we are hollow—and I did that in my spirit for far too long. Now perhaps it is time for the expedition into my soul. Though I admit that I am afraid of the unknown parts of myself. What will the voyage reveal?

In contrast to the mannequins, not long after my little visit to the mall, I attended an Alcoholics Anonymous meeting with the girl I mentioned earlier. She needed to attend one for her master's degree in counseling or something like that, so I said that I would go with her. I would go wherever her blonde hair went. It was the only way.

Anyway, sitting in AA was like being in the upper room at Pentecost. Being there in that smoky trailer in a tiny town in Georgia, surrounded by hungry, thirsty, shattered souls who treated community and God like the alcohol they craved, gave me the feeling that this was exactly the way Jesus intended the church to be. As I sat in that room, as each person who stood up admitted that he or she was an alcoholic, as those who had gathered said, "Hello, ____" to the alcoholic—accepting them for who they were and giving the broken soul dignity in calling them by name—and as the speaker that evening talked, teary-eyed, about the warm, smooth burn of Smirnoff vodka that tore up his esophagus and his family, I felt like a mannequin in a room overflowing with life. Yes, life.

They were genuine. Authentic. Transparent. Unashamedly themselves. At the bottom of their pain, they found joy. In their brokenness, they found hope. These people were not prideful people, too embarrassed to admit their shortcomings, too worried about looking good in a department store window. These people were broken, beautiful people who needed each other and needed God, people who were held together by the enemy they all had in common.

The Pharisees in Jesus' day looked good like a window display. But it was the prostitutes and adulterers and tax collectors who could admit their need for Jesus, their need to pursue the way of love. The Pharisees had religion. But the "sinners" had the living Christ. Religion without relationship—without union— both with God and each other, is nothing more than a plaid button-up. Religion is a headache of a thing. Relationship—union—is quite messy ... and life- changing.

It is stories like Bobby's, and so many others, that make Roanoke feel like I am back in that smoky trailer in Georgia. It is why I feel so alive here. Sure, it's no surprise—perhaps from the start of this book—that I hardly align with Church of God doctrine, but this tournament is not about theology. It's about oneness. Never have I seen so many men in one place displaying such weakness; but in this vulnerability God is strong in them. It is almost as if a requirement to attend this tournament is to take any facade that you might have and crucify it before you arrive.

The culture at this tournament reflects what the mountains were saying to me this morning: The valley is alive. And it is the *stories* at this tournament that bring it to life. As I look down at the fields following my interview with Bobby Roe Jr., it's as if I'm seeing a gigantic banquet table, a feast of sorts overflowing with love and relationships, perhaps a slight glimpse of what we'll all one day experience in heaven, when Jesus will be sitting at the head saying, "Welcome home, old friends."

Stories and songs,
take me in, take me home,
the only place that I belong,
lost in these stories and songs.

20

THE UMPIRE'S DAUGHTER

Coach and I have a good routine on this Saturday. He brings people up, I talk to them, then they leave, and I reflect on their stories in solitude. Writing and thinking. To work is to pray.

Spirit, won't You absorb my soul—the negativity in my mind, the chaos in my intellect, the bitterness in my emotions—like the whale that swallowed Jonah and spit him out a changed man? Swallow my Soul, Spirit. Then spit my Soul out forty days from now, and may it be forever changed. And then, when I die, the transition will be seamless, because the Spirit and the Soul will already be dancing. And at this time, the Body will find that it is better for the two of them to be together, for it to no longer complicate their undeniable chemistry, their radical love, and it will willingly leave. Then the Spirit will absorb the Soul once more, and instead of plunging deep into the ocean like the whale in the water a lifetime before, it will take flight like a dove and hover above the waters, just like the start, before souls carried chaos. Did this Soul even stand a chance, my God? I do not think so. But I also know it is not doomed. You did not have to infuse Your Spirit into the lowly, but You did, and therefore there must be hope. Hope for the coming of the redeeming whale in this life.

———

A man walks into the press box. He is an umpire, dressed in black slacks and a red polo like all the other umpires. He takes a seat. He is sweating profusely on this hot, summer day, and he removes his black cap and sets it on the tabletop, revealing a great head of thick, dirty-blond hair. I decide that I am not going to go outside for the remainder of the day. I will stay in the press box, in the air-conditioned monastery.

Since Coach Briscoe did not escort this man or introduce me to him, I know that I am not expected to interview him. Besides, I have whales to think about.

Ten minutes pass. The man remains.

"These players are kind of tough out here," the man suddenly says.

"Oh yeah?" I say, removing my headphones. "Are they giving you a hard time?"

"I won't name any names," he says, laughing. "They're good guys. Just getting a little competitive."

"Yeah, looks like the competitive-side of them is coming out a little," I say awkwardly. "You come here every year?" I ask him.

"Nah," he says. "First year."

The man is probably in his forties. I can't tell if he wants to talk or would prefer that I leave him alone.

He looks down at his phone.

I put my headphones back on.

Five minutes pass.

"You reading any good books?" he suddenly asks me.

We start talking about the books we are reading, and he eventually runs down to his car and brings back a copy of *Jesus Calling*, a devotional book.

"This is for you," he says, handing me the book and introducing himself. We'll call him Ryan.

"Thank you," I say, a little caught off guard. In other cases, I might think that a man who handed me a book with the word *Jesus* on the front was attempting to evangelize to me, which is a common occurrence in the South for a long-haired, sloppy-looking person like me. But he actually seems to be genuinely kind.

The exchange of a book is all that it takes for us to open up and become vulnerable. We begin talking about Jesus and spirituality and pain, like we are old friends picking up where we left off. This kind of stuff happens all the time in Roanoke.

Then Ryan begins to tell me a story.

"About six years ago," he says, "my daughter was born without the left side of her heart."

I stare at him, speechless.

"The nurses held her," he continues, "and they immediately knew something was wrong. They thought something might be wrong already because she had been born three weeks early, but by the look on their faces, I *really* knew something was wrong. I could hear healthy babies crying in the room next door to us."

The stench of death and loss in that hospital room.

The sounds of beautiful new life on the other side of the wall.

"I could hear the radio softly playing in the background," he continues. "I noticed that it was the Christian radio station. I went over and turned it up, louder than everything else. It was Chris Rice's song, 'Untitled Hymn.'"

It was as if the radio was meeting him where he was, just like the story Marcos had shared with me last year.

The nurses handed to him and his wife their dying baby daughter.

"I think my daughter took her last breath in my arms," he says.

The last verse of "Untitled Hymn" is about death, kissing the world goodbye and entering into eternal peace.

"It was beautiful," he continues. "She lived a life without any suffering."

———

It is interesting to hear Bobby's song and Ryan's story within hours of each other. Both involve the birth of a daughter. One, the crescendo of a story and the glorious display of grace and redemption after a year where alcohol nearly ripped his family apart; the other, the very depths of a story that makes you even question the existence of God. Both, somehow, involve some element of death and resurrection. For Bobby, the death of his sin and the rebirth of purpose. For Ryan, the death of his daughter and her rebirth in eternity. Isn't this the cycle of the seasons and of the spirit and of the seeds?

"It was beautiful. She lived a life without any suffering."

What profound depth of perspective, for death to become beautiful, for this life to be a thorn. Was Ryan the Umpire some sort of angel? Or some sort of saint reincarnate? The saints, after all, had upside-down worldviews because they were following a man, Jesus, whose home was in another world. Ryan gave me a glimpse, a reflection, of that man! Much like Norberto's words, Ryan's words must require immense faith to say and even more faith to believe.

In hearing Ryan's story, and other stories like these, I cannot help but find a certain wonder in the Christian God, this Jesus who became man and was born where the pigs feed, then lived in a place where the prize of his creation acted like pigs, yet pursued them anyway, and then bled on the cross, and, in doing so, provided the world with a scandalous, beautifully absurd picture of God, crying out on a cross while overcome with doubt and despair, "God, why have you forsaken me?" There is a smallness to this Jesus that draws me to God. How can I resist this God who pursues the lowly, who runs toward the undeserving prodigal and kills the fattened calf for him, who gravitates toward the rejects and the marginalized, who arranges divine appointments at coffeehouses, and communicates through radios in lonely hospital rooms?

21

"ONE DAY CLOSER"

Coach Briscoe walks through the press box doors. Usually he is bringing someone with him for me to interview, but this time he is alone. He takes a seat next to me.

I notice that his face is marked by exhaustion.

His joy and enthusiasm can only mask his pain so much.

I have yet to mention this, but two-and-a-half months ago, his wife, Jamie, was diagnosed with breast cancer. The fact she has cancer is difficult to fathom. She is so young—only two months shy of turning thirty-three when she was diagnosed—and extremely healthy. As difficult as a year it has been for me, I know it has been even more trying for Coach Briscoe.

"You doing all right?" I ask.

"I'm doing OK," he honestly says. "It's just been a wild year."

Though Coach and I rarely get the chance to share any one-on-one time at this tournament because he is so busy, what transpires is a fifteen-minute conversation about all that he and his family are currently enduring....

———

The Briscoes' last couple years have been difficult enough, as their transition to Indianapolis has been anything but tranquil. Not only did they miss the good people of Winona Lake and were often agonized over why exactly they had felt called to leave, but they also struggled to sell their house and consequently had to live in a small, two-bedroom apartment with their two daughters. Almost every day, Coach tells me, he and Jamie would text one another Bible verses to encourage one another's weary souls. Why in the world did they ever feel the urge to leave Winona Lake?

Little did they know that things were about to get even worse.

The cancer diagnosis came in May.

Coach tells me that two hours before Jamie received a call from her doctor making her aware of her diagnosis, she was scrolling through one of her social media feeds when a Bible verse seemed to jump off the screen: "She does not fear bad news, she confidently trusts the LORD to take care of her" (Psalm 112:7). Jamie shared the verse with Coach, and it was as if they both knew that they were in for a long battle. The verse was a foreshadowing, yet also a reminder of truth—that, in the worst of times when there are no words to explain the innate brokenness of reality, the message that God is with them does not lose its relevance.

Of course we will never know what might have happened had they been living somewhere else, somewhere other than the biggest city in Indiana with convenient access to some of the best doctors and oncologists in the state, but Coach has faith that this was perhaps one of the reasons why they were pulled south from Winona Lake. What's interesting about that theory is that, at around this same time, there was a vacancy in the athletic director position at Grace College, and Coach was once again offered the job. He accepted it. Following Coach's theory, it was almost as if God was saying, "OK, you came to Indianapolis for its doctors. Now you can return to Winona Lake for the job you love." Who knows? It is always worth thinking about the mystery of God's direction in our lives—whether God's sovereignty extends into situations like this or not—because it helps us to ground ourselves in a divine love and cultivate a lifestyle of gratitude.

A month after Jamie's diagnosis, doctors concluded that the cancer had not yet spread to anywhere else in her body. But because she was so young, they were going to pursue all forms of treatment—surgery, chemotherapy, and radiation— just to be safe. It would be a long journey, but it was the right thing to do.

Coach says that when Jamie started to lose her hair a couple months ago, instead of keeping their daughters—Kate (five) and Kinley (three)—in the dark of unknowing, as innocent as they may be, they invited their hairdresser over, and Kate and Kinley each took a turn shaving Jamie's head. Instead of the cancer dividing the family, they used it to bring them together. Instead of cancer having the upper-hand, they shaved her head before the chemo could run its course and turned it into a party. Instead of allowing the cancer to shatter their "normal" and disrupt their lives, they accepted that this was their new normal and showed no hesitancy, no fear, in adapting to this new phase they were stepping into. They turned something that was typically somber and shocking into a family event.

"One day at the start of Jamie's treatments," Coach says, "I went on a run and felt like these words were placed on my heart: *With each day, we are one day closer to well.*"

Coach's words resonate deeply with me. What a positive perspective to adopt in the waiting room! No matter what the day's challenges might bring, no matter what despair Coach and Jamie might feel in the turmoil of the trial, no matter how heavy the burden, by the end of the day there is this practical perspective that remains true to them: *They are one day closer to well.* I must apply this hope-filled thinking in my own waiting.

"These last few years have just been so chaotic," Coach says transparently. "I'm looking forward to the day when Jamie and I can just go on a cruise and leave all of this behind us." He lets out a lighthearted snicker when he says this, probably because the mere thought of going on a cruise feels like an eternity away.

I decide that I will, yes, pray for healing when the Briscoes cross my mind … but also for a cruise.

22

CHRISTMAS EVE WITHIN

It is always nice to be back in this place, this amphitheater in the mountains, for the annual church service.

Just last year I was standing in the back next to Rudy, listening to the rain pounding the rooftop, as he revealed to me the specifics of Norberto's car crash. My faith was pulled out from under me that day, and my heart fell onto the floor. My faith has since been restored, but my heart has been here on the amphitheater floor ever since.

All of today, and especially in this place, I find myself thinking about what it might be like to one day meet Norberto. It's been a little over a year since the tragedy that took Julie and Timothy, and, though I don't personally know Norberto, I have some days when I can't stop thinking about him.

Sometimes it's in the morning when I see the pinstriped Paraguayan soccer jersey, draped over my dresser mirror, that his brother, Marcos, gave to me last year. I keep it there to remind myself to pray for the mission and the Kurrle family. Most of the time, I think about Norberto while I'm driving. I keep a red-and-white cloth wristband, two of Paraguay's national colors, wrapped around my steering wheel at all times. I think I keep it in my car to remind myself that this was where Norberto's life changed: in a vehicle. I'm reminded of the frailty and brevity of life, of how quickly everything can change. And I'm also reminded that, if life can change in an instant, then it would make sense for me to devote myself to meaningful things, like Paraguay or relationships or things that are far more constructive than spending hours on social media or getting drunk at the bars, attempting to escape reality.

I thought about having Coach Briscoe arrange a phone interview with Norberto for me this year, but I don't think it's the right timing. I know I must attempt to interview Norberto at some point, for there isn't one story associated with this tournament—of all of its incredible stories—that has impacted me quite like his. But Norberto must grieve before he talks. Until then, I will continue clinging to his words from last year's video.

Whenever something doesn't go the way I want, there's still work to do.

Whenever a loved one dies unexpectedly, there's still work to do.

Whenever a relationship ends and I have loved all I can, there's still work to do.

If Norberto can say it, someone who has gone through more than I can even begin to imagine, then surely, I can too.

There's always more work to do.

And not work in a treadmill sense, but work that has the potential to help others to feel loved and less alone. As long as this crazy world is spinning, people will always be hurting, and therefore there will always be more work to do.

It is Norberto's pain, and his reaction to pain, that inspire me to do more work, and therefore I, too, must share my pain with others. In sharing our pain, we share ourselves, and there is nothing more valuable than sharing our very self with someone else. Yes, love is at the core of who we are in our spirit, but pain is baked into the realities of our souls. In sharing our stories, we Christians often flippantly pronounce that God is good and that He has a plan, which is a big view of God that might be necessary, but it is in our brokenness, in the depths of our pain, that God becomes beautifully small.

There is no resurrection without death; no grace without pain; and no magnitude without smallness. Maybe in this messiness, we encounter something such as love and union—the undergirding stream of all reality.

———

We arrive at Charlie and Twila's house. It is eleven o'clock or so.

The church service was good, as always. And the late-night dinner afterward at IHOP was good as well. The Briscoes, just like last year, still would not let me pay for my meal.

Coach directs me up the stairs and down the hallway to a green-carpeted room on the left.

"You're sleeping with Grandma," Coach says.

"Grandma?" I ask, confused.

Coach smiles and points to a magnificent portrait of a gray-haired woman hanging above my bed. Apparently, this is Grandma.

"She died a couple years ago," Coach says of his Grandma Tucker, Twila's mother.

"Oh, OK," I say, unsure of how I should comment on the matter. "I guess I'll sleep with Grandma."

"I'm heading to the fields early tomorrow morning," Coach says, switching the subject. "You can either come with me or meet me there later."

"I'll go with you," I say, resting my bags next to the bed.

"All right, sounds good," he says enthusiastically. "Thanks so much for being here. Let us know if you need anything else. I'll see you in the morning."

"Good night, Coach," I say.

———

I awaken in a haze. The alarm on my phone is ringing.

I do not always remember my dreams, but this one—the one I had last night—is crystal clear. Even now, as I get dressed, I find myself fighting through the cobwebs in my mind, wondering if I am stepping out of a dream or if I myself have died or if the dream I had was perhaps reality. It feels like the latter.

In my dream, I was at my Aunt Chris's farmhouse, where we always go for Christmas Eve—that cozy three-bedroom home where she has lived since before I was born, surrounded by all those Indiana cornfields, where the wind dances and tumbles and swirls across the openness, whistling outside the walls of that quaint place like a passing train. Both my immediate and extended family were there—that's what leads me to think it was Christmas Eve—but family members were still arriving, one by one, letting in a gust of wind each time they entered. We were all communing in a circle around my aunt's island in the kitchen, as we usually do, and I was on the other side of the island, with a clear visual of the entryway, where people were arriving. Each time someone walked in, they would be greeted by joyous hellos. It was a very believable scene, one that I experience every single year.

Standing on the other side of the island, I saw the door in the entryway open. That's when an elderly man hobbled in with a cane, wearing a black coat and a bucket hat, holding onto his wife, my grandmother.

It was Papaw.

The room fell silent.

We all thought that he had died. Most of us had even been at his funeral; seen him in the casket; wiped our eyes during the three-volley salute at his burial; and said our goodbyes as he was lowered into the ground.

Now he was here, with us once more.

While everyone else was frozen, shocked, I was pulled toward him like a magnet. Next thing I knew I was hugging him, burying my face in his neck, tears dampening his skin like a gentle rain.

————

Caroline, my dear,
won't you tell her where I am?
It's been a year of wandering,
but I think I understand
why the winds had their agenda
when they pulled me from my feet
and blew me south to salty shores
far from the jacaranda tree.

Tell her I miss those golden braids,
her rhythmic music in the sun,
the simplicity of slow Sundays,
all the summers come and gone.

You might find her in the silence
asleep in autumn's purest air,

or in a snowfall's innocence,
frosted treetops, glowing glares.

Please baptize me in memories
of rolling, rustic countrysides,
or laughs of love around the tree
at Grandma's house on Christmas night,
of long drives through her spacious place,
past rusty hoops in cracked driveways,
where time exhales and rests and waits,
where I was born and loved and raised.

Please forgive this odd adoption,
and tell her fields I said hello—
this soul of salt and heart that pines
for Indiana, my only home.

23

FOG II

I am in a reflective state this morning. Probably because of the vivid dream I had last night. Why did I have such a dream? Why did it feel so real? Maybe it had to do with sleeping under the watchful eye of Grandma Tucker, as I had gone to bed thinking about how I was sleeping beneath the picture of a woman who had passed away, which was weird, yet also symbolic of the saints watching over us and praying for us in our struggles. But maybe it was deeper than the picture. Was this dream my subconscious revealing my deepest longings in a year that was filled with loss upon loss? Maybe the dream was a revelation of what I longed for the most: being reunited with all I had lost. Whatever the case, I liked the dream. It was a gift, a splash of heaven.

I do not tell Coach Briscoe about my dream as he drives us to the fields, but I know I will journal about it later.

———

Coach and I arrive at Botetourt.

The rising sun is asking us to join, to follow in this glorious awakening within, as the tarp of night is lifted and the colors of God's painting are revealed. How often I have taken for granted this revelation, this invitation to enjoy and experience and rest in the masterpiece that is God's love. Most days I am hardly aware of this external and internal rising and therefore I am blind to the color— of the grace displayed in the world and the beauty of my true self.

This morning, however, it is all too symbolic.

As the tarp is slowly being lifted in the most mysterious of routines, yes, there are colors that are revealed in the valley, but all is blurred this morning, as we are confronted with one of the thickest fogs I've ever seen. From home plate, the shallow outfield is barely visible. The distant fence behind home plate is nonexistent.

Not long ago, I may have found this fog beautiful, but this fog means something different to me now. It has dawned on me this morning that it was this same thick veil of vapor 4,500 miles away that took the lives of Julie and Timothy two years before. Now when I see fog, I think of Norberto and Anahi, and I'm reminded to pray for them, though I usually don't because I'm not sure what prayer can do in a situation like that, in something no one can explain but a God who is somewhere, in the cosmos, in some alternate dimension I cannot fathom. God is in the mountains, I think, in the colors of creation. But I no longer think He's in the fog.

Now when I see fog, I have a deep, longing desire to hug Norberto and bury my nose in his neck—just as I did with Papaw in my dream—freely allowing my tears to moisten his skin, as if the one most affected by the tragedy is the only one who can possibly give *me* any sort of comfort—that if he can still believe in God, though his faith may be shaken, perhaps I can too … that if he can acknowledge that God is still mysteriously somehow benevolent, perhaps I can too … that if he can pray, perhaps I can too.

Funny thing is, I've never met Norberto. And yet I've never known of someone I have not even met having such a profound impact on my life.

I hope I meet Norberto one day. And when I do, I hope Norberto will be able to tell by the look in my eyes how much he means to me because I know I'd sound stupid explaining it. And I hope he'll be able to tell how much I love him, and how much I love his country of Paraguay, and how much I hate the fog.

YEAR IV

24

THE FOURTH DRIVE

There's still a stigma in the Christian community that anything like depression or anxiety can be solved with a spiritual solution. That's not to say that there aren't spiritual ideas or tactics that can help, but I've come to think that anyone who projects the idea that these emotional tumults are strictly spiritual issues is dead wrong. This false notion usually makes people feel even more alone, often only reaffirming the lie they are already telling themselves: that there is something deeply wrong with them. My story is proof that this notion is wrong.

Here I was, in the midst of a great spiritual awakening thanks to Dave Hickman and these stories revolving around Paraguay, having *finally* found who I really was at the core of my being, my spirit, and yet when it came to my soul— where things like anxiety or depression reside—it felt as if I were still journeying through the wreckage of heartbreak and loss from the year before with no idea how to rebuild. Just as I had to awaken to the underlying truths in my spirit, I also had to do so in my soul: my heart and my mind. I needed healing.

And for that, I needed help.

———

But before I could even begin to realize that I needed help, first I needed to press forward, as many must do in the fallout of something that shakes them. I needed to experience meaning and purpose despite the confusion within. It was Norberto's words "There's still work to do"—among other things that reflected this notion—that helped me to believe there was still beauty in life despite the internal chaos rising from all the loss and rejection I was wrestling with. When one is wandering through the desert of despair, it seems that he or she must first sometimes be reminded of his or her inherent worth—that "there is still work to do," that the world still needs you even though you do not think much of yourself.

And so I created things.

For the four months following last year's softball tournament, I poured my emotions into writing. I put up personal boundaries, such as getting rid of some of my social media accounts. I disappeared into my art chamber. I made my home in my loneliness.

The result of all of this was positive and what I needed—working, writing, pouring myself into something that was meaningful—but unfortunately, I became so busy, so distracted, that I never dealt with the existing pain. So it was always there. I would feel as if I made headway, but then the depression—which I'm fine calling it now, because that's what it was—would return once more, uninvited.

I began to realize that, though I was embarking on a journey of God-discovery, I never appropriately dealt with the complexities within my heart and my mind. I never adequately processed the pain. And then, when I acted out of my insecurities, my false self would emerge. My true self—the one that is united with Christ, the one that rests in, and is perfectly content with, God's love—would take a back seat, still *in* the car, forever in the car, just no longer in control of its direction, for a time, as my false self would drive the car toward self-centeredness and conceit and destruction. The false self always wants to keep driving from place to place. He is never content. His Tower of Babel is never high enough.

I realized that I needed to live more out of my true self, even if that meant acknowledging the existing pain that was there, which had become a part of me, whether I had a say in that union or not. Awakening to who you are always ushers in a new journey because you realize that who you are must become all of you—that the truths in the spirit must permeate through the soul and the body, that wholeness must spread. So at the start of the year, having had another family scare that led to the resurfacing of all my pain from the year before, I decided to finally listen to what my closest friends had been telling me all along—for a number of years, actually—and schedule a counseling appointment at a local church. *Counseling*: that horrifying word for a man to utter! But the church was only three miles away. I had no excuse.

Nervous about my first session, I remember arriving at the church early, before the counseling staff was even there, and sitting in the quiet calm of my car that wintry morning, sipping my coffee, watching the steam rise from my coffee cup, hoping my burdens might also rise from my soul. As scared as I was, I knew I was in the right place.

At nine o'clock I proceeded up that red-brick path that curved beneath a clutter of mature frosted trees, toward the three-story counseling building that looked like an old-fashioned schoolhouse. I walked up the steps and twisted the knob of a stately white front door. I was surprised at how heavy the door was and how difficult it was to push open. And isn't it true that the things we carry are almost always heavier than we can possibly imagine? It isn't until we recognize the heaviness that we are finally able conjure up the necessary strength to open the door to our internal self. This was what I was doing the moment I entered that building: opening the door to my internal self. The false self would prefer that the internal doors of my soul remained shut, for these are the doors to the temple, where the true self, united with Christ by the mystery of the Holy Spirit, resides. The false self, however, is too arrogant for introspection. Too prideful to enter into helplessness and pain in order to find truth.

Over the next several months, my counselor helped me to sift through my pain and the heaviness spawning from the year before. I always found myself trying to downplay the loss, as if hypersensitive about not coming across as too dramatic. After all, what I had endured was nothing compared to Norberto, losing his wife and son, or Coach Briscoe, whose wife was still in the middle of a fight against breast cancer. But my counselor—a middle-aged man with a gentle face and welcoming demeanor, who always sat with his legs crossed in his airy second-story wainscoted office, which had kind of an old, dusty smell reminiscent of the Biblical Studies building at Grace—would stop me whenever I began to downplay my pain and affirm all I felt by saying, "Stephen, you've been through a lot this past year. It'd be a lot for anyone to deal with." I cannot tell you how freeing it was for someone else, an outside source, to confirm how heavy a year it had been, to affirm that the complex emotions I felt were entirely warranted and normal.

Counseling helped me to have an understanding and awareness of the doors guarding the rooms of pain in the deep recesses of my soul—rooms that I did not even realize were there. And my counselor was arming me with mental and emotional strategies to confront the pain head-on, to enter into those dark rooms. With curiosity. Without judgment. With grace. All of this was a game-changer for me. Without any awareness of who I am and how pain has shaped me, I would have perhaps continued to lash out, against myself and against others, as if scrambling through life with a blindfold, recklessly swinging at anything that threatened me.

What's most interesting about journeying inward is that you move from exhausting yourself attempting to manipulate and control the "exterior" things in your life and instead venture deeper into the exploration of your "interior castle," as St. Teresa of Avila called it. Instead of being a victim of the things in the external world, you take ownership of the healing in your internal world, as you awaken more and more to wholeness. Here, in the castle of the soul, you might find dark rooms filled with pain and complexities ... but in exploring these rooms, there is also found an awareness, and perhaps a joy. Here, you might find your insecurities ... but one cannot develop emotional and mental "truth constructs" to combat them without first confronting them. You become awake. You begin to understand yourself.

———

One day, at the end of one of our counseling sessions, my therapist said to me, "Didn't you say that you love Brennan Manning?"

"Yeah, he's one of my favorite authors," I said.

"You will *love* this book," he told me, handing me a thin, white paperback book called *Life of the Beloved* by Henri Nouwen.

I read the whole thing on a flight to Austin, Texas.

And I think I underlined every sentence.

———

I suppose the reformation of my spirit the year before was perhaps more cerebral—through the study of theology and the eradication of unhealthy doctrinal ideas—and the reformation of my soul this year has been heavily experiential and exploratory—most notably through counseling. It was ultimately a paradigm shift of the spirit that ushered in a process of healing for my broken soul.

And broken, I was.

From the previous year's losses.

From the insecurities that were only deepened by the feelings of rejection and betrayal.

And from the current drought I was experiencing in two important areas of my life that seemed to cut me deepest: my creative life, where I was struggling to get a collaborative project through the publishing doors, and my romantic life, where I was unable to get a woman to go on more than two dates with me, thus inducing a toxic inner dialogue where my enough-ness seemed to be on trial. I knew that God no longer—nor did He ever—hate me. But why wasn't my writing good enough? And why wasn't I good enough for a relationship?

Henri Nouwen's *Life of the Beloved* was the perfect book to complement my exploration—and the healing—of my soul, as his words challenged me to confront the lies that I was telling myself in the fragile areas of my life and to claim that I was the Beloved—one who was deeply loved by God and chosen by God, one upon whom God's favor rested—even in those dark forlorn rooms within myself that housed my deepest insecurities. My deep sense of shame at my core had largely been eradicated thanks to the theology of union, but now the spiritual journey seemed to be about accepting and claiming my inherent Belovedness in the spaces in my life where I felt most insecure, where it was most tempting for me to let my ego run the show.

Nouwen profoundly wrote, "I kept running around it in large or small circles, always looking for someone or something able to convince me of my Belovedness … Self-rejection is the greatest enemy of the spiritual life because it contradicts the sacred voice that calls us the 'Beloved.' Being the Beloved expresses the core truth of our existence."

Truth is, I had been looking for someone (a romantic relationship) or something (completing a book) to convince myself that my life was worthwhile, that I was enough. And as these two aspects of my life hung in the balance, self-rejection was the most accessible reaction. My inner dialogue, often rooted in perception, which usually led to a feeling of rejection, contradicted the core truth of my existence—that I was the Beloved, that on me God's favor rests, no matter how much romantic rejection I experienced, no matter if I ever published another book or spent my entire life trying. There was nothing in this world, romantically or professionally (though our culture has made these two things into the cornerstones of happiness and success), that could strip away my identity as God's Beloved.

By now I am convinced that what Dave Hickman taught me last year is true. God is closer than close—in me and with me. Brennan Manning and Henri Nouwen have affirmed all these truths. It was all too fitting that I would stumble upon these two authors, Manning last year and Nouwen this year—authors with Catholic backgrounds who were part of a tradition that I had abandoned and even previously condemned in my narrow-minded thinking—who would help me to remove my blinders and to see myself for who God says that I am. As Thomas Merton wrote, "The spiritual life is, then, first of all a matter of keeping awake."

As my therapist guided me into those far-off rooms and healing arose from understanding, I found myself beginning to live more out of the mystery of wholeness and fullness rather than incompleteness and emptiness. In exploring those rooms, I was able to see the depth of the lies I was telling myself. Sanctification has suddenly taken on a different meaning. Instead of exhausting myself trying to check off a long list of do's and don'ts, I am now curiously and nonjudgmentally exploring my interior castle and finding within myself the underlying lies that often lead to my actions. Introspection was a practice that had been lost in my previous paradigm where I elevated doctrine and a sacred text above self-examination and inner experience. Introspection has a way of weeding out ignorance and arrogance because you begin to see the motives of your false self. This is healthy spirituality. I'm learning that the things I do or don't do are often mere symptoms of my inner dialogue, the story I am telling myself, often subconsciously. The more *aware* I can become in these rooms, the more power there is for healing, for surrender, for abiding, and for allowing who I am at the core—my inherent union and Belovedness—to permeate every corner of my soul, to light up the castle.

Dave once told me that growing spiritually is much like getting a tan. There is nothing exhausting or stressful about getting a tan. You simply go outside, lie down beneath the sun, rest, and *enjoy* the rays. This internal posture of *being* (faith) almost always ultimately reveals itself in *doing* (works) because service naturally flows from union, from rest, from enjoyment, from *being*.

I am beginning to become more comfortable with the idea that, even if I never am to find a spouse or see another book that I've collaborated on in a store, it is well with my soul, for by the grace of God I have already been gifted with that which is most important, and foundational, in this life: being the Beloved.

———

Dave once told me that whenever he goes to the beach, the first thing he does is stand quietly on the shoreline, praying something like "God, You are the painter. You have painted all this. Now enjoy Your creation through Your life that lives in me." Then Dave sprints into the ocean and dives into the painting.

That is my prayer as I enter yet another weekend in Roanoke, Virginia—that God would enjoy His painting, and the stories He has authored, in and through His life in me as I dive into them.

I look forward to this weekend each and every year. It has become a sort of retreat for me, as I've mentioned, where I allow the stories I am gathering to lead me into introspection and transformation. But this year might be the biggest weekend of all of them.

That's because Norberto will be there this year.

Yes, *the* Norberto, the one who has impacted my life so profoundly from afar, though he doesn't even know who I am. And Coach says that I will have the opportunity to interview him.

I confess I'm a bit nervous about talking to Norberto. It has recently dawned on me that, though I tell stories and interview people for a living, I've never interviewed anyone who has been through as much hell as Norberto has. I'm a bit afraid to look into his eyes—eyes that have seen so many things no one should have to see—and merely carrying on a halfway normal conversation with him.

What was it like for Thomas to place his hands on the wounds of Jesus, to touch the scars and gashes of the Savior who endured incomprehensible rejection and pain?

25

MEETING NORBERTO

I pull into the Botetourt Sports Complex.

It is Saturday morning.

I breathe in the mountain air, silence the static of the world, mute the voices in my head, and I allow myself to hear the mountains' gentle whisper. Like the year before, it is as if they are once again saying to me, "Welcome home, old friend. We have not changed, but we can see that you have."

There are people all around—players on the fields competing, teams in the parking lot relaxing in lawn chairs between games, and families in the bleachers. Each person has his or her own story. The element in each story, whether the protagonist of the story realizes it or not (and, yes, each person is worthy of being a protagonist!), might be the idea of change. Some have changed for the better this past year. Others have changed for the worse. Some lives have changed on the exterior: professional, relational, or material; *all* have changed on the interior. Changing for the better reminds us that we are going somewhere good that we might not understand. Changing for the worse reminds us that we need Someone to help us go toward that mysterious "somewhere."

Walking through the parking lot toward the Botetourt entrance, I begin to wonder what a book of each person's life might look like. Would the plot progress? Would the character develop? Would significant change for the better take place? All this thinking about plots and characters makes me think of Norberto, which makes me think about the book I'm working on, and this thinking about the book I'm working on makes me become momentarily depressed that it's taking me so long to complete. So I decide not to think about books anymore, and I conclude that Norberto's life looks more like a song anyway. This makes me feel better, and then I conclude that songs are better than books.

Coach sees me walking toward the press box and rushes out to embrace me.

"Hey, bud! So good to see you! How are you?" Coach says, wrapping his arms around me.

"I'm great. Thanks," I say, turning to give his wife Jamie a hug.

What a year.

Jamie Briscoe is cancer free.

"Oh, God bless your little heart!" Coach's mother Twila says, rising from her chair to give me a hug. "Can I get you something to eat, dear? You must be starving."

"I'm fine, thank you," I laugh, giving her a hug.

"How about something to drink? You've had such a long drive. God bless your little heart."

Twila is so genuine and caring you'd think I had been to war, not driven for three-and-a-half hours through the gorgeous Blue Ridge Mountains.

"It wasn't bad," I say, smiling. "I should be fine for now."

"Cope," Coach says, getting my attention.

I turn around.

"This is Norberto," Coach says, putting his arm around a thin man to his left who is just under six feet tall. Norberto is wearing a gray Interstate Softball T-shirt and dark green cargo shorts. He is wearing black sunglasses and has short brownish-blond hair.

Without hesitation—or social etiquette, I suppose—I feel no need to shake his hand, and I embrace him tightly. I can't explain it, but it's as if Norberto and I already know one another. It is as if our souls are already one.

———

"Well," Coach Briscoe says, his right hand on Norberto, his left hand on me, "I was thinking you guys could spend some time together up in the press box."

Norberto and I both nod.

And then we make our way up the three flights of stairs to the top floor.

To most, the building centered at the conjunction of the four surrounding softball diamonds is nothing more than a press box. But to me, it is a hub of beautiful memories and stories. I can point out the spot where a player from Alaska opened up to me about his alcoholism, the corner where an umpire told me about holding his stillborn daughter, the table where Coach Briscoe and I shared tears together over his wife's cancer treatment, and all my favorite spots to sit in silence and converse with the mountains.

"This good?" Norberto says, pulling out a chair.

"Yeah, this is perfect," I say, taking a seat next to him.

"What's this?" I laugh, pointing at a Barbie doll that is sticking out of a cargo pocket in his shorts.

"Well, Anahi puts all her toys in my pockets," he laughs. "I'm basically her traveling toy box. I've got all kinds of things in here."

Something about this image of Norberto carrying around his daughter's toys is impactful to me. It dawns on me that he is not only Anahi's father; he is also her mother. I ask Norberto if I can take a picture of the Barbie in his pocket, he approves, and I imagine him thinking to himself, "Does this guy always take pictures of Barbies?"

Norberto laughs and sets the Barbie doll on the counter. He then removes his sunglasses and sets them next to her … or it … or whatever it is. For the first time, I notice the warm gentleness in his green eyes. Though I had predicted there'd be a darkness in them—scarred by all he had been through, all he had seen, the depths in which he had journeyed—I see none of it. I suppose I thought his eyes might reveal hopelessness or exhaustion or emptiness—reflecting the kind of story I had once seen in the eyes of an alcoholic at a nearby bar. You know, a story that had little to do with the future and everything to do with the past. There is real joy in Norberto's eyes, however, and something youthful about his demeanor.

"Wow," he says, taking his eyes off me and gazing out the gigantic wall-to-wall window in the press box toward the mountains in the distance. "This is inspiring up here."

Norberto's accent is not nearly as strong as his younger brother Marcos's, and his English is smoother. His voice is also softer and much higher pitched.

"You could write up here, man," he continues.

"It's one of my favorite places to write," I say. "I love looking at the mountains."

"Next time I'm in the States," he says, still looking out at the expanse, "I'd like to hike part of the Appalachian Trail. I've heard it comes through here and stretches all the way up to Maine."

"Next sabbatical, huh?" I say, as I know his current sabbatical is what has brought him to the States.

"Yep, next sabbatical," he laughs.

Norberto and I begin talking about everything from his sabbatical to his love for the outdoors to the connection between his family and the Briscoes.

The more we talk, the more Norberto reminds me of Coach Briscoe—from his gentle laugh to his soft-spoken nature to his general willingness to enter into joy despite what is going on around him or within him. He is truly present, interested in one thing: the unfolding moment.

And, as I talk to him, it is as if his gentle green eyes are welcoming me into his story.

26

RESURRECTION DAY

"This past April was the two-year anniversary of the accident," Norberto says to me.

I look down at the floor, and then back up at him, surprised that he is already talking about the accident. We have not been talking for more than fifteen minutes, and he is already opening up to me about the worst day of his life—and, by far, the worst day I've encountered in my years telling stories as a journalist. As selfish as it sounds, I'm not sure if *I'm* ready to talk about it.

"The anniversary fell on Good Friday this year," he continues. He pauses, "So this past Easter was very symbolic for me."

Norberto tells me that there has been a great deal of symbolism in the last three Easters.

Ten days before the accident in April 2012, Norberto celebrated Easter with Julie, Timmy, and Anahi. Since they had just adopted Anahi, that was their first Easter as the four of them … and also their last.

Though Norberto's life was still "normal" at this point, it was a very abnormal Easter. The power went out at their house on Holy Thursday and didn't return until Easter Sunday, the same day that Christians believe Jesus rose from the dead in a display of God's power over the worldly constructs of sin and death.

In one of her blog posts around this time, Julie wrote that it was "a quiet and dark Easter." Though Norberto didn't know it at the time, quiet loneliness and dark depression would characterize his life for the next two years.

Ten days later, on April 18, 2012, the Kurrles woke up at five o'clock in the morning to drive to Asunción, the capital of Paraguay, to finalize Anahi's adoption papers. Not long after they left home, the crash took place.

In the months after the crash, Norberto lost complete sense of time, floating aimlessly each day through the darkest of waters on a lifeboat of memories and pain—a lifeboat because memories and pain were the only things that connected him to Julie and Timmy, though he was floating further into the stormy abyss.

"You don't want to suffer," Norberto says, "but it's the only thing that connects you to them." He pauses again. "And to love."

"The next Easter after the crash, I didn't even know what day it was. I didn't care. I used to buy the paper every week, but I didn't buy the paper anymore. The Pope came to Paraguay that year. We got a new president that year. But I tuned out everything. I was wrestling with so much pain."

To compensate for the pain—and perhaps fill the void of meaning in his life—he plunged into work and ministry throughout the year. He started working harder than ever. Sound familiar?

"I was getting exhausted and losing my love for what I was doing," Norberto admits.

Wisely, Norberto eventually decided to slow down.

This brings us to this year.

For the first time since becoming a missionary, he took a sabbatical. He visited relatives in Germany. He went to France. He went to a conference in Switzerland for missionaries who had experienced trauma and loss. He traveled to the United States. Everywhere he went, Anahi was by his side.

"That little girl has been to so many countries as a three-year old," Norberto laughs.

Healing began to take place. Real healing. He slowed down for the first time. He talked to a counselor for the first time. He stepped into the terrifying realm of darkness and complexity within himself and, by the strength of God, somehow found peace. Though the pain will forever exist, Norberto started to hope again.

He started to experience the power of the resurrection and live in the reality of, what Brennan Manning called "present risenness."

The week leading up to Easter this year, about four months earlier, Norberto woke up every day at five o'clock as a remembrance of his family's early-morning drive to Asunción the day of the crash—to be alone with God and step into the stillness of the Almighty, to listen for the whisper of the only One who could possibly breathe hope into his broken world and shattered life. Good Friday this year just so happened to fall on the two-year anniversary of the accident.

"God loved His Son but allowed him to die ... and my son also died that same day," Norberto says. "I started to think about the pain God might have felt. Then I realized that Sunday, when we celebrated the resurrection, was a time of joy. The disciples rejoiced. Everyone rejoiced. And everyone is still rejoicing.

"For me, I took that Resurrection Sunday as my own resurrection day to start believing that life is not about death. Yes, pain will happen. Yes, death will happen. It's not like I no longer felt the pain, but I started to focus on the hope of the gospel—more so than before. I started to cling to the hope of the future instead of the pain of the past. It was very symbolic to me, and I told myself it was time to live in this new hope. It was time to live my life like I had never lived it before."

————

I'm currently working on a book project with a former Division I college basketball coach who now lives in Texas. Over the course of the project, we have become incredibly close. Today, I call him "Coach." In the wake of my Papaw passing away, Coach has become somewhat of a grandfather figure to me.

One thing Coach shared with me is something he said his friend, Paul Young, author of *The Shack*, once told him: "What you focus on expands."

Focus on grace, and it will expand. Focus on hope, and it will expand. Focus on your identity in Christ, and it will expand. This is the only thing unfathomable things can do: expand. And, eventually, this expansion becomes all of you.

A couple months ago, I spent a week in Texas with Coach, and I remember gazing out the window and marveling at the gigantic Texas sky as he drove me back to the Austin airport. I thought about what Paul Young had said— "*What you focus on expands*"—and I wondered if God's love and grace were like the sky

I was looking at. It was only when I had dared to set my eyes upon the sky that I was pulled deeper into the mystery of the sky's immeasurable expanse. East became west, and west became east. Awe and wonder began to bloom.

Maybe anything of divine love and grace, like hope, is like the Texas sky. And Norberto has made me want to focus my gaze upon the mystery of hope more and more. Very practically, I figure that if there is something that can bring a man, who lost everything, some sense of transcendent hope, then that thing would be worth discovering. If a man, who tragically lost his wife and only son in a foggy moment, when God seemingly turned His back, can still talk about hope for the future, then surely, I want what that man has. That's a hope I can believe in. That's a hope I can trust. Just as my grandparents' fifty-year marriage inspired me to believe in love (not Nicholas Sparks novels or Hallmark movies), Norberto inspires me to believe in hope—because his type of love and his type of hope have weathered the worst.

Norberto, more than anyone I've ever met, has participated and *is* still participating in Christ's sufferings. He has become like Christ in his death. And this past Easter, Norberto somehow began to know Christ and the power of his resurrection and the hope that it brings.

I find myself looking at Norberto like I looked at the Texas sky that day: in awe and wonder of the hope he displays, captivated as I watch his hope expand.

27

ANAHI, ANAHI, ANAHI

Norberto and I have been up in the press box for a couple of hours. We've talked about a lot of different topics, and whereas we have yet to dive into anything that has left either of us teary-eyed or choking on our words, we have discussed some pretty deep things considering we just met this afternoon. I know that, at some point this weekend, I will need to ask him about Julie and Timothy. I'm nervous about that, but I also know that it's essential in order to preserve their legacies through this book. Plus, I think Norberto finds it therapeutic to talk about his journey.

The door to the press box suddenly opens, and two little girls dressed in purple and pink come running around the corner. Jamie Briscoe follows them.

"Hey, Kinley!" I say to Coach Briscoe's youngest daughter.

"Hi," she says adorably, twirling around in the press box in her white saddle shoes, navy blue shorts, and bright pink shirt. I figure she's probably five years old now, but, considering my utter ignorance when it comes to child development, she could also be three or seven or nine.

The other girl playfully skips over to Norberto and wraps her arms around his leg, which is dangling from a stool. I figure that this is Anahi.

Norberto looks down and smiles, then picks her up and sits her on his lap.

"This is Anahi," Norberto says. "Anahi, this is our new friend, Cope."

"Well, hello, Anahi," I say, grinning.

It'd be easy to think that Kinley and Anahi are sisters, though they are different nationalities. Both have blonde, sun-kissed hair and a similar complexion. I figure Anahi is three years old, but she could also be one or five or seven.

"She's the cutest little thing," I say to Norberto.

"She's my little girl," he says.

Anahi looks at me—this strange man with floppy hair—smiles shyly, then looks down at the bag of Skittles she has in her right hand. She reaches into the bag, grabs a handful, and puts them in her mouth. It's easy to see that she has already done some damage on the bag of Skittles because she has colors smeared all over her face. She definitely tasted the rainbow and liked it.

She looks up at Norberto and guiltily smiles. It's as if she already knows that she has consumed way too much sugar but also knows she can get away with it because she is in America and this is what Americans do and she and her daddy are on vacation and that sugar should be consumed on an American vacation.

"I think that's enough for you," Norberto laughs.

It is a precious thing to see Norberto and Anahi interact. It's as if they not only have a father-and-daughter relationship but are also already best friends—because they are all that the other has.

Anahi reaches for the bag of Skittles.

"Okay, one more handful," Norberto says.

———

It is late afternoon, and we are now resting at Charlie and Twila's house before the annual church service.

I'm sitting in the basement with Charlie, watching football. He is telling me about a hundred different things, and in between each thing he is inserting all kinds of strange commentary like "You gotta be careful eating vegetables, Cope. It'll put hair on your chest!" or "I tell you what, Cope. That was more fun than a train wreck!"

Gosh, I love this strange, joyful man.

Charlie and I hear a *pat-pat-pat* in the stairwell, and before we know it, Kinley is standing at the bottom of the stairs wearing a pretty pink dress. She looks up at her grandfather and grins bashfully.

"Did your mom give you a pretty pill today? Because you look *awfully* pretty," Charlie says.

I shake my head in disbelief. Does Charlie ever run out of sayings?

Kinley giggles and curtsies for us, then runs into the center of the room. She throws her hands into the air and twirls, as if she is a ballerina, then curtsies once more.

Charlie and I clap for her and shower her with compliments.

Kinley twirls around again, giggles, then runs back up the stairs.

We go back to watching football, and, for some reason, I cannot stop thinking about Timothy. I guess I am not around children very much, and Kinley's youth and innocence have made me wonder what little Timothy might have been like.

Timmy was six years old when he died.

———

"Would you like anything to drink?" Charlie eventually says.

"I think I might go upstairs and get a root beer," I say.

Charlie and Twila's refrigerator is always stocked with off-brand root beer, probably from Aldi, which is the best place to grocery shop because soup is fifty cents.

"Do you need anything?" I ask Charlie, standing up.

"Nah, I'm fine, Cope. Thank you," he says. "You make yourself at home, now, and eat or drink anything you want up there. We're so happy that you are here."

"Thanks so much for having me," I say. "All right, I think I am going to get a root beer."

Charlie looks at me as if to say, "I know. You already told me that."

I make my way up the stairs toward the kitchen and look to my left—past the wooden railing on the stairwell and into the Briscoes' living room, which is filled with antiques, fine china, and old family photographs hanging on the wall—and that's when I see something that makes my insides feel all tangled and my throat feel as if I've swallowed a golf ball.

Norberto is fast asleep on the living room sofa, lying on his back, and Anahi is peacefully sleeping on his chest. Norberto's right arm is holding Anahi, as if she's a teddy bear, and his other arm is dangling from the sofa.

There were times, earlier today when Norberto was sharing his story with me, that I once again grew angry with God because of Norberto's hellish reality. The incomprehensible depth of his suffering is still an unresolved spiritual issue in my mind. In this moment, however, watching the two of them nap together on the couch, I am filled with joy and gratitude and all sorts of emotion, thankful that Norberto has Anahi, thankful that Norberto has *someone* at a time when he lost everyone.

———

My little Anahi,
I do not find it a coincidence
that your favorite place to sleep
is upon my chest,
for you are the closest thing
in this world to my heart.

Only now am I free,
in the stillness of your sweet innocence,
removed from all my weeping.
As I feel your breath,
it's as if my soul sings
a song that heals my scars.

Anahi, Anahi, Anahi,
Did you hear me crying in my sleep?
I'm thankful you're beside me, Anahi.

My little Anahi,
how divine and strange is the mystery of your
arrival in all my seeking—
conceived in the mind
of a mother unknown
to you but loved by me.

Oh, the complexity—
it's as if she knew I'd need more
of her and him upon leaving.
You were right on time,
and now you're mine to hold
'til seeing them again in eternity.

Anahi, Anahi, Anahi,
Take one more step into my dreams.
Kiss Julie and Timothy, Anahi.

Anahi, Anahi, Anahi,
Did you hear me singing in my sleep?
I'm thankful you're beside me, Anahi.

28

THE FINAL PROPANE TANK

It is Sunday. I wake up to the distant sounds of early-morning shuffling out in the hotel hallway—people leaving their rooms and making their way down to the lobby as they pull their suitcases past the maids pushing their cleaning carts.

I am looking forward to today. Norberto's faith shines like a lighthouse in the thick of night on an empty beach. Though surrounded by darkness and the mystery of an endless, terrifying expanse, it still shines brightly, piercing through that which tries to shroud the source of its glow. I find myself captivated by the light, and all I want to do is stare in wonder, there on the lonely shore, with no understanding at all, just wonder. I am excited to continue gazing at the light of Norberto's faith today.

———

At the softball diamonds, Norberto and I once again convene in the press box.

"So," I say, "today I was thinking that we could really dive into your and Julie's story and how you both ended up together and also ended up in Paraguay."

I pause a little bit, hoping that my request does not sound too impertinent.

"I know that some of this might be tough to talk about ... so don't feel like you have to ... but it sounds like you two had an incredible family ... and I'd love to tell your story ... and I can't imagine how tough it must be to talk about, but—"

"Oh, I love talking about Julie," he says, silencing my apology. "Where do you want me to start?"

———

Norberto first gives a brief overview of their dating history.

They met at Anderson University, and Norberto says that he could tell right away that she was mature, strong-willed, independent, and purpose driven. He felt drawn to her and she, to him. They began dating.

As they dated, however, a question about their future always seemed to hang over them: Did Norberto see himself living in Paraguay to continue his parents' mission or living in America and seeing what that might be like—and if he did indeed see himself continuing the mission in Paraguay, would Julie be willing to leave the States behind? Though Julie, like most college students, had gone to school unsure of what her future might be, moving to a small country 4,500 miles away *for a guy* was something she couldn't have ever fathomed.

When Norberto obtained his undergraduate degree (Julie was still in school at Anderson), he returned to Paraguay (this was when he and Marcos oversaw the church in Obligado for a year), hoping to gain clarity about both his future in ministry and his future with or without Julie.

"From January to June, we would talk once every two weeks on the phone," Norberto says. "It was hard because it was at least $1.50 per minute. One time we talked and talked and talked, and before we knew it, we had spent $100 … That's when we realized our relationship would take a lot of sacrifice."

Carrying on a serious relationship, with limited communication, with 4,500 miles in between them, pushed them to the very edge.

"One day when we talked, we actually said to each other, 'If God brings someone else into our lives, pray that it happens now,'" Norberto says.

They ended up going two months without saying a word to one another. They only wrote letters.

"In October, it hit home," Norberto says. "I realized that I was done searching. Everyone I met didn't compare to Julie. I felt like she was the person I could commit to forever. She understood me. She trusted me. She inspired me. She intrigued me."

After he completed his yearlong commitment to help the church in Obligado, Norberto decided to return to Anderson to attend seminary and be with Julie.

They began dating seriously once more.

While attending seminary, Norberto arrived at two conclusions: one, he wanted to continue the mission in Paraguay; and, two, he wanted to not only be with Julie but also to marry her. Could he have both? Or would it be one or the other?

As he and Julie discussed their future, Norberto knew that they needed to have a talk. "I remember never wanting to have it," he says.

One day Norberto met her at her job and remembers sitting with her on a bench near a pond. It was time.

"I love you so much that I want you to be happy," Norberto said to her. "My heart is in South America in missions, and I want to be with you, but I don't want you to be miserable. If you don't feel like God is calling you to missions or ministry, then we need to think hard about our future."

Julie grew quiet and murmured, "Give me some time."

One week later, Norberto received a long letter from Julie. Though Julie had a business degree, she admitted in the letter that she found ministry and missions to be something that captivated her. Then she quoted what Ruth had told Naomi, her Israelite mother-in-law, in the Bible: "Where you go I will go, and where you stay I will stay. Your people shall be my people and your God my God. Where you die I will die, and there I will be buried."

Soon after, they decided to get married.

"I believe, looking back today, that she had a deep understanding of her mission in this world," Norberto reflects. "She wasn't just looking for a family, a marriage, or a job. She understood, at age twenty-two, that she was here for a purpose. She said no to a lot of other opportunities. Her faith was very deep. She understood deep, godly principles. When I told her I felt called to South America, she said, 'That made me respect you more because you knew what you wanted.' But when I told her that, I was really scared I would lose her."

He didn't lose her.

And for twelve years, he wouldn't.

———

The couple was married the morning of August 12, 2000, in an outdoor auditorium in Seymour, Indiana. In a blog post by Norberto on August 12, 2012—four months after the accident—he reflects on their wedding day as he celebrated what would have been their twelfth anniversary: "Your face, your dress, your eyes said everything. You were radiant, pure, beautiful, gentle, and ready to begin the journey of a lifetime."

During the ceremony, they washed one another's feet, symbolizing their commitment to serving one another for the rest of their lives. Norberto continues in his post: "It was not so much about what you or I could get out of it, but about how we could help each other to become the woman and man that God intended."

After the wedding, they rode a paddleboat to the reception, and after the reception, their friends surprised them with a hot air balloon ride.

It was always Julie's dream to fly in a hot air balloon.

Norberto and Julie boarded the balloon, and under the pilot's guidance, they floated away.

The sun was beginning to set, the day was cooling, and, as they looked out at the horizon across the rolling southern Indiana hills, it seemed to symbolize how they had their whole future ahead of them, filled with peaks and valleys, but perhaps more than anything, beautiful views.

"It was like we were getting ready for an incredible life and adventure," Norberto says. "I knew I was in for a ride. Being with the woman God prepared you for, we had a sense of oneness. Just flying above everything, how would I describe it? It was perfect," he pauses. "Almost."

That was when things got interesting.

The wind, apparently, was gustier than the pilot expected and pushed the balloon into territory he'd never been. He was forced to load the second of three propane tanks, which heats the air in the balloon so that it can stay in flight.

Eventually the pilot thought he spotted a place where they could land, and they floated toward the ground.

Hovering twenty or thirty feet above the ground, traveling much faster than the pilot intended, the pilot told them that they might need to jump out of the balloon once they got a little lower. Norberto and Julie braced to take a leap of faith when the pilot screamed, "No! Hold on!" because he realized they were now flying over marshland.

That would have been one way to ruin a wedding dress.

The balloon once again took flight, and the pilot was forced to load the third and final propane tank.

By this point, Norberto thinks they might have drifted all the way into Kentucky.

With no propane tanks left, they really didn't have a choice but to force a landing. Luckily, they spotted a patch of farmland below and began their descent. This landing attempt was much more graceful.

They landed in a farmer's backyard, and his entire family, amazed by what was transpiring, left their house and greeted them with a bottle of champagne. It's not every day a bride and groom fall out of the sky and into your field.

The next day, Norberto and Julie were featured in the tiny town's newspaper.

————

Norberto and Julie's wedding day and their near-traumatic hot air balloon ride set the tone for their marital journey, where they embraced life's imperfections fully and did not allow life's typical curveballs to drag them into a frenzied and anxious state, for these curveballs were to be expected. Imperfections, rather, were to be embraced because it made for a more interesting and adventurous story.

When you try to control the story, you end up exhausted; when you let the story come to you, you end up on an adventure. And the only way to truly allow a story to come to you is to live fully in the present and not attempt to micromanage the future or haphazardly react to insecurities.

As crazy as their balloon ride was, in the end, they got nearly two extra hours of flying time, shared champagne with some new friends, and were featured in a local newspaper.

All because something went wrong.

"It was very symbolic," Norberto smiles. "We felt like the journey we were beginning together was going to be wild. We loved it. The more adventurous, the better."

Yes, I think I will start praying for a relationship like Norberto and Julie's— one that is flexible and open to the unexpected pull of the winds; one where imperfections—in myself or in her or in life—are not feared or micromanaged but are rather embraced and celebrated because they are gateways to growth and transformation; one that goes somewhere into mysterious lands; one that has a deep understanding of service and mission that quiets the American Dream and the selfishness it breeds. I want to float through the air, my beloved in my arms, as we glide over hillsides and hover over marshlands and share champagne with new friends in a farmer's field.

———

Somehow, I've become lost in this idea of hope;
as if I am some masochist,
I've convinced my soul that loneliness is
where I uncover art in its transcendence,
as if this island is my home—
His presence revealed through the salt and waves
as I walk this shoreline alone.
"Loneliness births hope," I think to myself,
and I write it on my wall,
believing these outlaw's footprints toward nowhere
are fulfillment in fullness, in and through,
and maybe they are, or maybe they're not,
and maybe we are, but maybe she's there, too,
clapping along, awaiting to join the dance.
You say it is not good for man to be alone,
then why must he be?
The shoreline and dance are my home,
then why the in between?
Contentment on the shore, exhaustion in the dance,
but the dance is what I need.
Somehow, I've become lost in this idea of hope,
and today I'll be an optimist,
hopeful of this dance,
this art reflecting You.

29

12,000 MILES

"So, when did you guys fly down and start serving in Paraguay?" I ask.

"Well," Norberto grins, "we actually *drove* down."

I smile suspiciously, wondering if he's joking. I have never thought of Paraguay being accessible by anything other than a plane. In my head, I try to determine whether it is physically possible to even make such an ambitious drive. I do not want to exclaim, "Did you really?!?" only to feel sheepish and gullible when I realize he is joking.

"Did you really?!?" I exclaim.

"Yeah," he says nonchalantly.

"How many hours is that?" I ask, astonished.

"It took us seventy days," he laughs.

"You're kidding me," I say, embarrassed that I believed a drive like that could even be measured in hours.

"It was something we always wanted to do," he says. "We drove through fourteen countries total."

Norberto and Julie actually decided they would make the drive to Paraguay while they were on their way back to Indiana from—you guessed it—the softball tournament in Roanoke. This place has a knack for inspiring people to do crazy and uncomfortable things—and that is one of the many reasons why it is a sacred place. So Norberto and Julie committed themselves to making the drive of a lifetime *to* Paraguay *on* a drive *from* a tournament that happened to be Paraguay's financial lifeline.

As he tells me all of this, I again find myself inspired by how Norberto and Julie viewed the world, both as individuals but also in the context of their relationship. Whether it was the life-changing decision to become missionaries in Paraguay or the once-in-a-lifetime opportunity to drive down to Paraguay, it was as if they felt so free in their calling that fear was abandoned and adventure was welcomed. They had enough heaven in them that the world did not matter; yet while they were in this world, they were dedicated to enjoying and experiencing heaven *in* it.

———

The following summer, Norberto and Julie sold everything they owned and used $4,500 to buy a white and blue 1988 Chevy Suburban with 150,000 miles on it.

They loaded their Suburban with fifteen plastic crates full of supplies for the journey and necessities for their future home in Paraguay. Norberto, who managed Spanish production for the Christian Brotherhood Hour radio program while he was obtaining his seminary degree, happened to have business contacts in each country in Latin America that they would be driving through. If anything went wrong, they at least would not be stranded without help. They estimated the 12,000-mile journey through fourteen countries would take approximately two months.

The morning of September 3, 2002, exactly one year after they made the commitment to drive to Paraguay while returning from Roanoke, Norberto and Julie met with their friends in a church parking lot in Indiana for a sendoff. Everyone surrounded the truck, laid hands on it, and prayed for it. They even anointed it with oil. This was fitting, since the truck would need seven oil changes over the course of the trip.

"We really had our reservations about the trip because we knew we needed a good vehicle," Norberto says. "But we just didn't have the money."

But by this point, there was no turning back. The couple got on the road at eight o'clock in the morning, leaving both the Midwest and the American Dream far behind.

In many ways, their drive to Paraguay would perfectly encapsulate and represent the life they had chosen: Though the journey would be undoubtedly beautiful on the way, it would not be easy.

There were bumps in the road, literally, almost immediately.

In Mexico, Julie rammed into a "sleeping cop," which is essentially a speed bump on an open road. Norberto says that when Julie struck the bump, the book that he was reading flew out of his hands. Astonishingly, the Suburban didn't even suffer a scratch.

"Julie was used to driving in the States, and I warned her that she would need to slow down once she crossed the American border," he laughs. "She didn't."

In Honduras, they witnessed a head-on collision when an oncoming truck lost control and crunched into a semi that Norberto and Julie had been following on their way out of the capital of Tegucigalpa. Glass flew all around them as Julie slammed on the brakes—the Suburban, again, unharmed. They stopped to help the men in the fragmented pickup truck. One had already died; the other had broken glass protruding from his skin.

In Nicaragua, it took them an entire day to travel fifty miles … because they were traveling on a small, sandy road in the middle of a rainstorm. Norberto was afraid that they might float away when they crossed a stream that had a water level rising above their tires. Julie videotaped the whole thing and laughed.

After these early challenges, their journey through Central America settled down in Costa Rica, where they stayed for a week and treated like a second honeymoon.

But then their journey grew difficult again

Venturing deeper into the mainland of South America, they had to travel through Ecuador with a cop in the passenger seat while Julie was scrunched in the back between their storage crates. Law enforcement feared foreigners would bring cars into their country, sell them, and leave them there, which would have a detrimental effect on their struggling economy; therefore, anyone passing through had to be escorted by a cop.

It was also in Ecuador that dangerous, violent strikes were taking place, so they listened to the radio to find out when the nearby strikes were dying down.

They would then get on the road while it was safe, which was usually in the middle of the night.

As strenuous as Ecuador might have been, it led to the most breathtaking drive of the trip: the Pan American Highway on the coast of Peru, the South Pacific Ocean to the west, the Andes Mountains to the east. One day they drove 600 miles south toward Chile and didn't see a single soul on the road. Overcome by the beauty of it all, Norberto remembers spending much of the drive in prayer with Julie.

They made a left turn in Chile and headed east toward Paraguay, a route that included a seventy-mile drive over the Andes Mountains and an elevation that reached over 15,000 feet. During the trek up the mountain, they noticed that the Suburban was beginning to struggle, as if it were gasping for air. Norberto suddenly remembered that diesel vehicles struggle in elevation because the air is so thin. He admits it was a miscalculation and something he never considered. Their speed decreased to twenty miles per hour the remainder of the day, and as the sun began to fade, they knew they were in trouble.

Whereas they began the day believing they'd make it through the Andes and across the Chilean border while it was still light, they would now have to break up the trip and sleep in the freezing cold, high in the mountains. On top of that, Norberto had always been prone to suffer from altitude sickness at anything higher than 8,000 feet.

"We were so cold, and I was so sick," Norberto says. "We would run the truck for an hour or two during the night, turn it off for a little so that we wouldn't run out of gas, then start it again. I started to feel so bad that I began to think, 'I'm going to die up here.' I told Julie, 'If I stop breathing, just drive down the mountain.'"

Norberto obviously made it through the night, and, though it was difficult to enjoy it at the time, they witnessed the most beautiful sunrise of their lives, from 15,000 feet atop the Andes that morning. Julie drove the car down the Andes, and they crossed the border into Argentina that afternoon—their final country before crossing into Paraguay.

Home free.

Well, after their car got robbed in Argentina. But that's another story. You get the point by now.

Overall, their drive to Paraguay not only reminded Norberto and Julie of the risk involved in abandoning the American Dream but also strengthened and reinforced their decision to begin a new life in Paraguay.

"Everything in life, there is a risk," Norberto says. "You can stay home and never do anything but miss out on living. An earthquake can just as easily wipe away your home. I think that trip set the stage for us to go and be bold and do things that are unconventional."

———

The great lie in America is that safety exists. In each phase of my life, I have experienced pressure to arrive at this fantasized place, this safe haven—whether it be financial, relational, professional, or geographical. It seems that most conversations revolve around this arrival.

"If only I can get that raise ... "

"If only I can find a spouse ... "

"If only I can buy that house ... "

The idea of safety is really only a mirage in the desert. It appears to exist way out in the distance, but once you have journeyed through the empty land to the place it ought to be, you discover it does not exist as you envisioned or sometimes does not exist at all. These fantasies are comparable to the fruit that hung on the Tree of the Knowledge of Good and Evil in the Genesis poem, the sacred-object (as philosopher Peter Rollins calls it) that Adam and Eve elevated in their minds because of prohibition, believing it could satisfy them. Our obsessive search for these sacred-objects only seems to end with an even more haunted feeling. And, ironically, we feel very *unsafe* and empty when we bite the fruit and realize that it does not fulfill. It's interesting that the highest suicide rate in America is among white middle- to upper-class males. Perhaps they grab hold of the American Dream and find it to be horrifically empty.

But it seems that Norberto and Julie never bought into this comfort-focused way of living. In fact, they didn't just resist America's materialism. Quite the opposite was true. Striving for safety wouldn't have been *living* to them. And consequently, this openness to adventure freed them to live in the moment and do things that most of us would consider crazy, like driving from Indiana to Paraguay simply because ... well, because they could. They did not seem to be affected by the manipulative systems of this world, because, in following Jesus—the adventurous path toward love and selflessness—the world was void of manipulative systems.

————

Maybe this is all there is to life:
enjoying God's love in different ways,
swimming in this magnificent grace.
How freeing. How simple.

Oh, how we work and strive
trying so desperately to prove our worth,
wrestling with grace amidst our own perceptions
when all I must do is fall and swim.

30

TIMOTHY

By now Norberto and I have left the confines of the press box and are walking laps around the softball diamonds, just as I did when I interviewed his brother, Marcos, two years before.

"When did you and Julie start thinking about having kids?" I ask Norberto.

"Well," he thinks. "That's a story in itself."

Since her youth, Julie had an odd, reoccurring dream of twelve children of different races all holding hands and dancing around a tree together. She didn't know what the dream meant. All she knew was that she had a deep desire to nurture children and that kids kept showing up in her dreams. Perhaps the tree represented her and Norberto's love; its shade, their care; the children's different races, their Paraguayan life.

For their first three years in Paraguay, however, there in Obligado, it looked as if Norberto and Julie wouldn't be able to have kids. Infertility became their reality: Pregnancy tests came back negative month after month; barrenness continued year after year.

Norberto tells me that Julie took it very personally. They were around teenagers in their community every day who had mistakenly become pregnant, who viewed their growing stomachs as terrible burdens and curses, crosses to bear. And here was Julie, a loving woman with a devoted husband—the type of parents a child would be blessed to have—and yet *they* were the ones who would be denied a child? It didn't seem right. Or fair.

Julie eventually had surgery at a hospital because she was getting blood clots between her uterus and organs, increasing her chances for an ectopic pregnancy (where the fetus is outside of the uterus). They hoped the surgery would help.

Several months went by, however, and the pregnancy tests continued to come back negative. What more could they do?

————

"So when did Julie become pregnant with Timothy?" I ask.

"Oh, wow!" he grins, joy bursting from his eyes. "That was an amazing week."

That particular week, Norberto and Julie decided they should probably get away from Obligado and relax. Full-time ministry can be a rewarding thing, he tells me, but it can quickly lead to burnout and a workaholic mind-set if you never give yourself time to recharge and renew your mind.

So they decided to take a bus to South Brazil and spend some time on the coast of Ipanema, their first time going to the beach since moving to Paraguay four years before. They spent a whole week away from their to-do lists in Paraguay and simply enjoyed one another's company.

One evening they went out for dinner and then took a walk on the beach. That's when Norberto heard Julie say something he had never heard before: "Norb," she said, her eyes about to burst with joyful tears, "I'm pregnant."

In their two years of trying to get pregnant, it was the first time her test came back positive. This was the last thing he expected.

The two of them embraced, tears mixing.

"That was the beginning of Timothy," Norberto says, smiling.

Timothy was born nine months later in Obligado.

"Ohhhh, it was life-giving," Norberto says, shaking his head in disbelief. "We were both in tears. Timmy was everything to us. He was really a miracle."

————

Dave Hickman says there are all kinds of illustrations for our union with God. The most profound, perhaps, is pregnancy. The child is *in* the mother's womb, and wherever she goes, he goes. The baby within is also entirely dependent on the mother's nutrients to survive, and there is no work that he must do to absorb the nutrients. He does not need to convince his mother to feed him, work for her attention, or maintain his mother's approval. All he must do is rest inside his mother's womb, connected to the only source that will allow him to grow. It is where he is most safe.

In the womb of his mother, it is not his life to live. It is ultimately her life living through him. It is in the womb that the child is in his most natural state because she is all he needs. He does not even realize it, but she is all he wants. Inside the mother's womb, a child cannot sin: He cannot steal, cheat, or lie. He has no sense of arrogance or pride, selfishness or rage. There is no ego in the womb. All the child can do is abide in the one who gives him life and helps him grow. Resting and being lead to maturation. The true posture of worship is *resting in who we already are.*

I know that, as long as we live on this earth, we will each have our own set of struggles and temptations. But I cannot help but wonder if perfect union can be reclaimed more and more, as we slowly awaken to how united we already are with the divine, to how loved we've always been. As Henri Nouwen said in *Life of the Beloved,* "That is the spiritual life: the chance to say 'Yes' to our inner truth."

31

THE MYSTERY OF ADOPTION

A year and a half after Timothy was born, Julie and Norberto decided to try for another child, and Julie became pregnant almost immediately. It almost seemed too easy, considering how difficult it had been to have Timothy.

They soon found out, however, that the embryo was growing outside of the uterus. Her blood clots had returned. Since ectopic pregnancies are life threatening for the mother, especially in a developing country, surgeons had to go in and remove the embryo two months into her pregnancy.

Norberto says the entire experience was traumatic for Julie. Her thorn in the flesh—the inability to have children—had returned. She once again faced the same lack of worth and the same self-doubt she had experienced for two straight years leading up to her pregnancy with Timothy.

They began discussing alternative options for having more children.

One day Julie asked Norberto, "Have you ever thought about adoption?"

———

Norberto and I drift from the softball fields and begin to walk down a gravel path that winds its way through an undulating open field toward a maintenance shed in the distance. He begins to tell me about his journey with adoption, the gravel crunching steadily beneath our feet.

He shares with me that when Julie first asked him about adoption, he was completely against it. It was hard for him to imagine having a child that had a different biological mother and father.

As they were trying to decide whether or not to pursue in vitro fertilization, Norberto attended a missionaries' conference in Miami, Florida. He noticed a workshop titled "The Miracle of Adoption" and thought it sounded interesting. He decided he would go—a decision that would forever change his life.

When it was time for the workshop, Norberto shuffled into the back of a conference room that was filled with eighty people or so. The Colombian woman who was teaching the workshop began talking about "the miracle of adoption"— how all of us, technically, are adopted by God. It is the truest thing about us: our belonging to the divine ... our spot at the table with the Father, Son, and Spirit ... our place in the ongoing dance of the Trinity. The choice, really, lies in whether or not we accept this adoption to be true in faith and then live in the flow of this inherent belonging.

Then she asked a question that made Norberto feel as if he were the only one in the room: "Who are we, as Christians, to close our hearts to adoption when *we* ourselves are adopted by God?"

It was as if God had brought him from Paraguay to Miami, an entire day's flight, for this beautiful, lonely, convicting moment. It was once again a *question* that propelled him into a new realm of understanding.

"I started bawling," Norberto tells me. "I had never cried like that before."

After the workshop ended, Norberto gave Julie a call. He told her, "God has been working in me here in Miami about adoption."

———

We stop walking. We have ventured far down the gravel path into a field and begin talking beneath the shade of a tree. Behind the tree is a barbed-wire fence surrounding a pasture of thick weeds and grass. All is quiet; the sounds of the softball games have faded in the distance.

Norberto tells me that he and Julie decided to go through an adoption agency in Asunción; they figured that if the agency didn't contact them within a year, then they might still pursue in vitro fertilization. An entire year passed, and they were about to begin their in vitro when the agency gave them a call.

"We think we have a little girl who would be perfect for you guys," the agent told them over the phone.

Norberto and Julie eagerly made the seven-hour drive up to Asunción. Upon their arrival, the agency showed Norberto and Julie a photograph of an eleven-month-old Paraguayan girl with blonde hair. "Her name is Anahi," the agent said, handing the picture to Norberto.

"I held my tears back," Norberto says to me. "The same emotion I felt at that workshop in Miami suddenly returned in that moment I held the picture. It was like I couldn't escape—this was *my* girl. Without knowing her or anything about her life, I knew she was the one."

This was whom God had chosen for Norberto and Julie, in whom their waiting had come to fruition, in whom their pain and heartbreak were found worthwhile—there, in the eyes of this little girl named Anahi.

"Would you like to meet her?" the agent said.

And, in minutes, Norberto and Julie were driving to the foster home to meet their new daughter.

"It was the last day of August 2011," Norberto explains.

He pauses.

"Oh my gosh," he says. "That's today … isn't it?"

I reach into my pocket to check the calendar on my phone.

It's the last day of August. Tomorrow is Labor Day.

"You're right," I confirm.

Here we are, on the anniversary of when Norberto first met Anahi, and it's as if this realization pulls us both deeper into the mystery of Anahi's arrival. Norberto becomes even more reflective, as if meeting Anahi happened minutes ago, not years ago.

"We walked into the foster home, and I saw Anahi playing on the ground," Norberto says softly. "I walked over to her, and she immediately stretched out her arms … as if she had known me forever."

He pauses.

"She's my little girl," he says, smiling.

———

I remember going on a family vacation to Disney World when I was eight or nine years old. One afternoon while we were at Epcot, a summer storm rolled through central Florida, so we took cover in a theatre at the theme park. We sat down to watch whatever film was playing and, to my parents' dismay, endured a thirty-minute animated feature about reproduction. Seriously. I specifically remember hundreds of animated sperm racing through "tunnels," like little fishes in a sea, to be the first to fertilize the egg. At one point, I remember, one of the animated sperm looked into the camera and exclaimed, "I hope I win so I can make a baby!" then scurried off to find the egg thingy. I found all of this very interesting because I liked racing … and I wondered what was in the egg.

All this to say, I learned at an early age that it takes two things—an egg and a sperm—to make a baby. Profound, I know. And I also learned that a sperm is a light blue tadpole with a high-pitched voice and a Mario Andretti-like desire to win. As I grew older, of course, I learned that conception wasn't always as simple as the animated sperm race I saw at Epcot.

The only reason I mention all of this—and I understand that it's quite unnecessary for me to mention all of this—is to talk about the uniqueness of Anahi's adoption. I admit that as I watched Norberto and Anahi interact yesterday, part of me *did* wish Anahi had a piece of Julie in her, that someone might pick her up and say, "Aww, she has her mother's eyes" or "Wow, she's growing up to look just like her mom." After losing Julie (whom he saw nearly every day for twelve years), Timothy (who had Julie in him), and the tiny fetus (who was inside Julie at the time of the car wreck, which not many people know about), I couldn't help but feel as if Norberto lost every possible remembrance of the love of his life in an instant—in a single second where hell met earth. I wished Norberto might have some physical, living reminder of Julie, that he might be able to feel her presence through another, that her genes might live through another. This, however, would never be the case.

Julie: gone.

Timmy: gone.

Caleb, if the fetus was a boy; Lilly, if the fetus was a girl: gone.

What I find most interesting about Norberto and Julie's adoption of Anahi, however, is that the entire idea of adoption was conceived in the *mind* of

Norberto—*by Julie*. It was Julie who brought it up, Julie who prayed, Julie who was patient with him, and Julie whom Norberto called from the missionary conference in Miami. And in Noberto's mind-womb, Anahi was conceived.

Anahi might not have Julie's eyes or hands or hair, but Julie is more present in her daughter than biology could ever accomplish.

32

BLUEBERRY PANCAKES

One of the main characters of the 2005—2009 television series *Prison Break* is a man named Lincoln Burrows. He was framed by the government for killing the Vice President's brother and was sentenced to death. Leading up to his scheduled execution, Burrows is asked what he would like to eat for his final meal.

At first, Burrows doesn't care. He had turned bitter and lost all faith in humanity—understandably so. However, as he sits in his cell each day, locked up in solitary confinement, he begins to accept his fate—that the nightmare he is living is actually his life. He begins to have flashbacks, good and bad, and accepts that the end is nearing.

One of his fondest flashbacks involves his only son, L.J.—how the two of them used to make blueberry pancakes together and eat them at the kitchen table, when life was actually life, beautiful and simple, love-abounding and meaningful.

A few days before the execution, one of the prison guards delivers Lincoln's lunch to his cell.

"Boss?" Lincoln says to the guard. "I've thought more about my final meal."

"All right," the guard says quietly, empathizing with him. "What would you like, Linc?"

"Blueberry pancakes," he says.

As Norberto and I continue our conversation there beneath the shade of the tree near the gravel path, he pulls his wallet out of his back pocket, opens it, and removes five or six pictures of his family. His wallet is more like a photo album. It is a reminder to me that, especially for those who have experienced unfathomable trauma, their memories are a part of their daily lives. The trauma is not in the past. It is ongoing, stretching into the present.

"This picture was taken a few months before the accident," he says, handing me the family photo.

As I stare at the photo, I notice that Norberto's smile is vibrant. Joy, as I've noticed in talking to Norberto, is one of his most noticeable qualities, even after all he has been through; but in the picture, he is *happy*, and there is certainly a difference between happiness and joy. His glowing smile reflects a sense of contentment, that he has everything a man could ask for—his arm around Julie, his newly adopted daughter resting against Julie's leg, and Timmy next to Julie, wearing a blue Disney *Cars* shirt and looking into the camera with a goofy, awkward grin.

"One of the things Timmy always wanted was a BB gun," Norberto reflects, as I remove my phone to take a picture of the photo. "Julie didn't want me to get him one, but I told her we would just shoot branches … and then from there we would just shoot ugly birds … and then we would just go up from there." He laughs.

"My brother, Marcos, has a BB gun, and one weekend while we were visiting him in Asunción, I set up a target that was about twenty-five feet away. Out of ten shots, I remember Timmy hitting the target seven or eight times. He was a natural. I bought Timmy a BB gun."

That March and April, Norberto shares with me, he and Timothy were working on building a model rocket. They built it from scratch, and they built it together. The goal was to complete it by the time Timmy turned seven in November.

"Timmy was very studious, very active," he continues. "One day, he said, 'Daddy, I have an idea.'"

His idea was to somehow build a trigger-like device that, whenever you shot a toy soldier with a BB gun from afar, the rocket would ignite. It's obvious that Timmy was innovative and brilliant, especially considering that he was only six years old.

So Norberto and Timmy worked on building a gas-driven lighter that could be attached to their model rocket. They found an instructional YouTube video and built the entire thing from scratch until it was complete.

One evening, Norberto returned home from work after a tiring daylong ministry meeting. Norberto and Julie had originally planned on leaving for Asunción that night to finalize Anahi's adoption papers, but by the time Norberto returned home at nine o'clock that night, he was exhausted.

"How about we just leave early in the morning?" he suggested.

Julie agreed.

Timmy, however, was—as always—bursting with energy.

"Daddy," he said, "let's go outside and shoot."

It might not have been what Norberto necessarily *felt* like doing, considering the long day he had just endured, but Norberto placed Timmy's needs before his own, allowed Timmy's enthusiasm to trump his own exhaustion, and agreed to go outside and shoot.

The rocket wasn't complete, but they set up the toy soldier and gas-trigger in order to practice for the scheduled rocket launch on Timmy's birthday in November.

"We shot, like, thirty times at the soldier, and on the thirtieth time, Timmy shot it," Norberto remembers. "He shot the soldier, saw a little flame ignite, then handed me his gun, and said, 'Daddy, thank you.' Then it was time for bed."

Norberto tells me that Timmy was at an age when he often got in trouble because he would crawl into Norberto and Julie's bed in the middle of the night. He was sneaky, too, and sometimes wouldn't be discovered until the morning. They gave him a rule: *He had to sleep in his bed all night, every night.*

On this particular evening, however, Timmy decided to push the boundaries of that rule. He woke up in the middle of the night and wandered into his parents' bedroom, as he had many times before.

Norberto groggily awoke.

"Daddy," Timmy said, "Can I sleep with you and Mommy?"

Since they were going to leave for their four o'clock-in-the-morning drive to Asunción in merely a couple of hours, Norberto agreed.

"I told him, 'Okay, Timmy, you can sleep with us tonight since we have to travel tomorrow. But you have to stay quiet.'"

Timmy crawled into bed with his parents, and Norberto went back to sleep.

An hour or so later, Norberto remembers waking up and feeling someone clinging to him.

It was Timmy.

He was hugging his father.

Half asleep, wondering why someone was touching him, Norberto unconsciously tried to push Timmy away and roll over to go back to sleep.

"He hugged me again," Norberto says. "It was a 'good night' hug, but he wouldn't let go. It was a longer hug than usual. I woke up and hugged him back and held him close to me. It felt like he wanted to stretch it forever, as if he knew something was going to happen to him."

The next morning, Timmy died.

That November for Timmy's birthday—and every November since—Norberto shoots Timmy's BB gun in remembrance of the wonderful last night they had and the rocket they were supposed to shoot.

Blueberry pancakes.

———

Talking to Norberto has only reaffirmed the internal direction that I must continue to take. I must journey inward to carry on. The spiritual life used to be a desperate scrambling to somehow get close to something that felt entirely separate from reality—a God who was up there, somewhere, detached from my lived experience, bothered by the complexity of my thoughts and emotions, my questions and my doubts, looking down on me with disdain—but now the spiritual life seems more about diving deeper *into* reality, into Life itself, into my heart and my mind. God is already here. I am already the Beloved. There is nothing left to be gained. Yet there is so much more for me to see! Especially in the darkest rooms of my interior castle.

Shortly after the tragic accident, the fact that "there was still work to do" helped Norberto to carry on and experience some sort of meaning and purpose. He had no hope, so he had to choose it and declare it. But he also knew that work could only take him so far, and so eventually, once he was ready—and only *he* could decide when he was ready—he decided to venture into those dark rooms within himself. He got away from work. He went on a sabbatical. He found a therapy group for missionaries who had experienced trauma.

Ever since I first saw that video at the tournament, I was inspired by Norberto's resiliency, by his choosing hope, by his continuing to do the work that he knew God had for him. But now I am also inspired by Norberto's willingness to discover hope in the places within himself where hope is most difficult to find, there in the darkest places in his soul.

As Norberto opens up to me—which he can only do because he has already ventured into those fragile spaces within himself—it is as if I am standing in those dark, empty rooms with him, there in the unexplainable horror of his deepest wounds, where all words fail, where God feels absent, where unknowing prevails … and yet there is something of a light bleeding slightly through the cracks of his soul's floorboards. Our feet seem to be mysteriously aglow.

YEAR VI

(Yes, Year 6)

33

THE FIRST FLIGHT

It is mid-May. I am on a plane right now, flying from Charlotte, North Carolina, to Newark, New Jersey. There, I will meet up with Chad and Jamie Briscoe, and then we will fly through the night to São Paulo, Brazil. We will then begin the final leg of our journey and fly to Asunción, the capital city of Paraguay (yes, you read that correctly, I'M GOING TO PARAGUAY!), where we'll stay for a week and hopefully not get malaria or yellow fever or Zika, a new virus born in Brazil that I saw on the cover of *Time* magazine at the Charlotte airport this afternoon. Comforting.

It is hard to believe that this trip is really happening. I have long dreamed of going to Paraguay. It has been four years since I have seen Marcos and two since I have seen Norberto. Never have I met their parents, Martin and Tabita, or their sisters, Priscila and Nila. I suppose it is a fitting way for this journey to end: in Paraguay, the reason for the softball tournament ... visiting the Kurrles, whom the softball tournament supports ... with Chad and Jamie Briscoe, whose family started the tournament and welcomed me into this story.

Though I travel quite a bit for my day job, I have not been out of the country since going to Honduras a decade ago. Whenever I leave town, I usually throw some clothes in a bag right before I leave. This trip, however, required packing a week before, getting shots a month before, and visiting a travel agency in March. I have already messed up the taking of my oral typhoid fever vaccine. I thought the labeling said that the first of four pills should be ingested a week before leaving the country when in actuality it said that the *fourth pill* should be ingested a week before leaving the country. Of all the things that I could have screwed up, I don't think misreading the label on a typhoid fever vaccination is the cleanest mistake. Couldn't I have just forgotten my boxers or something?

———

You might have noticed that I jumped from Year IV to Year VI. Do not worry! You did not receive a defective book. Sorry for the gap. To echo the words of a girl I once dated, "It's not that I don't care about you. I just need to figure myself out first." Well, I've spent the last two years trying to figure myself out, discovering who I am in the wake of opening my eyes to my truest reality as one who is in union with the divine at the spirit level and who recognizes my identity as God's Beloved at the soul level.

It's funny what happens when you get off the treadmill. When shame is left behind. When performance is no longer the thing carrying you into religious activities. When you start to realize that you're already there, right where you are supposed to be, having accepted your own belonging. What happens is that you start to see those same inherent realities in others. You start gravitating toward those who are most different from you because suddenly there is so much to learn from them rather than so much to change in them, for they, too, are the Beloved and have something to do with your continued awakening. Everyone becomes your teacher. Just like the stories of those Paraguayan missionaries, the stories that are most different from yours—especially those who are on the margins of society or those who are suffering—have everything to do with your salvation. You start considering different ideas that you had always rejected. You start opening your eyes to systematic problems that before you could never see. You leave dualism behind and enter into non-dualism. The gates of mystery open up, and you start to dance in your unknowing.

Of course, this can sometimes be as lonely as it is freeing, for this often involves leaving some things behind. But I'm determined to keep venturing deeper into the ways of this Jesus who captivated my heart years ago. Some have judged me and thought I've lost the plot just because some of my doctrinal views have changed, but the opposite is true: I'm going deeper *into* the plot, the mystery of orthodoxy, the heart of love. An inner experience is unfolding. Like Mary, there is something being born within me.

————

The last two years, this inner experience has revolved around my surrendering to Love's gentle permeation throughout those far-off rooms in my soul. When I first went to counseling, that surrender meant entering into those rooms that were filled with pain and allowing healing to take place. Lately, however, that surrender to Love has involved entering into rooms that are closest to my heart—which are often the parts of my life that my ego fights tooth and nail to control—and allowing Belovedness to infiltrate those spaces as well. As Henri Nouwen said, *being* the Beloved means *becoming* the Beloved.

This struggle to surrender has mostly revealed itself in my professional life as a writer: I have been forced to confront the idols that the inner waves of my Belovedness have washed up to the shoreline of my consciousness. Writing is where I invest most of my energy and my time. And because it's a pursuit so close to my heart, it's where the lies of my false self are most prevalent. Work has been the thing that I run to whenever I am hurting; it's the thing that I think I can control. In many senses, writing is a healthy outlet, but it can also become an idol—the thing that so easily defines my worth and, in doing so, can rob me of my joy. My relentless doing can often rob me of being—of presence, of surrender.

It's interesting how, just as being unaware of your innate power and wholeness at the spirit level can affect the well-being of your soul, being unaware of your innate Belovedness at the soul level tends to affect the body. When something is elevated too high, like work, my thoughts and emotions form a vicious feedback loop—issues of the soul. My mind is already in a general state of unrest, constantly processing and evaluating, but this only worsens when I elevate something in my life to a consuming place, as I drift into obsession or fantasy. And it reveals itself through the third component of my being that is a temple for my soul and spirit: my body. Through sleeplessness. Through anxiety. Through the lack of self-care.

About a year ago, this unhealthy elevation of work—pursuing my dreams at all costs and being unable to rest until I accomplished what I had set out to do—ultimately birthed something of perfectionism. My days were often miserable, frequently hijacked by a mere smidgen of negativity—a mistake, an email, something that someone said, an expectation that was not met, lies that I was telling myself, yes, mostly lies that I was telling myself—and in the evening, the negative thoughts would have their way in my head, carving deeper pathways of uncertainty and anxiety in my mind. It is a fine line between passion and perfectionism, and my relentless pursuit of writing and of checking things off my endless to-do list had resulted in my mind falling into the tangled mess of perfectionism. It was as if I had simply moved the treadmill to my professional life. Trapped in my mind, my body didn't stand a chance.

There's this haunting scene in the award-winning movie *Inception* where the protagonists of the film—those who have been contracted to invade people's dreams and implant thoughts and ideas into their minds—are led into a dark, foreboding basement. In the basement are beds lined up like in a military medical ward, where people are hooked up to "sleep machines" so that they can dream. They are purposeless and zombie-like. That's when an old and decrepit man with empty eyes and a worn, wrinkled face says to them, "They come to be woken up; the **dream** has become their reality." Their bodies were there, but they weren't really *there*. They were trapped in their souls, in the thoughts and emotions associated with their dreams. A false reality had fallen upon them.

This is often the world of a perfectionist. Meeting my internal demands was the world I hung out in the most, the world where I devoted most of my thoughts and emotions—just like those in that dark basement who decided to live their lives in their dreams. Remain in any mind-set long enough, and it eventually becomes your reality, even if it is a false one. Though I had found healing within myself in some of those lonely spaces that were filled with pain, now I had to fill those rooms in my soul that were closest to my heart with *right-thinking* patterns and less reactive emotional cycles.

And so, about six months ago—a year and a half after my previous counseling session that helped me to confront the wreckage of that heavy year—I decided to go *back* to counseling, and I had no shame doing so. Whereas the last time I went to counseling, my therapist helped me—in my pain—awaken to self-worth and purpose as God's Beloved, this round of counseling had a more narrow focus: What did it mean to live out of the reality of *being* God's Beloved while I worked?

My therapist spent several months helping me to identify the vast differences between pursuing excellence and perfection. Instead of living freely in a beautiful world, I had become controlled by the demands of the tiny world in which I lived. Instead of working freely, enjoying the challenges of the artistic process, I had become intoxicated by the pursuit of a finished project. Work and life had become less about embracing opportunities and more about meeting internal demands. My counselor helped me to introspectively become aware of the story that I was telling myself, moment by moment, throughout each day. Was I living in a realistic world or a fantasy, a dream? Was I living freely in the pursuit of excellence, or was I living as a slave in a prison of perfectionism? Was I focused on the process or the product? Was I believing the lie that said, "You're not enough," or was I allowing my enough-ness to joyfully overflow into other aspects of my being and my life? What were the lies I was telling myself that contradicted my core reality as the Beloved?

––––––

I recently read a parable from philosopher and Author Peter Rollins about a man who was undergoing intense psychoanalysis because he was convinced that he was a seed. The man was eventually released to return home because he finally began to believe that he was not a seed. However, when the man saw his neighbor's chickens, he ended up back in psychoanalysis, crying hysterically and having a mental breakdown. His therapist asked him, "What happened? You know that you aren't a seed," to which the man responded, "I know that! But do the chickens know?"

This is an absurd parable, but I relate to it deeply, probably because I'm an absurd kind of guy but also because it's a darn good parable. When my enough-ness is on trial, I think I'm a seed! And the professional and romantic avenues of my existence are the chickens! Like the strange man in the parable, I freak out, believing that the lies I'm telling myself are truest of me—that perhaps my hard work is meaningless professionally speaking or that I'm too different to belong romantically speaking, both of which are lies that contradict my core reality as the Beloved.

I must continue to explore these rooms that are closest to my heart. Though I still fall into that tangled mess of perfectionism from time to time, gaining an awareness of my tendency has helped me to manage perfectionism whenever it shows its face. Still, there is much to explore as it pertains to the lies I tell myself in this arena of writing and creativity. As for my romantic journey, after taking a much-needed hiatus, I have entered into another committed relationship—with someone who knows me and understands me and accepts me as I am. Still, there is much to explore there too. The beautiful messiness of romance and intimacy has led to the resurfacing of all kinds of wounds and insecurities, but I've a feeling that confronting these lies is the next stage of my journey.

Contemplation, as my new favorite author Thomas Merton wrote about, is the next stage of the journey.

Writing my own love story is the next stage of the journey.

But perhaps all of that is for another book.

I have not arrived and don't think I ever will arrive, but I feel each day as if I have tasted of something glorious, something of arrival. I am in transit yet at the same time already home.

———

We are on a plane now from Newark to São Paulo. Coach Briscoe is sitting directly to my left, across the aisle. Jamie is beside him, sitting in a window seat. Oh, how rejuvenating it was to see the two of them walking through the terminal toward our gate in Newark! A glimpse of Indiana, a piece of home, in New Jersey of all places. I could have spotted them from a mile away—Coach, in his baseball cap and Grace College sweats; Jamie, lovely as always, looking much more sophisticated and put together than Coach and me. I was in my gym clothes, probably looking just as disheveled as I always look, pleased with myself that I was there.

When Coach and Jamie saw me walking toward them, Coach threw out his arms, and we embraced there in the terminal. Then we all looked at one another as if to say, "Is this really happening?!?"

Being with Coach on this flight has sent me into a state of reflection. I remember walking into his office nine years ago when he had first become the athletic director at Grace College. I had no idea at the time that the joyful man I was talking to would impact me more than anyone else during the next four years. He is the one who challenged me to change and to grow and to transform.

"Come back changed" were words of his I'll always remember. And four years later, it was he who helped to propel me into the beautiful, freeing, scary Narrative of Change when the opportunity to move to Charlotte showed up uninvited at my door. He knew that leaving everything I knew behind was the gateway to transformation, to the abundant life. And, once I moved to Charlotte, it was Coach who invited me into a story that has *changed* me more than any other story during my journalism career.

Well, I'm still changing, perhaps more than ever before.

And I will not stop.

Because to change is to live.

All this to say, if we return to the States unchanged, then the trip will be a waste. Coach Briscoe taught me that. And I will never forget it.

———

Speaking of change and transition, my goal on these different flights en route to Paraguay was to finish *The Alchemist* by Paulo Coelho. Change and transition are underlying themes in the book, but these themes flow out of the reality that there is something deep within each person—like a voice, like a true self, like a union with the divine, like love—that carries us into liminality and transformation.

I meant to read it a while ago, but then I got distracted reading Brennan Manning which led to Henri Nouwen which led to Thomas Merton which led to Richard Rohr—all Catholics! Anyway, I just finished *The Alchemist* an hour ago, here at the São Paulo International Airport. Soon we will board our flight to Asunción, Paraguay. Like *Ragamuffin Gospel* and *Life of the Beloved, The Alchemist* is speaking to me in a profound way.

It's fitting that *The Alchemist* was given to me by Dave Hickman, probably the single-most person in Charlotte who has influenced my spirituality throughout my twenties. And fitting that I've been reading it on my way to Paraguay, the single-most story that has captivated me in my twenties. And also fitting that I finished it in the São Paulo airport, since its author, Paulo Coelho, is from Brazil, and São Paulo is in Brazil and I am in São Paulo.

Like so many other times in my life, it was as if God, a sort of divine librarian, knew that I needed this book before I knew that I needed this book.

The Alchemist—a parable about a Shepherd Boy who journeys to the Pyramids (because he thinks there is treasure there) in the pursuit of his Personal Legend—has brought to the surface a lot of the things that I've been feeling for a long time but am just now expressing....

The parable challenges me to listen to the voice within—my heart—as I proceed down the path in the pursuit of my dreams. And yet Coelho's point of the parable—in my interpretation of it—is not to inspire its readers to find treasure at the Pyramids, but rather to discover one's internal treasure *on the way* to the Pyramids: to find one's true self, one's own Personal Legend. It's all about uncovering what you already have and awakening to who you were created to be. The question is not "Will I find the treasure at the Pyramids?" but rather "How will the journey toward the Pyramids—how will following my heart—remove the dirt atop the already-existing treasure within?" The question is not "Am I doing the right thing?" but rather "How can I continue pursuing that which makes me feel alive?" It is not "What will become of this journey?" (results) but rather "Who will I become on this journey?" (discovery). It is not about the life that I live—the journey of my own feet, the potential to have treasure in my hands—but rather it is the life that God lives in me and through me. As Frederick Buechner once wrote, "It's as if my hands are gloves, and in them other hands than mine, and those the ones that folk appear with roods of straw to seek."

I think *The Alchemist* resonated with me so deeply because for the last several months I have felt a restlessness to begin something anew in my life. To perhaps leave the faith-based sports magazine that I had worked at for over a half-decade and pursue a new creative outlet: books. To write less about certainty and more about mystery. The magazine in which I am employed had long been a dream job for me, which has perhaps led to the end of not one but two romantic relationships. But released from the burden of my perfectionism and the constant taunting of my to-do list, it is as if I can see more clearly: I am no longer sure if I belong at the magazine creatively and spiritually. That's nothing against the magazine. It's run by great people, some of the best people I know, and is having a positive impact on the world, hopefully inspiring positive, intangible aspects like hope and joy in the hearts of its readers. But I feel that same pull that I felt six years ago—a voice, a groaning, rising up from a mysterious space deep within me. Interestingly, the deeper I've gone into answering the Roman guard's first question in the parable— "Who are you?"—the more my answer to his second question— "What are you doing?"—has continued to change. The internal influences and empowers the external, which makes all of life as sacred as a prayer.

I suppose it is time to begin again.

Time for me to quit.

Time to put something to death so that something else can be born.

Time to die so that I can truly live.

No, it is not the simple life. But it is the artist's life. The Christian life.

The Pyramids are calling.

In the desert, we might groan. But it is also where we will grow.

————

May life be a marvelous exploration of that which we cannot understand, of stepping into another level of learning, of exploring a boundless sea yet always realizing that the horizon, though it looks like the edge of the earth, is only the beginning, only the very brink of our awareness of what is already true within, which, like the glistening waters beneath the sun, can reflect the flaming ball— hanging there in the blue, naked sky—in portions, yet cannot reflect all its light, and does not try to, for these waters know that they are not the sun and cannot be the sun and therefore never cease to reflect sparkling slivers of its magnitude.

Forgive me for believing I can see the edge.

Forgive me for thinking that just because I see the ball in the distance, I can therefore hold it in my palms. If I want to continue the voyage, if I wish to reflect the incomprehensible, then surely, I cannot throw You at others as if I am flinging a baseball. You are not that simple, and I am not that athletic.

If no eye has seen and no ear has heard, then I am therefore blind and deaf—yet also free from dotting the i's and crossing the t's of mystery, for mystery has no alphabet, no words that can adequately describe the unfathomable, which is You ... and You in me ... and me in You. Won't You forgive my ignorant simplicity?

34

"WELCOME TO PARAGUAY"

Norberto—yes, *that* Norberto! —and I are sitting next to one another on a big black bus that is making its way across the Paraguayan countryside. Coach and Jamie are sitting in front of us.

We are taking this bus from the capital of Asunción, where Norberto met us at the airport, to Encarnación, a port city where Norberto lives, just across the Paraná River from Posadas, Argentina.

I cannot believe that I am really here ... in Paraguay. After more than a half-decade of exploring this story, I am finally here—in this country that I have always longed to see. After discovering this story at a distance for all these years, here I am, *in* the story.

My heart was overwhelmed with joy when I saw Norberto walk through those doors at that gray, muggy airport terminal in Asunción. When Norberto and Coach Briscoe hugged one another, I felt as if I had witnessed the fullness of friendship—brothers separated by thousands of miles with an unlikely history and an unbreakable bond, now reunited. Their mothers roomed together at Anderson College fifty years before. They, too, went to Anderson together. And now here we were, in Paraguay.

When Norberto and I embraced, I noticed that his pearl green eyes were more full, more alive. Yes, two years ago when I interviewed him in Roanoke, I could sense that there was joy deep within them—deep within *him*—but now I felt like there was a tangible happiness. His face was glowing.

While at the airport, Norberto had arranged for a couple of taxis to take us to a nearby church in the city. The streets of Asunción were like New York City … that is, without stoplights or rules or drivers with car insurance. Our taxi driver tailed the bumper of every car that was in front of us while other commuters whizzed by on their bikes, in our lane! We were told that whenever there is an accident, the two drivers simply assess the damage, then hand over some money.

When we arrived at the church, we were greeted by a fat, white dog that wildly wagged her tail upon seeing Norberto.

"This was Timmy's dog," Norberto said to me. "Her name is Sandy. Timmy loved that dog."

Though Norberto smiled thoughtfully while saying it, the statement stung my heart. This dog had outlived Norberto's son.

———

On the bus Norberto has been telling us about his new family.

About a year ago, he married a woman from Encarnación named Nancy. Her spouse tragically passed away too. She had two children from her marriage: Marcos (of course his name is Marcos, the same name of Norberto's brother), who is fifteen, and Nicole, who is eleven. And now Norberto and Nancy are expecting a child of their own sometime here in the two or three weeks: a boy. What unlikely timing it is that, though our flights were booked a year in advance, we are here in Paraguay on the brink of the birth of Norberto and Nancy's first child together.

For the last three years, our hearts have agonized over the deaths of Julie and Timothy, and, though the pain Norberto experienced will never go away and the tragedy will never be explainable, there is a feeling—when listening to Norberto's excitement as he talks about Nancy and his family—that *some* of what he lost has been redeemed. Like the story of Job, when God doubled all that Job had lost, it did not change the fact that Job had still lost what was most important to him … but it also did not change the fact that aspects of our deepest pains can be redeemed.

———

Though Asunción seemed to be a bustling city when we drove through it an hour or so ago, with its chaotic streets and even more chaotic drivers, it now feels as if we are out in the middle of nowhere. Norberto says that there are only twelve main roads which run through Paraguay. This is one of them, Highway #6. We will take this road all the way to Encarnación.

Sadly, this is also the same road where Norberto's accident occurred four years before, that fateful foggy day. What is it like for Norberto to be on this highway where his life was stripped away from him? I use the phrase "life stripped away" because what he endured was worse than death.

I cannot speak for Norberto, but a few years ago, driving down this road would have made me unbearably angry. I can still remember sitting in the back of that amphitheater in the mountains in Roanoke four years ago and cursing God when I saw Norberto and Anahi appear on that screen. I was angry because I hated the idea of a God who planned things and allowed things. It didn't make any sense to my finite mind. I still have not found a suitable answer or explanation to the unexplainable suffering in this world—but lately I have wondered if the extent of God's involvement in our sufferings might be found in the mystery that God is *with* us in it. The Christian God, if epitomized in Jesus, seems to be a lot more about powerlessness than power; more about *being* with us and *entering into* our sufferings than trying to explain them intellectually. I find it interesting that, according to Christian tradition, the most accurate picture of God that we have is a bleeding, naked, suffering, powerless, impoverished, and rejected Savior who hung on a cross.

I recently heard a parable that was originally written by writer and filmmaker Phil Harrison about a man who dies and is greeted at heaven's gates by Saint Peter. The man is welcomed into heaven but notices that hovering behind him are his dear friends of all different religions. The man asks Saint Peter if his friends can come into heaven too, and Peter, with a pain on his face, says, "You know the rules. I'm sorry, but that's the way things are."

Before taking another step into heaven, the man thinks about Jesus, "the bastard, the outsider, the unacceptable, the drunkard, the fool, the heretic, the criminal," and suddenly knows exactly where he belongs. He takes his one foot out of heaven and says to Saint Peter, "I'll just stay here then too." That's when the man witnesses "something like a grin break across St. Peter's face." A voice from inside whispers, "At last."

It was Mother Teresa who wrote: "If I ever become a Saint, I will surely be one of 'darkness.' I will continually be absent from Heaven—to light the light of those in darkness on earth."

———

The sky has an orange and purple hue spilling into the thick smoky clouds this evening. Though it is only five o'clock, we are already approaching dusk. It is autumn down here below the equator. Shorter days. Longer nights. As the sun sets, I am awed by Paraguay's beauty—her fields of gold contrasted with her lush green grasslands, and the dark, waning eastern hills on the horizon contoured into the cool-white clouds. All is vibrant. Without contrast there is no vibrancy. It seems that few find vibrancy in this life because they are too afraid of contrast, which involves stepping into the world of another—changing, realizing that you have much to learn, becoming. We cannot become without contrast. Anyway, all is vibrant for me on this drive.

It is interesting to be on this bus today, making this journey with Norberto, Coach, and Jamie. The last time I was with Coach and Norberto at the same time was two years ago, at the softball tournament in Roanoke, when Jamie was merely months removed from her cancer treatments and Norberto was in the middle of his grieving. Now, here we all are. In Paraguay. Together.

Coach and Jamie are sitting in front of me, and I cannot help but think about how, not too long ago, they would not have been able to fathom a moment like this: sitting next to one another on a bus in a foreign country, side by side, healthy, smiling. Together, they have emerged from the grasp of death. Jamie is cancer free. This, in a sense, is their cruise that Coach had envisioned years before.

Norberto is sitting beside me, and I cannot help but think about how, not too long ago, he too would not have been able to fathom a moment like this: sitting with all of us, talking about the *blessings* in his life revolving around his *family*.

"Oh my gosh," I suddenly say. "Look out the window."

We all look out to see the most majestic of rainbows, no more than a hundred yards away, stretching across the expanse of that Paraguayan sky and hanging above her caramel fields. The timing of the rainbow is indelible, almost spooky. The rainbow has historically been a sign that God will not leave us or forsake us, that God lives in the frailty and brokenness, in the floods and catastrophes of our lives. And perhaps tonight it is a reminder that what Norberto endured on this road, what Jamie and Chad endured in the desolate hours in a lonely hospital room, what we all endure as humans in this broken place, will never be okay—and will never be able to be explained—but that God is *with us* through it all.

Emmanuel.

"God with us."

Norberto leans over and quietly says to me, "That's God saying, 'Welcome to Paraguay.'"

———

(As continued from Chapter 9 ...)
I threw a brick from the bridge when my friend was driving by.
He asked me why from his bedside,
and I revealed the intricacies of my plan,
how the pain would bring us closer,
how the suffering would make us stronger,
how I loved him beyond all measure,
enough to bring him to surrender.
And now I'm in the psych ward
surrounded by walls of bricks.

I took my child to the candy store and watched the man walk in.
He said he needed a companion,
then took my child by the hand.
Authorities found the tapes peculiar,
how I consciously turned my back
how I allowed this sick transaction,
how I enabled the attack.
And now I'm his companion in the courtyard, wearing matching clothes.

Do You really have a plan, some road map, some knowing?
Do You really allow the terror, as if blind to the suffering?
If the plan is to prosper, not to harm, then what about the slave?
If You allowed the Holocaust, do they curse You from their graves?
Am I supposed to believe
that You'd shape my life
but neglect the refugee,
that You'd hear my cry
but turn a deaf ear to missionaries?

Yes? No? Maybe?
I call myself a mystic,
but I'm again creating categories,
thinking words can somehow capture
that which cannot be attained,
thinking I can find a formula
for that which cannot be explained.
Maybe we find You on the fringes,
in the heartbreak, in the storm,
when we're forced to start all over,
when we're broken to the core,
in the dying breaths and helpless cries,
in grave unrest and last goodbyes,
when faith and doubt and grace collide,
in this mystery of union.

The suffering Savior takes a knee to wash my feet and smile.

35

THE BOY WHO
BELONGS TO GOD

I wake up to the thrum of motor bikes and loud Spanish conversations in the streets. It is morning in Encarnación, Paraguay. I open the curtains and peer down into the city from my hotel room. Below are a man and a woman getting situated with their child on a single motorbike. None are wearing helmets. They speed off up the hill into the busy city traffic, next to vehicles that are merely a couple feet away, the rumbling crackle of the motor bouncing off the city buildings and fractured pavement.

We stayed in the De La Costa Hotel in downtown Encarnación last night, an elegant hotel on the river. Staying in a nice hotel like this is probably not what many would consider an authentic experience in a developing country but considering how the Briscoes have helped the Kurrles over the years, I assume that the Kurrles want to do everything they can to make the Briscoes' stay enjoyable. I have not really done anything for the Kurrles or the country of Paraguay, but I hope to. I will send them some royalty checks, and then they will be very disappointed and saddened that the checks total about a dollar, and then the Kurrles will start giving me money from the softball tournament as a part of their mission.

Anyway, today we are eating breakfast with Norberto and Nancy at the De La Costa (they live only a couple of blocks away); then I am told that Martin and Tabita (Norberto's parents, the founders of this noble mission in Paraguay) are going to pick us up and take us to Obligado, the epicenter of the mission, ninety minutes north of here. I am excited to spend time with Norberto and Nancy … and meet Martin and Tabita for the first time … and explore this splendid country.

Norberto and Nancy arrive at the De La Costa around nine o'clock in the morning. Nancy is a lovely, soft-spoken lady with a gentle smile. She is slender (especially considering she is eight months pregnant!), and she has brunette hair and a narrow face. She is light-skinned, like Norberto, and of Ukrainian descent. Nancy cannot speak English, so Norberto translates our words for her throughout breakfast. It is beautiful to watch them interact: they have each been through hell but found a piece of heaven in one another.

Norberto shares with us that he and Nancy are going to name their son Dominick, which means "Belonging to God." I remember Norberto telling me two years ago in Roanoke that his realization that Timothy belonged to God helped free him from the entitlement he associated with being Timothy's father.

All belongs to God, and all will be brought back to God. I must become more and more aware of my belonging if I wish to become who I am supposed to be, which is found in uncovering who I already am.

Throughout breakfast, I find myself thinking about Norberto's heartbreaking journey toward parenthood. He and Julie struggled to get pregnant for years; then, one miscarriage later, they had Timmy; then, one miscarriage later, they adopted Anahi; then Timmy and the unborn baby in Julie tragically died in the car accident; and now Dominick rests in Nancy's womb, which is a type of heaven, free from the broken, sinful world and all its hardships, as God knits him together and we all wait expectantly for the Boy Who Belongs to God.

Norberto is now the father (or stepfather) of eight children—four of them in heaven, three of them here on earth, and one in between. And one day, in the afterlife, all of his children will meet one another. And perhaps they will dance together around a tree, just as Julie had dreamed.

———

Martin and Tabita arrive at the De La Costa in a red Volkswagen pickup truck.

We convene in the lobby, as I meet them face-to-face for the first time. Tabita has short, curly, bronze hair, a cowlick above her forehead, and is wearing a pair of wide-framed glasses, resting on her nose beneath her eyes, like a distinguished professor. She has a lighter complexion and is probably five feet, seven inches. It is apparent that Tabita is the talkative one—the planner—as she is already directing us to put our suitcases in the truck bed and rattling off all that is on the schedule today, occasionally pointing at her watch. Tabita is not your typical seventy-two-year-old; she has bundles of energy, and it is easy to see why she and Twila are the best of friends. They are practically clones living 4,500 miles apart. Firecrackers. Chatterboxes. Yet very intentional in everything that they do. Planners. Achievers.

As Tabita talks, Martin stands quietly behind her. He is tall—about six feet, two inches—and slightly darker skinned. He is German, balding on the top of his head, with white sideburns beginning at his big ears, running down his cheeks, and joining his thinly trimmed chinstrap and horseshoe mustache. He does not know English like Tabita does, but he still seems quieter and more reserved. Also, he is drinking a Sprite, an overall wholesome choice.

From what Norberto has told me about his parents—how they are hard-working, blue-collar, Type A planners who stick to a rigorous schedule and find little value in rest or sleep or relaxation—their entrance does not surprise me. There are things to do. People to see. Places to be. Norberto is quite the opposite, very South American in this regard, and I can tell that it drives his poor mother crazy.

We eventually say goodbye to Norberto and Nancy in the De La Costa parking lot. We will see Norberto again later in the week, but Nancy we will not. I wish there were no language barrier between Nancy and me. I would tell her how much her husband has impacted my life and how he has inspired me. I would tell her that, though I hate the circumstances that took her first husband and the fog that took Julie, I am happy that she found Norberto and that Norberto found her and that God found both of them in their sea of pain. And then I would tell her that I love her family and wish that she would hurry up and have Dominick while we were in Paraguay so I could hold the Boy Who Belongs to God.

36

QUIET DREAM

We've been riding around in Martin and Tabita's pickup truck for the last few hours, visiting different churches and talking to pastors and missionaries whom the softball tournament has benefited, encouraging them yet knowing all along that we are the ones who are most encouraged.

Being with Martin and Tabita brings with it the feeling that you are in the presence of saints—people who approach the world through the lens of heaven, not this world and its schemes, schemes that are especially prevalent in America where it's all about accumulating things and attaining some level of importance.

I've heard so many stories about this selfless couple who quieted the American Dream so that they could meet the needs of the Paraguayan people ... and now I get to be *with* them. Tabita could have stayed in America, and Martin could have stayed in Germany. But they never lost sight of that which makes them feel most alive: missionary work; serving others; meeting those who are on the margins of society—the poor, the oppressed—right where they are. And something tells me that they'll serve the people of Paraguay until the day they die. For people like Martin and Tabita, there is no such thing as retirement. Their faith frees them from the monotony of man-made systems. The real tragedy in America is not its wealth; it's that its people abandon that which makes them feel most alive for the comforts of a system.

The American Dream is a damning thing. The pursuit always requires some level of selfishness. We neglect the well-being and needs of others, which in turn involves the shedding of our souls, since our souls are fueled by their union with the spirit, which is one with God and with others, which means we must give of ourselves to gain anything at all that is transcendent—like hope, which is blessing someone else, or peace, which is forgiving someone else, or joy, which is the most life-giving of all. But the American Dream forces you into self-absorption and brainwashes you with fear-based lies like "I need this," or "I need that," or "I want more."

Anyway, the world spins on its axis, and the naive North Koreans go about their days—their lives—thinking their dictator is their god … and the naive Americans go about their days—their lives—thinking the Dream is theirs.

————

Now we are in the town of Obligado, the epicenter of the mission, still riding along with Tabita and Martin. This is where we will spend the next few days. Located here is the mission's first church, the radio station that Norberto started called Radio Alternativa, and Timothy's School, a Christian grade school named after Norberto's late son. This is also where Marcos and his family now live, having recently moved here from the capital of Asunción, which I am told is a story in itself.

Here in Obligado, Paraguay feels like more of a developing country—with its cluttered yards and littered streets and the smell of garbage hanging in the muggy air. The houses in this area are more dilapidated and askew. Children are playing in the streets. Some are selling goods from woven baskets, probably *chipas*, a type of Paraguayan bread-roll filled with cheese, which we have been offered constantly the last couple of days, whether it was on our plane ride to Asunción or our bus ride to Encarnación or in the city or, well, just about everywhere except the bathroom.

They're Americans; they like food, especially cheese.

Let's sell them chipa *after* chipa *after* chipa.

Tabita turns onto a side street, and our car rumbles and jolts atop the bumpy surface. She parks the car next to a small brick building on the right. We walk toward the place, open the front door—which is next to a small sign that says, in Spanish, "Church of God, House of God,"—then walk inside. The room is mostly empty. There are some chairs scattered throughout the place, disarranged on the brown, tiled floor, and a few tables in the back with mounds of clothes piled on top of them.

"Elena?" Tabita hollers.

A paunchy white woman with glasses emerges from a back room. "Tabita!" she smiles. They embrace and begin speaking in Spanish.

"This is Elena," Tabita eventually says to us, smiling widely. "Elena helps the children and families in this community."

Tabita shares with us that Elena's ministry began with her meeting six kids from the neighborhood, each day, under a tree. She would feed them food that she had cooked, comfort and nurture them, and teach them about God. We are told that this not only is a poor community but is also a broken community consisting of shattered families. Lots of absent fathers. Apparently, it is unfortunately common in Paraguay for husbands to suddenly leave their wives and children behind and start all over elsewhere, thus leaving a void in a child's life.

Tabita explains to us that, over time, more children kept coming to the tree to be with Elena. Physically, they liked being fed. Emotionally, they liked being loved. Spiritually, they liked her teaching. Could there be anything more vital for young children than realizing that there is someone who is *for* them, someone who affirms that they *belong*, not because of what they do, not because of their performance in school or athletics or in the household, but simply and profoundly because of who they are?

Eventually the gatherings became so large that the Church of God constructed this building, under Julie's direction, for Elena—a forty-by-twenty-foot open room with a kitchen in the back so that she could continue preparing food for all who gathered there.

Julie's fingerprints are all over this mission, this country.

As Tabita talks about Julie, Elena's eyes become glassy.

————

What's most unique about the "Church of God, House of God" is Elena's business plan. Elena is not a wealthy woman, but she obviously somehow pays for the resources she provides for the people in this community. So she gets wealthier people, the upper class, to donate their clothes; then she sells those clothes to the middle-class people who can afford it; and then she uses the money she earns from selling clothes to buy food and water for the lower class, the poor.

I want to think like Elena. This life is not about acquiring all that I can for myself, as America tells me to do; it is about doing all I can to help others. This is the source of meaning in this life: entering into others' pain and sufferings.

Right when we are about to leave, a little dark-skinned boy in a blue Nike shirt walks into the building. He politely shakes our hands and then asks Elena if he can have some water. The boy is thirsty. She goes to the kitchen and fetches him a bottle of water. The boy smiles and walks into the streets, balancing a basket of bread on his head.

37

TIMOTHY II

It is almost dusk. We are walking through the campus at Timothy's School in Obligado, Tabita leading the way. She guides us toward a tiny house, still intact, across from the church, where the Kurrles used to live in Marcos and Norberto's youth, when the mission was just beginning. The house is small and battered. It is vacant, sitting there like a museum, commemorating a family who spent their lives, not accumulating things *for* themselves, but giving *of* themselves.

The fact that their former home is a rock's throw away from the church symbolizes the cost of being a missionary: It requires all of you, affecting every intricate detail of your life, down to where you live and rest your head. Maybe this was what Jesus meant when he said that the Son of Man had no place to sleep. There was no missionary like him. Yes, even Jesus found value in solitude (Isn't this the great challenge of anyone who is passionate, anyone who bleeds ambition, anyone who has dedicated their lives to someone or something: to still find solitude?) but when it came to his ministry—his mission—all that mattered was his proximity to the people he was serving and loving. Similarly, the Kurrles wanted to be as close as they could be to the people whom they served and loved. Fifty feet away from the church, to be exact.

Tabita then guides us into a yellow church across from their old house, at the center of campus. We walk through an old sanctuary, which is now the youth room, and into a new, tiled sanctuary with rows of blue plastic chairs. Centered behind the altar is a hollowed-out, cross-shaped window, the soft glow of twilight dimly lighting up the stage. Soon it will be dark; the cross too will be dark through the thick of the opaque night. Only the flicker of passing headlights and the glimmer of distant stars will penetrate the mold of the cross. And tomorrow morning the light will blast through the window with the force of the rising sun, lighting up the sanctuary. Unless it is overcast, and then the light of the cross will also be subdued.

Though the brightness of the cross might change by the hour, never does the cross cease to be a window. It meets the day, or the night, wherever it is, no matter how light, no matter how dark. Yes, the cross is a beacon of hope. But it would not be a beacon of hope if it were not a symbol of pain. Maybe this window, like the rainbow yesterday, is a profound metaphor for the God who did not come to explain our suffering but rather to enter into it with us, to let us know that we are not alone.

———

We exit the church and walk down a stained, broken sidewalk toward a long, yellow, two-story building running perpendicular to the church. The outside of the entrance is draped in colorful thin cloths: red, white, and blue—Paraguay's national colors—on the left; and light blue, orange, yellow, and green—Obligado's colors—on the right. That's when I look up to my right and see it: a green sign reading "Timothy's School" in elegant cursive.

To the young children here, I am sure that they do not yet understand the meaning behind the name of their school, but maybe one day they will. And surely, they will be inspired to live with purpose like the Kurrle family, for life is far too short and death is too criminal and heaven is too close to live any other way; to care for others the way Timothy's parents cared for others; and to embrace those we love, each day, in some way, like Timmy did, clinging to Norberto and wrapping his little arms around his daddy in the middle of the night, hours before he died.

I find myself thinking about that illuminating cross.

38

THE TREES THAT NORB PLANTED

"Brotha! Brotha!" we hear while marveling at the sign from the sidewalk.

It's Marcos. He is running toward us like a drunken monkey, wildly pumping his knees up and down, his arms extended. It has been four years since I have seen Marcos, but I am once more reminded of his contagious enthusiasm. Coach laughs heartily as he and Marcos embrace. Coach's eyes once more water up in this blissful reunion with a best friend, who, before this week, had been separated by over a thousand days and thousands of miles.

First, Marcos gives us a tour of the school. In one of the classrooms, we talk briefly with his wife, Cristiane, who is teaching a class, and then we are guided into a preschool classroom where the children preciously sing "Heads, Shoulders, Knees, and Toes" and "Itsy Bitsy Spider" for us in broken English. Whatever burdens I might have carried into Paraguay seemed to slide off my shoulders in the presence of those innocent children.

Marcos then leads us a couple of blocks from the campus of Timothy's School, down those dusty, red-stone streets, and into a three-story radio station, the station that Norberto founded. There are multiple offices, a control room, a recording studio with a large table for three on-air personalities, and a production room on the other side of the studio glass. There is even a room that they are planning to turn into a television studio. Marcos says that the station's new $23,000 transmitter, which the softball tournament helped purchase, allows the station's radio waves to travel all the way to the border of Argentina, about an hour and a half away. Overall, Paraguay seems to be where America was about two generations ago, with the explosion of radio and television. Marcos and his team are uniquely shaping culture. Bringing hope and inspiration to people over the airwaves.

———

Nothing epitomizes this idea of sacrifice in Marcos's life more than his and Cristiane's most recent transition from Asunción to Obligado.

Sitting in his third-story office at the radio station, Marcos begins to tell us about the series of circumstances that led to his and Cristiane's life-changing move. The last time I interviewed Marcos, after all, he and Cristiane were overwhelmingly happy in the nation's capital. They were running a youth outreach ministry called Youth Planet in the center of the city (thanks to the Miracle of the 666) and were both taking the necessary educational steps in their careers—Marcos, who had hopes of one day running a radio station, and Cristiane, who had hopes of one day starting a school. But they wanted to do all of this in Asunción, where they were hoping to establish their family's roots, not Obligado. What happened?

Two years after I interviewed Marcos in Roanoke, he found out that Youth Planet, which had since moved to a bigger location due to its growth, would once again have to relocate because the landlord no longer wanted to rent out the space. This was unforeseen. What were they to do? Should they find another place to rent? Should they discontinue Youth Planet indefinitely and finally start a radio station and a school? Leaving Asunción to do something different did not cross their minds.

In October, Marcos received a call from Norberto, who was still working at the radio station and serving as a pastor in Obligado, asking Marcos to come to Obligado one Sunday to preach. Marcos agreed. Upon visiting, Marcos felt an odd longing to possibly work at Norberto's radio station one day. He had always been intrigued with radio and media. He certainly had the personality and the voice to be on air. And now he had the training too. Marcos returned to Asunción and mentioned the idea to Cristiane.

"What do you think about working with Norberto in Obligado?" he asked her.

Flustered by the mere thought of leaving a city that they loved, Cristiane responded: "Don't talk to me about Obligado again. Don't you believe in the dreams God gave us in Asunción?"

Marcos respected Cristiane's request and did not bring up Obligado to her again. She was right. They had risked so much moving to Asunción. And now it had become their home. Wouldn't it be a foolish thing to leave?

Meanwhile, Marcos and Cristiane's future hung in the balance. As weeks passed, they received no clarity about Youth Planet or launching a school or starting a radio station in Asunción.

One day Cristiane said to Marcos, "Wherever you feel we should go, I will go," an echo of what Julie told Norberto years before when she decided to open herself up to the idea of moving to Paraguay.

It was as if all that the universe needed to know was her openness to an alternative plan. God saw that her arms were extended and her hands were open, ready to receive alternative possibilities, unexpected blessings.

And by January, in the wake of Norberto's marriage to Nancy and their move to Encarnación, Marcos and Cristiane had moved their family to Obligado so that Marcos could take Norberto's place at the radio station. And, much to Cristiane's surprise, the Church of God was *also* looking for someone to open a school. Cristiane said that she would do it. Today Marcos is running a radio ministry that Norberto built, and Cristiane is running a school named after Norberto's late son.

Do Marcos's and Norberto's paths ever fail to intersect?

Marcos stands up from his desk and walks over to a pair of sliding glass windows on the far end of his office. He opens the windows and looks outside. There are two South American pines no more than an arm's length away.

"Sometimes in the morning I open these windows," Marcos says. "The other day I watched a bird build its nest right outside this window on this tree. He would get one twig, then get another twig. It was peaceful to watch."

Marcos pauses. "I said to myself, 'Thank you for planting these trees, Norb.'"

Norberto had planted the pines outside Marcos's office fifteen years before.

39

100 BLESSINGS A DAY

We are at a quaint, brightly lit restaurant in downtown Obligado with Marcos, Cristiane, and their children, Mateo (twelve), and Alheli (nine). It feels like a cafe in Italy, with its stone structure, thin wooden tables, and red-and-white checkered tablecloths. Then again, I've never been to Italy.

I just finished one of the best meals I've ever had: some variation of *la hamburgesa* consisting of two thin eight-inch-long steak burgers, topped with egg, cheese, ham, and tomato. Four dollars or something. I'm not sure if portions are always this big in Paraguay, or if the chef just supersized our entrees since we are Americans and are therefore out-of-control fatsos.

I wish today was not ending. It has been so life-giving to be with Marcos and his family these last several hours. How cursed we all are by the grip of time! The ticking hands of a clock, the ever-changing digits on our phones—they're all a reminder that we're wearing away, that good things always end, for even the most purposeful people in the world must sleep. Time is the most valuable resource that we have, yet it is the one thing that is constantly decreasing. Money can increase. Possessions can increase. Influence can increase. Even love and charity and justice can increase. But time will always decrease. How I wish we were not bound by it! But we are, and that's what makes life special. That's what makes the present so vital, so essential to truly living.

I don't think it's normal for Marcos and his family to go out to eat on a weekday evening, especially at nine thirty at night. They must be tired. Cristiane is running an entire school, for heaven's sake, entrusted with a hundred children, and Marcos is managing a radio station, carrying around the burden of its direction. They both have to be at work early tomorrow. Not to mention they are parents. But Marcos and Cristiane do not act like they have anywhere to go or anything that they must do. Sleep is the last thing on their minds. They make you feel as if nothing is more important than the current moment, and therefore nothing is more important than you. They do not look at their phones. They do not act like they have places that they must be. They are human beings, not human doings. "Which one are you?" my therapist once asked me. I looked down at the floor. That was my answer. He did not feel the need to ask me a follow-up question.

Marcos and Cristiane seem to be experts in living in the Mysterious Now, which I capitalize because that is where the divine resides. People in South America are typically better at this than Americans. The South Americans' apathy toward time has made them less bound by it, which seems to be an appropriate attitude toward something that is wasting away. In the South American's mind, *being* with people trumps enslavement to a to-do list; *living* in the present trumps constantly fantasizing or obsessing about the future. The correlation between being and living might be the most forgotten thing in America today. Maybe a divine call, while sometimes a vocation or specific task, is usually more about simply *being*.

The great challenge of the abundant life is to awaken more and more to the beauty of the present moment. Here we all are, in a restaurant, having been separated by 4,500 miles forty-eight hours before ... all because two women named Twila and Tabita roomed together five decades before—and because they continued to pursue that friendship. Though this is an extreme story, I've a feeling that each communal instance that we experience in this life is more miraculous— more magical—than we have ever dared to realize. The more we become aware of the awe and wonder in each bestowed moment, the more present we will be. We will find this life to be drenched in the divine, always inviting us into the flow of Reality, the dance of the Trinity. And becoming more aware of the magic unfolding around us will surely move us to gratitude.

———

Gratitude is something else that I've noticed today, specifically in my conversations with Marcos. In the last three hours, I've heard him say some variation of "Thank You, God" or "Praise Jesus" probably twenty or thirty times. He said it in reference to the big things, like when he was telling us about Cristiane and her work at Timothy's School, or their children and their transition from Asunción, or his job and how he felt like radio was what God had been preparing him for all of his life. But I also heard him say it in the small things, like when we arrived at the restaurant safely or when he took a bite of his food.

Maybe this is why he and Cristiane can be so present ... though they are exhausted ... though there is chaos swarming around them ... though so many people depend on them and they work their tails off to collect monthly paychecks that are merely $300: because whenever your framework for life is thankfulness and gratitude, which flow from awe and wonder for the mystery and gift of life, the most natural thing to do is to enjoy the moment you are living in.

I read something the other day that it is now scientifically proven that our brains automatically cling to negativity or uncertainty. It makes sense. That's why I go to bed thinking about the typo I found or that negative email I received or my uncertain future or the mistakes of my past instead of the one thousand blessings that occurred that day. The negative is the harness in each seat of the rollercoaster: It locks us in, then whips us around however it chooses.

Richard Rohr, who has written some profound things about the contemplative life and how it pertains to the brain, writes this in *Essential Teachings on Love*: "Neuroscience can now demonstrate the brain indeed has a negative bias; the brain prefers to constellate around fearful, negative, or problematic situations. In fact, when a loving, positive, or unproblematic thing comes your way, you have to savor it consciously for at least fifteen seconds before it can harbor and store itself in your 'implicit memory;' otherwise it doesn't stick."

Similarly, I was listening to a podcast the other day where the host was interviewing a man called "Rabbi Joel." Rabbi Joel was talking about the Hebrew word *kavanah*, which basically means "intention." Prayer, Rabbi Joel says, begins with intention. And for him, intention is rooted in gratitude. So to develop a lifestyle of thankfulness, Rabbi Joel has adopted the spiritual discipline of intentionally identifying one hundred blessings a day. I find all of this interesting in this stage of my life where I am trying to abandon my perfectionism and develop new thinking patterns.

This profound idea reminds me of Marcos—how I heard him say some variation of "Thank You, God" or "Praise Jesus" multiple times throughout the day. Could it be that Marcos's framework of gratitude in his approach to life is what allows him to be present despite his exhaustion, joyful despite the struggles he is facing, and overwhelmingly positive despite the negative things that have the potential to infect his mind?

———

As I lie in my bed at our hotel in Bella Vista, about ten minutes away from Obligado, I find myself thinking about a moment that I experienced earlier— one that seems to encompass the present and intentionality and gratitude, all the inspiring things that Marcos and his family represent …

After leaving the radio station, we went to Marcos's house, which Norberto and Julie had actually built years before (this is a story in itself, but I will delve into that later). While Marcos caught up with Coach and while Jamie caught up with Cristiane, I bonded with their thirteen-year-old son, Mateo. Mateo was quiet and reserved and stoic, not as enthusiastic as his father, yet seemed to be just as genuine, even though he was young. I tried to talk to him in Spanish, but he mostly looked at me like I was speaking Chinese, which I might have been. Still, we kept trying to talk to one another. He showed me his room and his Xbox games and his drum set. I noticed a keyboard in the corner of his room as well.

"*Te gusta la música?*" I asked.

"*Sí,*" he said, followed by a sentence that I did not understand.

"*Sí,*" I said, acting like I understood the sentence.

"*Te gusta juegas los … eh … ?*" I asked, pointing at the drums.

"Drums (pronounced *drooms*)?" he asked.

"*Sí,*" I said. "Drooms."

"*Sí,*" he said, followed by a sentence that I did not understand.

"*Sí,*" I said, acting like I understood the sentence.

"*Te gusta juegas el ... eh ... ?*" I asked, pointing at the piano.

"Piano (pronounced *piano*)?" he asked.

"*Sí*," I said. "Piano."

"*Sí*," he said, followed by a sentence that I did not understand.

"*Sí*," I said, acting like I understood the sentence.

Mateo sat down and started playing the piano. It was as if he had had enough of my idiocy and our pointless conversation. Regardless, I added *drooms* and *piano* to my Spanish vocabulary.

In a matter of seconds I realized that Mateo was playing Beethoven's popular "Für Elise." As I stood there in his room, all seemed to slow down for me. Tears welled up in my eyes. I thought about how music was a universal language and how this boy whom I could not even communicate with was causing something to stir within my soul—all by playing a song.

It is time for me to take some different records off the shelf and play them in my mind's record player: to intentionally live in the now and practice gratitude like Marcos. Instead of waking up and thinking about all that I must do, I will play the record titled *What I Get to Do Today.* Instead of going to bed thinking about all that I did not get done, I will play the record titled *All That I Got to Do Today.* Instead of always thinking about the things that are not going right in my life, I will play the record titled *All That You Have to Be Thankful For.* Tonight, I will take a proverbial Beethoven record off the shelf and think about that scene with Mateo.

Yes, replaying the beautiful music of a deaf man seems like a good place to start. Yes, Paraguay seems like a good place to break ground in my mind.

———

I'm free again—
a speckle in this great expanse
lost in the mystery of the dance
that breathes peace in all my strife
where hands are gloves and I'm alive.
I was lost in the noise at sea;
now there's layers beneath my feet
whispering, "Rest and be."

"I'm enough for you, don't you see?
Let the noise fade into Me;
I'll turn it into a symphony
and help you be, to set you free
from the chaos in the winds,
the push and pull of sin again,
where noise runs deep."

In the noise is where I weep,
tossed by these things inside of me,
like a puppet on a string,
controlled by all these worldly things.
How can You run to who I am,
this forgotten, fallen man?
Won't You change my name?

"Come and rest just as you are;
I know your feet have traveled far
through these formulaic schemes
that they use to make you bleed,
not as you should be but for who I am,
for I know you're just a man,
and your name is Love."

40

ROMINA IN THE GAP

I can feel my heart sinking, aching, crumbling into a thousand pieces, then falling—quite violently and rapidly—like the incessant darts in one of those overwhelming summertime Roanoke rainfalls, forming puddles in the pits of my stomach.

It has been a busy day—from visiting Timothy's School this morning to attending a church meeting at Martin and Tabita's house this afternoon to touring the local Yerba Mate (a type of South American tea) after that—but this is the most eye-opening and shocking. I am not even sure if we should be in this place, here on the outskirts of Bella Vista in this community of dilapidated shacks, carrying around our cameras and phones, naturally curious and wide-eyed. We are completely out of our comfort zones, entirely unable to blend in.

We are at the house of a young teenage girl named Romina—an adorable, dark-haired, caramel-eyed girl with a mousy voice—whom we met this morning at the church meeting. We walk through her family's backyard of muddy red clay and see a couple of boarded, makeshift shacks. One shack is a kitchen. Another shack is where everyone sleeps. No bathrooms. No water. There's a crater behind one of the shacks where they are trying to dig a well, but it is yet to be completed. Apparently, Romina's father died while digging a well. I am unsure if it is this same well, but it might be. Regardless, the hole in their yard is a reminder of a grave. As for Romina's mother, she is hardly present in the lives of Romina and her three siblings. We are told that her mother is rather promiscuous in their tiny community, hopping from man to man, from place to place, leaving her teenage children to fend for themselves. Her method of coping with the loss of her love, perhaps, has resulted in the abandonment of her other love: her children.

Romina's grandmother, a paunchy, dark-skinned Guarani woman with a damp, sweaty face, and troughs of wrinkles beneath her eyes reflecting her years of sacrificial nurturing, is washing clothes on the back porch of the kitchen. She is the children's primary caregiver now. She greets us with a warm smile, then continues to labor along, accomplishing the day's tasks, for the sake and survival of her grandchildren. She will have a special place in heaven, I think. Her life is all about serving the "least of these." She is following the "Jesus Way," whether she realizes it or not. She understands.

Tabita is leading the way through their yard, as Romina and her two sisters and brother walk beside her. Clothes are hanging on lines that are draped from shack to shack, from tree to tree. We are constantly ducking our heads as we make our way around the yard. Dirty chickens and large roosters are wandering aimlessly around us, squawking at the lurking cats and pestering dogs. One of the roosters tumbles kamikaze-style out of an overhanging tree, then regains its balance and clucks along.

"This is where Romina's family sleeps," Tabita says to us as we peer into a small, dark, shack with clothes hanging from the rafters and trash strewn all over the floor. There are no shelves, no dressers. No room to put anything at all. Just beds. Junk and debris are everywhere.

"They sleep two or three to a bed," Tabita continues.

For Coach, Jamie, and me it is as if time has stopped in its tracks. Oh, if we were not in front of Romina and her siblings, surely we would fall onto our knees and cry out to God, "Why do poverty and injustice such as this exist, Father? What can we do to help?" Injustice, I've heard it said, is naming that which is not natural. This is unnatural. And it is impossible to ignore what is going on within me. My soul finds itself in an unfamiliar and vulnerable and frightening place, and therefore I'm scrambling around in the Garden of my mind, searching for fig leaves to clothe myself.

Shame.

I feel *shame.*

Not the kind of personal shame that had plagued my spirituality for years, rooted in thinking that I was an unforgiven and hopeless sinner or a failure at my core, only amplified by my wrongdoings or by certain ideologies. No, this is not the type of shame that I am talking about as I stare into this dirty shanty. This is more of a communal shame, as a member of the human race, as a broken piece in the mosaic of mankind. A shame that rises from anger—that poverty such as this exists in our world, that *this* is not right, that *this* is unfair, that *something* must be done.

Romina is crying now. I do not know why. Gentle tears are streaming down her little cheeks. Tabita consoles her. It's as if, in the presence of three Americans, Romina perhaps inherently knows how abnormal these conditions are, how shocking it must look to outsiders like us. She knows how wrong this is for them to have to live like this. She, too, is marked by *shame.* A different type of shame. A deeply personal sense of shame. Like the child who has a friend over only to witness the wrath of an alcoholic father or the kid who attends school hiding the scars and bruises of abuse by his or her parents, Romina looks up at us with her watery eyes as if to say, "I just wish things were different." Tabita has her arm around her. She bends down and says something to her in Spanish. Romina nods.

Yes, this is poverty. And that should be acknowledged. But what should also be acknowledged is the fact that this is her home. Her beautiful, wonderful home. This is where Romina and her siblings will learn and grow and mature, molded and guided under the careful watch of their grandmother.

As we leave, her grandmother gives me a wet kiss on my cheek.

It feels a lot like God.

———

In 2009 two authors and researchers named Kate Pickett and Richard Wilkinson published a book called *The Spirit Level: Why More Equal Societies Always Do Better.* The book, based on thirty years of research, revealed that for each of the eleven different health and social problems—physical health, mental health, drug abuse, education, imprisonment, obesity, social mobility, trust and community life, violence, teenage pregnancies, and child well-being—data is significantly worse in more unequal countries, where there is a large gap between the rich and the poor. The book also revealed that life expectancy is directly related to this gap. The bigger the gap, the lower the life expectancy is in that country.

I have not read the book, but I heard about it while watching a film called *Everything Is Spiritual* by Author Rob Bell. Bell's conclusion about the research was fascinating to me: that the natural progression of the universe is for it to become more *unified* and that anything opposite of that is unnatural. Whether you come to the same conclusions about the research or not, this principle—of moving toward unification—is a wonderful way to live and can inspire social justice. It is what Christianity is at its finest: serving those on the margins and gravitating toward suffering, narrowing the gap, affirming the value and worth of all people. It's why the Kurrles do what they do. It's why the Briscoes do what they do.

It starts with me, though.

And with you.

My mentality must shift from looking out for myself to looking out for others; from obsessing over the American Dream to helping others attain their own dreams; from entitlement to generosity, from privilege to focusing my gaze on the alienated and marginalized; from ignorance to awareness. The scales must fall from my eyes. Romina needs me to see her home and her shame and her tears. Seeing must lead to doing.

41

THREE SOULS, FOREVER INTERTWINED

It is evening now.

We are at Marcos and Cristiane's house, and Marcos keeps saying, "Tonight, we celebrate!" and then laughing wildly. Though today has been sobering in many ways, as we have been confronted with the sad realities of poverty in Paraguay, tonight we are going to do what Marcos says we are going to do: celebrate and fellowship with one another. Marcos has already opened a bottle of wine, and Cristiane picked up some steaks and sausages at the store for Marcos to grill. We are waiting for Norberto and his family to arrive.

"We never do this," Marcos says, "but tonight we must."

He says that we must, because tonight, for the first time in fifteen years, Marcos, Norberto, and Coach will all be together.

In the same room.

Three souls that have been intertwined since birth.

No, they did not choose their connection to one another. It all began with the matriarchs of their families, Twila and Tabita. The three of them were born into this story. But now they choose it. And love flows from their united devotion to the mission.

It's been such a long time since the three of them have been together because, one, the Briscoes hardly ever come to Paraguay, and, two, whenever the Kurrle missionaries come to the States, it's usually one at a time. Of course Coach saw Marcos five years ago (Year II of this book) and Norberto two years ago (Year IV of this book) when I interviewed each of them at the softball tournament, but it has been a long fifteen years since the three of them have been together at the same time.

The last time was Norberto and Julie's wedding.

———

Norberto arrives, and he and Coach embrace in the kitchen as Coach joyfully laughs. It has been a couple days since we have seen Norberto.

Just seeing Norberto in this place is a story of its own.

That's because this very home used to belong to, and was built by, Norberto and Julie. Now Marcos and his family live here. This might seem like an odd thing, but the Kurrles are resourceful missionaries who don't see any need to let a perfectly good house go to waste, even if it is a reminder of tragedy and what used to be.

"We haven't told them anything about the house, Norb," Marcos says to Norberto as he greets everyone in the kitchen. "We were waiting for you to get here so you can talk to them about it."

"Oh, OK. I will tell them about it," Norberto says.

He pauses.

"This was my and Julie's dream home," he begins.

Norberto shares with us that this house took them ten years to build. The lot was cheap, and they got the lumber for free from Martin's farm. As they gradually built the house, Norberto and his family would live in different closed-off sections of the home and then build onto it once they had the funds. In the end, they actually spent less money building their home than they would have had they rented a small apartment all those years.

Standing here in this home with Norberto, it is eerie to think that this was the house where Norberto and Julie planned on raising their family. Though Norberto seems to be in a better emotional state now, I am guessing there was a time when he could not bear to come into this place. Traces of Julie and

Timothy's spirits are here. I can picture Julie and Norberto having dinners in this place and playing with Timothy in this place and joyously organizing the room of their adopted Anahi in this place. Amidst the havoc of their lives as missionaries—moving from the United States and all around Paraguay in subsequent years—and amidst the pain they experienced in their marriage—their struggle with infertility and their countless miscarriages—this home was a symbol of stability to them. A safe haven. A hospital where they could nurse their wounds. A fortress where they could escape life's unexplainable attacks. It is where Norberto and Julie planned to grow old together, where they planned to live out the rest of their days, raising their family and serving this country that had captured their hearts. I guess it is only fitting that now perhaps Marcos and Cristiane can grow old together in this place.

It seems that Marcos and Norberto, brothers who have been joined at the hip since their childhoods, are incapable of journeying down separate paths. Their lives have always been interconnected, from the jungles of Raúl Peña in their youth to now. Even when it looks like they are heading in different directions, like when Norberto went to school in the States and Marcos went to school in Germany, they still ended up pastoring a church together—yes, here in Obligado—once they graduated; or when it looked like Marcos would raise his family in Asunción and Norberto in Obligado, well, here we are. How fitting it is that after all those years of Norberto picking up and carrying Marcos—whether it was when they were kids skinning up their knees while racing on bikes through the tangled jungle of Raúl Peña or when they went off to school in Argentina and Marcos was bullied and ridiculed—that Marcos now would be the one picking up the radio ministry that Norberto began and taking care of the house that Norberto built.

No, it is not the end of their story.

But it is a fitting conclusion to *this* story.

———

"Come here, friends," Marcos says, leading Coach, Norberto, and me out the back door of the kitchen. "I will show you how I grill steak!"

We make our way outside down a walkway of large, rounded stones beneath a couple of overhanging palm trees, toward a slab of concrete sheltered by a log tiki hut roofed with bamboo and palm. It is a comfortable, autumn evening, growing cooler as night settles. The colors from the sunken sun are barely hanging in the air.

Marcos fires up the rotisserie grill beneath the tiki hut and sticks two meaty hunks of steak and two ropes of sausages on the rotator. Marcos was not kidding when he said that we were going to celebrate. Money does not matter tonight. We will eat and drink and be merry. Also, we are passing around a glass of something chocolatey mixed with Baileys Irish whiskey. (Did I mention that these are some of the coolest, most relatable missionaries I've ever met?)

We eventually sit down at a wooden table in the hut and begin to talk while the meat is cooking. As we talk, it dawns on me that I am not only looking at the next generation—Coach, Marcos, and Norberto—of a mission that has brought life to numerous communities in this country, but I am also looking at three of the men who have impacted me the most in my twenties.

Coach, the man who introduced me to this story, a story that has spoken to me consistently these last six years; the man who shaped and molded me at college, ingraining in me the principles of servant-leadership, and who gave me the courage (and a gentle prod) to leave Indiana so that I could become a man in Charlotte.

Here Coach is, sitting with me.

Marcos, the man whose fiery passion and perspective on life, work, and ministry, has been inspiring me since I interviewed him in Year II, back when I was in the loneliest of states, unable to adequately process the dramatic changes in my life—in geography, in work, in my friendships, in my romantic relationship— yet gained strength from the profundity of his words, which propelled me into a deeper discovery of myself and of spirituality, so that I could perhaps one day personally experience the joy and passion that Marcos so acutely reflected.

Here Marcos is, sitting with me.

Norberto, the man whose faith somehow remained intact in the depths of unendurable pain, a faith that had been inspiring me since I saw him on that video screen four years ago, when he said those five mystifying words "There's still work to do"—merely four months after that hellish day when fog took Julie and Timothy. It was a faith that I was able to witness firsthand when I interviewed him in Roanoke two years later, when I was moving through my own valley of grief, a much lesser form of grief than Norberto but grief nonetheless, when I was hoping to emerge from my depression and found myself comforted and strengthened by Norberto's transparency in sharing with me his own story. It was a faith that propelled me into a deeper discovery of Christ's sufferings, where I found the Christ standing there in the valley with me, assuring me of perhaps the only absolute I've found in Christian spirituality: *"I love you, and I'm here with you."*

Here Norberto is, sitting with me.

———

Jamie joins us outside, and Coach and Jamie begin talking about the happenings of the day and their observations about Paraguay and the Kurrles' mission.

"Here's the thing … " Coach reflects. "Not only did Martin and Tabita throw their lives into full-time ministry, but they have *four* children walking with God and they are all serving and ministering in Paraguay. And that—*that's*—what is so powerful."

Coach is right. It is perhaps the most incredible element of this story, yet it's often overlooked because for some reason we have different standards when it comes to people from a different country or when it pertains to missionaries. But this would be the rough equivalent, in the States, of two baristas marrying and having four children who also became full-time baristas … all in the same area.

Marcos and Norberto could've pursued a different life, one that reflected the values of the American Dream, but they didn't.

"You could have stayed in the States after you went to college," Coach continues, pointing at Norberto. "And you could have stayed in Germany after college," he adds, pointing at Marcos.

Marcos nods. "I had three invitations to stay in Germany."

"And it was tempting sometimes," Norberto says. "Stay in the States, get a good job … it's easier."

"It's still a temptation sometimes," Marcos continues. "Sometimes when there are difficulties, when we are struggling, when finances are tight, we think, 'Hey, let's go for five years to the United States.' But that is really short-lived."

"We are working with everything we can here," Marcos says. "We don't have abundance. We have to measure everything. But it's such a blessing, the tournament. It gives us such a push. The tournament tells us: *Go ahead, do it.*"

Marcos and Norberto teach me that everything that a materialist culture elevates must be quieted, at least in some fashion, if we are to truly live a life that is marked by selflessness, love, and service. To live a life like Christ lived.

We suddenly hear the *pat-pat* of little feet making their way up the path behind us.

It's Anahi.

She finds Norberto, her father, and leans on his legs.

"*Papi,*" she says, in her adorable high-pitched voice, "*yo quiero comer el carne.*" *I want to eat meat.*

Norberto says something, but I'm not sure what it is. I'm guessing it's along the lines of "We will eat *carne* soon."

Anahi then runs off to go play with her cousins.

Oh, that precious child! She has little idea what she has been through—unaware of the tragic history of her family. But it is as if her innocence rescues us, momentarily, from all that we know, from all that we have seen Norberto endure over the last four years.

The interaction takes Coach to a place of introspection.

"This trip has been great, but this is the highlight," Coach says, his eyes watering. "There are times in my day when something happens, or I get mad or something, and then I stop and I think about you, and what you're doing here."

And in an instant, Coach had done what he has always done so well: turn the conversation into something that even goes beyond joy and laughter and ventures into the crux of our humanity—our true selves, our core selves, our spirit selves.

"And then the preciousness of the next two hours," Coach continues, choking up, his voice growing shaky. "I don't know when I'll be with you two again. So then you just think, '*What's heaven like?*'"

There is a pause, and then Norberto smiles.

"We won't have to get up from the table," Norberto says.

"I *long* for that day," Coach says, wiping his eyes.

"We'll have 1,000 years to catch up," Norberto adds.

"And thank *you*," Marcos says to Coach and Jamie, "for continuing the tournament. There's not much around the world, stories like this."

"You took the torch," Norberto says.

———

Dinner is served *Rodizio* style. Marcos makes his way around the table with the steak on a metal pole, asking each of us to point to the spot on the steak that we would like to eat, and then—*SLICE*—he cuts through the slab of juicy meat until it falls onto our plates. The faces of Marcos's children (Mateo and Alheli) and Norberto's children (Marcos, Nicole, and Anahi) are marked with awe toward the feast that we are all about to partake in.

Marcos blesses the meal, and then the feast begins.

Parts of the table are speaking Spanish.

Parts are speaking English.

Children. Adults.

Different nationalities.

A diverse collection of people with all kinds of different pasts, cultures, and experiences.

I keep thinking of Julie's dream about the children dancing around the tree.

———

The night is winding down. It is almost time for Norberto to leave with his family and return to Encarnación. Before they leave, however, Jamie has a brilliant idea: for me to interview Coach, Marcos, and Norberto on video. Who knows when the three of them will be together again? If another fifteen years pass before they are all in the same room together, they will all be in their late fifties. It is once again a reminder of the fleeting nature of time, of the importance of living *for* today and *in* the moment.

We sit down for the interview in Marcos's living room. The three of them sitting together (Marcos on the left, Coach in the middle, and Norberto on the right) and facing me.

As I interview them, I find myself thinking about how this book just happened to unfold at the most pivotal of times in each of their lives: Coach, in his and Jamie's moving to Indianapolis and then back to Winona Lake and then, most importantly, enduring the biggest test of their lives, the dreaded curse of cancer; Marcos, in his and Cristiane's moving to Asunción, where they felt as if they would spend the rest of their days, and then being unexpectedly pulled to Obligado, perhaps the biggest test of their lives; and Norberto, in his losing of Julie and Timothy, a tragedy where words like *test* or *trial* do not suffice, and the journey of grief he had to travel before finding his beloved Nancy and her two children on the other side.

So, yes, here they are together, which is historical, no doubt … but it is more than that. In the last half-decade, each of them has been thrown into life's most fragile places, into the garden of their own Gethsemane at the foot of the Mount of Olives. And, like the Christ, in sweating drops of blood, they have comforted me that it is OK for faith to be messy and agonizing and complicated; in crying out, "Take this cup from me!" they have comforted me that it is OK to question and to doubt and to scream; and in saying, "Not my will, but Yours be done," they have inspired me to surrender to something that transcends my existence, to let go of what I can't control.

At the end of our interview, as we have moved from their personal journeys to the mission, from their individual trials to their communal focus, Norberto is the last to speak. His closing words are all too fitting.

"There's still work to do."

————

What is a dream?
Was it in those burning embers?
Red, the fire in my soul.
Did it wave to me that day?
Blue, the promise in its skies.
Am I more than my performance?
White, the emptiness that I feel.

It left me scrambling in the void.
It left me drowning in the noise.
In its systems I had no choice.

I come to You with questions,
and You answer me with a story.
How fitting it is for You to answer me with a story!
Just like the parables of old,
You have no answer, no absolutes.
Just a spectrum of awareness.
Just the expanding hue of Your love.

Just a journey You're inviting me into.
A journey where I find what's true.
I lost my shell when I ... found ... You.

What is a dream?
No flag, no system led to fullness.
My body, my soul left me helpless.
"A dream is a desire," You say,
"Of the true self, not the false self.
Of the spirit, nothing else.
In the nothingness, I am."

And so I found my desire, my dream,
through a story that You gave,
about two families
and two countries
united by You, in You, through You
symbolized by three colors:
red, white, and blue.

I found my dream, my desire,
in the passion of a man whose fire
burned with the reds of joy and love.

I found it in the glassy eyes
of a man who lost his son and wife,
the white emptiness of lost love.

I found it where the colors blend,
where grace begins and never ends,
in the shadows of the Blue Ridge.

I found it beneath a violet sky
on a Paraguayan countryside
where everything within me died
so I could truly live again.
So I could swim in union.

42

FOG III

We are standing on a street of wet, red clay, overlooking an open field, just down the road from Marcos's house. Today, Marcos is going to shuttle us around the southeastern part of Paraguay, where most of the Church of God *Iglesias* have been planted. So why are we standing on a road and looking out at the field?

Well, no more than a couple of hundred feet into our journey down one of those long, muddy Paraguayan roads, we felt inclined to pull over.

It is seven o'clock in the morning. The sky is gray, and the air is damp. A morning fog hangs like a cloud above the openness of this emerald field, absorbing the tops of distant trees as they fade into the smoky silver of vapor.

We stand there in solitude. We do not talk about it plainly, but we are all thinking the same thing.

"Of course it's foggy this morning," Coach eventually says.

Just last night we were with Norberto, and he talked transparently about his journey the last five years. And now, here we are: presented with a heavy fog in the early morning. It was only four years ago—almost exactly—when Julie and Norberto had left this exact house, which I can still see in the distance, no more than eighty yards away, with Timothy and Anahi in the backseat. Norberto eventually returned to this house with two people ... instead of four.

As I gaze out, I notice a lone tree out in the middle of the field. It is a mighty tree, its bare branches climbing a hundred different directions, spider-webbing into the sky, its dark outline stenciled into the smoky gray.

The fog is in the background, but it is still part of the scene. The lonely and bare and mighty tree stands tall, extending its hands into the air, hoping to make peace with the sky.

43

THE JUNGLE AND ITS PULSE

It has been an eerie morning. After such a joyous evening last night, this morning has been a reminder of how quickly things can change, and how quickly things *did* change for Norberto on that fateful foggy day.

We've been on the road for an hour or so, and the fog, instead of lifting, has only thickened. At one point, a parked truck emerges from the fog on the right side of the road. No one says anything, but I know exactly what we are all thinking.

Not long after passing the truck, Marcos speaks up.

"One time Alheli asked me, 'Why do we die?' after watching a movie. So I tried to explain to her why we die. She said, 'Can I die with you? Can we die together as a family?'"

―――――

"We're almost here," Marcos says, two hours into our drive, as we pull into a run-down gas station so that we gringos can use the *bano*. There's not a bathroom in the gas station. Just portable potties out back. I peed in a bush. It was the right thing to do.

This section of Highway 6 feels like a ghost town. Next to this rundown gas station is a dark, deserted tobacco shop, and that's about all there is in this area. How Martin decided to plant the second church of the mission here, I have no idea.

We get back into Marcos's car, and he turns onto a cobblestone road that stretches on for at least six more miles, taking us farther off the beaten path. We journey deeper and deeper into what was once a thick, tangled jungle, and it becomes even more absurd that this was where Martin decided to expand the mission. This would be the equivalent of Nike opening an outlet store in the middle of a desert. We are smack-dab in the middle of nowhere. There are no cars. No people walking on the side of the road. Very few houses.

"Everyone thought we were crazy for coming here," Marcos reflects. "I want to do things different at the radio station. Maybe I'm just crazy, too. Maybe it's in my blood."

Before we know it, we have turned onto the gravel road that leads to the heart of the Raúl Peña campus. Shaded by hundreds of towering trees, this remote area is the site of a church, grade school, high school, Bible college, and the Kurrles' old house, which is currently uninhabited. The dim of the early-morning light hangs in the shadows of the trees as if trapped beneath a blanket.

Upon arriving, we are greeted by the church's head pastor, a gentle, soft-spoken, gray-haired man named Nei Ohlweiler. Nei is accompanied by five young adults, all wearing T-shirts and jeans, who I assume work with him on this campus.

We circle up, and Marcos exchanges some words with Nei in Spanish. We learn that the two young white men are Nei's sons, and the other three are young men from the Dominican Republic. Apparently, a Dominican woman who attended the Bible college here in Raúl Peña married a man who also went to the school and then moved back to the Dominican Republic. Now there is a pipeline from the D.R. to this church in the jungles of Paraguay, which the softball tournament helped build. What a reflection of global unity this forested place is! It is what we should all long for: to join the dance, which has no bounds, which cannot be contained by geography or something so worldly as words or language.

Though Nei does not speak English, one of his sons (whose name I have unfortunately forgotten!) speaks basic English. He shares with us the story of his family—how Nei was in the first sixth-grade graduating class here in Raúl Peña … and how his mother went here too … and how he and his brother went here too. And now they all work together. Here. He is currently attending the Bible college. Here.

This place provides one of the most necessary ingredients for a flourishing society: education. I'm reminded of what Marcos told me back when I interviewed him four years ago: how he and Norberto used to ride their bikes to the local government school only to discover that their teacher was *no esta*. So then they would ride their bikes to the teacher's house and wake him up.

However random the location might be, people come to this place from all the surrounding rural communities. This is the only church and school in the area, not to mention the only college.

No, Martin moving his family here did not make sense from a business-standpoint—their ministry pursuits would have been more financially sustainable had they planted a church or begun a school in a big city like Asunción, Encarnación, or El Ciudad de Este—three of the biggest cities in Paraguay. And, no, it did not make sense from his family's standpoint: It would have been easier to raise a family near a city or town with a store and a hospital and all the resources that they needed. Living in the jungle required much more work. And yet the Kurrles' moving to the jungle was a reflection of the parable of the lost sheep. In the towns and cities, there might have been ninety-nine sheep, but in the density of the jungle there was one. And the one sheep was just as important, if not more important, than the ninety-nine. So they moved to be a loving resource for the one—for the people who were alienated and totally removed from civilization.

As Nei's son tells us about the education that his entire family received, I'm reminded that, though Martin and Tabita moved here to plant a church, they realized that the need was even deeper. (And, yes, there can be deeper needs than planting churches.) It is one thing to find the lost sheep, but it is quite another to put the sheep on your shoulders and bring it back to the flock, back to its home, back to where it can be healthy as it grows and matures. It is why they started a school: They recognized the need. And now there is not only a grade school, but also a high school, and not only a high school but also a college. And Nei's family benefited from all of it.

"This school here is much better than the government school," says the son.

We spend some time in the thirty-five-year-old church. The inside is made entirely of a tannish-brown European yew. It is beautiful. And then we are led down a gravel road and into a courtyard that is surrounded by school buildings.

All the children are out in the courtyard, banging on drums and making music. Apparently, the kids get out of school early today because of Independence Day tomorrow, a celebration of Paraguay's liberation from Spain, which they won on May 14, 1811. Today is May 13.

From what I understand, each community hosts a parade, and in each parade, the school children march and play the same ancient Guarani song, a basic tune carried by a steady drumbeat—*thump, thump, thump-thump-thump*—reminiscent of the standard war march: *left, left, left-right-left.*

It has been interesting being in Paraguay this week in the days leading up to their celebration of independence. Almost every town has been decorated with red, white, and blue, Paraguay's national colors, and it has often felt like we are in America on July 4.

Once the children in this courtyard realize that they have an audience, they decide to perform the song for us, from start to finish. The song begins with a single drumbeat, and as the song progresses, more students join in with their instruments. Once all have joined in, the instruments gradually begin to fade out until it's back to the steady drumbeat—*thump, thump, thump-thump-thump.*

Despite all of their varying backgrounds and stories, perhaps represented by all the different instruments involved in the song, they are unified—no, *we* are unified—for seven minutes, around the drum's repetition. And it is as if each of our souls cries out for us to become aware of the universal rhythm of our spirits—which is Theirs in us and us in Them—uniting us, ready to burst from within us and dance together in the sky.

———

We have been here for about an hour and a half. Marcos says that we should probably be leaving soon, considering we still have to drive across the entire southeastern side of the country, about seventy-five miles, and visit three more churches.

We walk back toward the heart of campus, where the car is parked, and gather together on a nearby porch, where plates of pastries and a thermos of coffee have been prepared for us.

As we eat and drink with Nei, his two sons, and the three Dominicans, one of the Dominicans nudges me and hands me his phone. We had tried to talk to each other while walking back here, but we kept hitting walls in our conversation because of the language barrier. All I know is that his name is Yasser, and he kept saying things like "escribir" (to write) and "Virginia" (Virginia). Yasser seems to be in his mid- to late twenties and is about five-foot-ten. He has a dark mustache, goatee, and patchy, scraggily sideburns.

I take his phone and look at his screen. On the left is a box that says "Spanish," on the right a box that says "English."

I smile.

"Do you like to write?" it says on the right.

"Sí, MUCHO MUCHO MUCHO," I type in Spanish.

Yasser laughs. Probably at the shallowness of my *Español*.

"I like to write too," he types.

"What do you like to write?" I ask.

"I like writing about lessons and stories from the Bible," he types.

As he hands the phone to me, we are both glowing.

Our conversation continues for another fifteen minutes or so. And before it is time to leave, I type a note to Yasser: *"I can see that you are passionate. You should keep writing."*

Yasser nods his head in affirmation.

"Gracias," he says, shaking my hand.

I give him my email address, and we agree to stay in contact.

And as we pull away, the campus of Raúl Peña fading in our rearview mirror, I pray for Yasser and for his writing and that I would somehow be able to believe my own words about my own artistic pursuits. And as the *thump-thump* of the cobblestone road shakes the car, I find myself thinking about the drumbeat and my heartbeat and the pulse of Raúl Peña—that its origin had little practicality, just a "feeling" from one man named Martin, who was willing to attempt what had never been done before; to follow and trust and surrender to that which does not make any sense, that which is not always God but is sometimes God and is therefore *always* worth the risk.

44

THE TABLE

We have entered El Ciudad del Este (City of the East), a city on the Parana River across from the Brazilian border, known for its many shops and malls that line its chaotic city streets. Here we will visit our final church of the day.

It has been interesting to see all the different churches today and meet with the people in their communities—all of which are churches Martin and Tabita started! First, the church and the school in the jungles of Raúl Peña, which we visited this morning, which feels like an eternity ago; and then the church in the rural area of Naranjal, a small church that we visited this afternoon, which is led by Norberto's sister Priscila and her husband, Enrique; and then the gigantic church in Santa Rita, a church in an extremely affluent community, its economy powered by wealthy Brazilians coming over the border; and now this church in El Ciudad del Este, which is by far located in the poorest community we have visited, here in the heart of the second largest city in Paraguay, nestled next to all the small houses and shacks, where stray dogs roam freely and there is trash in the streets, and there are flies, so many flies!

We are greeted by Pastor Raul, a heavyset dark-skinned man with short, black hair, a thick mustache, and a gentle grin. His wife and his six children also warmly greet us and welcome us to their church with big smiles and eyes that are filled with intrigue. Americans!

Even though Marcos called Pastor Raul ahead of time and told him that we were not very hungry, Raul and his family guide us into the sanctuary where we see a long plastic table that is covered with plates that are full of empanadas and *chipas* (always *chipas!*) and pastries. They also have for us multiple liters of El Pulp, a Paraguayan soft drink that Coach and I have recently become obsessed with, which we will continue to guzzle like the Pulpaholics that we have become.

It's interesting to me that, every church we have visited today, the people there have fed us. It is cultural, I think. Whenever there are guests, you eat together, *especially* if they are guests at your *church*. Most have never met Coach and Jamie, and certainly none of them have met me. I cannot even speak their own language. They do not know what I believe, what my theology is, what I've done, or where I've been. I have nothing to offer them. I might not ever see them again. I might not ever be able to repay them. But it is all irrelevant to them. The people at each church have welcomed us in with open arms and have asked us to take a seat at the table and enjoy the gifts that they have prepared for us. Their posture toward outsiders is one of inherent belonging to all who enter into their sacred space.

It seems that when you break down the general posture of the American church, there are many stipulations for outsiders. Though we might welcome guests into our sanctuaries, the exclusivity that is sometimes projected from the pulpit—deriving from dualistic, either/or thinking—makes the guests think that they aren't all that welcome after all, that they are too different to belong. I have spent much of my young-adult life feeling that way. As Richard Rohr says, the chief sin of churches in the West is that "we have not moved doctrine and dogma to the level of inner experience."

Philosopher Peter Rollins says that the church ought to mirror how a loving family raises a child: first, the family makes sure that child knows that he or she *belongs*; second, the family helps the child with his or her *behavior*; third, behavior moves toward *belief.* The American church, however, has seemed to start with belief (pray a prayer, get baptized, become a Christian), which moves toward behavior (read your Bible, pray, go to church, join a small group), which then moves toward belonging because that person has suddenly been conformed into the image of everyone else! This approach has robbed the church of diversity.

I need to be surrounded by people who are most different than me, not people who are exactly the same. Often times it's the alien—the person whose story is most different than my own—that reflects to me the mystery of the cross, blowing up all of my constructs and inspiring me to see in a new, different way.

Christ not only believed that there was room at the table for all (the only people group he had an exclusive attitude towards was the religious people!), but he also *went* to the tables, the dinner parties, himself. And when he broke bread at the Last Supper, at his table, his very betrayer, Judas, sat in their midst, and he knew who it was, and he not only invited him to break bread and drink from the cup, just like all the others, but he also washed his feet!

The Paraguayans' hospitality today has moved me, especially at this church in Ciudad del Este. It has been a reflection to me of Christ's mysterious inclusivity. As we sit at that table in the sanctuary in Ciudad del Este with Raul, his wife, and their six children, drinking El Pulp and eating empanadas and *chipas* and pastries, flies buzzing all around us, it is as if the church as it was intended to be is in our midst. We are all taking part in the mystery of the table—where *all* belong. And the fact that they have prepared such an extravagant meal for us with the limited resources they have feels as if they are washing our feet.

45

STEAM

We are sitting in traffic on a bridge over the Parana River, which connects El Ciudad del Este in Paraguay to Foz do Iguaçu in Brazil, home of Iguazú Falls (which means "Big Water" in Guarani), one of the "New 7 Wonders of Nature," which we are going to visit tomorrow.

Marcos insists that we gringos will be fine getting across the Brazilian border even without purchasing a visa or going through standard customs that Americans must go through, because he has snagged a sign from the radio station that says *LA PRENSA* (the press). He has clearly displayed the sign in the front-left corner of our front windshield. He says that no one will inspect our car, or the people in it, if they believe that we are the press.

As we wait in traffic, Marcos is hilariously rehearsing what he will say to the authorities if we *do* get stopped at the border.

"We have an important meeting with the Owner of waterfalls," Marcos rehearses. "The owner—His name is God—and we are going to see what He needs us to do, you know, talk to Him a little."

Marcos's humor is helping because I think we are all a little nervous. We're in a foreign country, after all. This isn't America. They don't have our backgrounds on file. For all they know, we could be terrorists!

We arrive at the border, which feels more like a gigantic New Jersey toll booth, with about fifteen different gates for vehicles to pass through, and I—surprisingly—do not see a single policeman or guard.

We make it to Brazil.

A few miles into Brazil, we see a ramp to the right with a sign that says "ARGENTINA." Apparently, the Argentina border is here too. Within five miles of us are three different countries—massive countries, by the way: Brazil (the fifth largest country in the world), Argentina (the eighth largest country in the world), and Paraguay (which is the size of California). Marcos tells us that the lower side of Iguazú Falls is the Brazilian side, and that the upper side of the waterfalls is the Argentinian side. I wonder if we will try our luck and sneak into Argentina, too.

"They are much more strict in Argentina," Marcos says.

We will not try to sneak across the Argentinean border.

————

We find a hotel, the Hotel Nacional Inn, about five miles away from Iguazú Falls. Fifty dollars. Seriously.

A nice hotel too. Probably a four-star hotel, by Priceline's standards, which are reliable standards, with a free breakfast, pool, steam room, game room, and workout room.

As a writer, I do not think that I will ever be in a financial position to retire. But perhaps I can retire here, in South America, when I'm ninety or so. Yes, I think I will retire at ninety and move to Paraguay or Brazil.

Marcos and I are rooming together tonight.

It has been a long day. A good day, but a long day. Four churches. Five hours of driving, all across the southeastern side of Paraguay, through the heavy fog at dawn, down those winding back roads near Raúl Peña, to sneaking across the border this evening.

I don't think anyone is as tired as Marcos, though. Not only has he been driving us around, but he was also our translator everywhere that we went. Poor guy. It is not a day off for a radio personality if he still has to talk all day. Bob Costas would never take a vacation day to be an auctioneer.

Marcos and I decide that we should unwind, so we make our way downstairs to the steam room. Marcos tells me that he has never been in one before. As we take a seat inside a small box, slightly bigger than our hotel bathroom, constructed entirely with turquoise tile, I tell him that it's a great place to sit in silence and relax.

"Let's do that," he says. "Peace and quiet."

He lets out an exasperated sigh, as if to decompress.

We hit the button, and within five minutes, the steam is so dense that I cannot even see Marcos. It reminds me of the fog that we experienced this morning, a fog that increased with each hour and hung lower and lower, slowly falling like a curtain.

I hate the fog, I think to myself, *but steam is OK.*

Ten minutes pass.

Fifteen minutes pass.

We have not said a word to one another.

I have been trying to pray, and what I mean by pray is my new way of praying, inspired by Marcos, where I basically thank God for all the blessings in my life that I can think of. I do not ask God for anything. I just thank God for everything. So, instead of asking God to help me publish some of my projects, which is a request that spawns from my aggravation with publishing, which is negative, I thank God for giving me the opportunity to write, which is positive. So it's basically cognitive therapy for my perfectionism and anxiety, which has all sorts of practical and neurological implications, which I think is why I like this new way of praying so much, because I *know* it's beneficial. That might sound sad to some who are reading this—that I have to have practical implications for something as central to the Christian life as prayer, so that I know I'm not wasting my time, but it is just where I'm at right now. It helps me to calm my restless mind. It helps me return to gratitude. It helps my heartbeat to slow down. It helps my body to relax. All I've ever really wanted is peace.

Plus, prayer has always confused me, and lately I've stopped asking God for things because it just makes me upset. What if God answers my silly prayer about finding a publisher for this book but doesn't answer the refugee's prayer whose life is on the fringes? My mind always wanders into these dark places when I pray, so for now, I will just thank God for things because I know that there is a lot to be thankful for, and I know that recognizing all these positive things can lead to a healthier life because the positivity can be the antidote to my perfectionistic tendencies.

Suddenly, Marcos speaks up.

But he is not talking to me.

"Ohhhhh, thank You, Lord," he says aloud.

A minute or so later, he says it again.

"Ohhhhh, thank You, Lord," he says. "Yes, Jesus," he whispers.

And then again.

"Ohhhhh, we praise You today, Lord. Thank You, thank You, thank You, Jesus."

It is as if Marcos could read my thoughts, and now, here we are, just having a gratitude festival in a steam room in Brazil!

But then Marcos does something that I do not expect, something that makes me a little anxious and uncomfortable.

He falls to his knees, lifts his hands into the air, and begins to pray aloud. I can only tell, here in the thickness of this steam, because I hear his knees hit the floor, and I can see one of his hands in the air, not much higher than my face.

I say "uncomfortable" because by praying aloud, Marcos is inviting me to join him. One does not pray aloud in a steam room with another man if he does not want that other man to pray with him. But there was no formal discussion about it. Marcos just did it.

But who am I to pray aloud with this inspiring, righteous, sacrificial man, who has surrendered the comforts of this life to be a missionary? *How* can I pray? I am a head case when it comes to prayer. Neuroscience is what brings me to God's throne room nowadays. Neuroscience! Not Jesus. Neuroscience!

Yet I decide to.

It would be rude not to pray with a man who is inviting me to pray with him.

The next five or fifteen or thirty minutes are somewhat of a blur.

I cannot recall fully what happened.

———

Marcos and I have our sweaty arms around one another in a brotherly embrace, standing in the center of the steam room. Had I entered into some sort of existential bliss? It's not like I had one of those mystical experiences where you lose your bearings, or one of those Buddhist experiences where you awaken to your oneness with the divine and enter into a purple light, but it is fair to say that it was the most charismatic time that I have ever experienced. I am not a charismatic person. No, I am practical to a fault. It is strange, isn't it, that someone who is so obsessed with learning from the great Christian mystics struggles to welcome Mystery into the everyday moments of his life? I am drawn to that which I do not understand.

All I know is that a moment ago, I was on my knees, in the opposite corner of where I started praying, and I had my hands in the air.

The other day Marcos taught me about gratitude, which has all kinds of practical benefits. But today he taught me of *surrender*—a liberating yielding to powerlessness and a belief that there is Someone bigger than us who can meet us in our struggles. An admittance that it's not all up to us.

I remember surrendering this book to God, my romantic life to God, my job to God, my future to God—all those aspects that consume my heart, my mind, my soul, and seem to, more often than not, create so much tension in my body. And as I prayed, I kept raising my hands higher and higher, as high as they could go, until my arms became sore … and I kept my knees on the tile … and I did not slouch back and sit on my heels … because I wanted God to know that I was serious, serious about surrendering; that, though soaked in sweat, tired and weak, my body was an outward display of what I wanted my soul to also be: not my own. And then I looked up into the hazy cloud beyond my outstretched hands, and I realized that I could not even see the ceiling. I thought about what the Blue Ridge Mountains taught me about *thin places*, and how this was a thin place, where you suddenly become aware of how heaven is meeting earth, how there is no bottom or top to anything, no ground or sky. Everything simply *is*. Heaven is *here*.

And I thought about how this place was constantly being filled with steam, just as God constantly breathes into us, and how it is up to us whether or not we choose to become aware of how, at the core of who we are, is the same breath of the divine, the same *ruach* ("wind" or "spirit" in Hebrew), that transformed Adam into a *living* being in the Genesis poem. And I thought about Marcos's internal posture of gratitude and surrender … and how I would take these two ideas with me back to the United States.

After showering, we head upstairs to our hotel room. Coach happens to be leaving his room at the moment we get back.

"Were you guys in the steam room this whole time?" Coach asks.

"Three of us were," Marcos laughs. "Me, my friend Steve, and the Holy Spirit."

46

FALLS LIKE MOUNTAINS

Today is our last full day in South America. Tomorrow afternoon, Nila Kurrle—Norberto and Marcos's sister—and her husband, Ricardo, will take us to the Asunción airport, where we will fly to São Paulo, and will then fly through the night to New Jersey. I do not want to leave this beautiful country.

————

Where are these waterfalls exactly?

For the last fifteen minutes or so, we've been on a green, double-decker tour bus journeying toward Iguazú Falls on a one-lane road that takes us through the Atlantic Rainforest, one of the few remaining inland rainforests in all of South America. Apparently, there are all kinds of wildlife in the thick of these trees: toucans and monkeys and jaguars, oh my! Already, it is a much different experience than Niagara Falls, which is a tourist trap with its casinos and bars and restaurants.

I keep closing my eyes and listening for the falls. You would think that you would be able to hear *something*, considering they are some of the largest waterfalls in the world, you know, some sort of tumbling, crashing water, but all I hear is the rumble of the bus engine. You'd think you would be able to *see* something, too—some sort of towering waterfall beyond the trees somewhere, like a far-off mountain or a distant castle that we are voyaging toward.

Nothing.

Marcos could not have picked a better day for us to do this, though. It's probably seventy degrees. The sky is clear—an opaque blue—and thin, white clouds are smeared across the dome-like expanse, fading into the blue canvas like airplane trails. I am sitting in an outside seat on the bus. A calming, early-morning breeze from the bus window is cooling my face, almost putting me asleep. What if I were to fall asleep and ended up missing the first sight of one of the world's seven natural wonders? Then again, maybe God *wants* me to wake up to the splendor. It is a metaphor for each day that is offered to us, when we awaken and arise from our slumber and enter into the day, a day that is filled with beauty and mystery and divine invitation. Anyway, I do not end up falling asleep. Though my body is relaxed, I keep playing with a dozen stories in my head.

Our bus eventually comes to a stop. Still, I cannot see anything. However, I *can* finally hear the steady rainlike pattering of crashing cascades in the distance.

People are exiting the bus and making their way down a railed walkway toward a lookout point.

We follow.

And then, upon arriving at the platform, we are confronted with the depths of the gorge, and—oh my, God! —we finally see it. *Iguazú Falls.*

It does not matter where you look, to the left or to the right or straight ahead across the river into the distance. The waterfalls are everywhere, in all shapes and sizes—some gushing over the edges like rapids, others trickling down in gentle streams—all painting the cliffside with a hundred stripes (apparently there are at least 275 drops). And we are on top of it all, looking *down* into the ravine, the lowest point of the river, which is where all the great waterfalls—Iguazú, Victoria, and Niagara—are located. Sometimes it is at our lowest points, it seems, in our powerlessness, that we experience the power of God in us the most.

We keep pointing at each of the individual waterfalls across the river, like little children pointing out their Christmas gifts beneath a tree, and exclaiming, "There's another one! Whoa, there's another one!" After a while, I lose count. You try to find numbers or statistics to contain what you see, but in the end, you are forced to come to the same conclusion that scientists have come to about something as foundational as gravity: "It is a mystery! We can try to explain it, but we cannot adequately and accurately explain it!"

Even if this is all it is—standing on this platform and marveling at the falls—it is worth every penny. I'm confident I could stand here all day and notice the differences of each waterfall, draping over the cliffs into the ravine, listening to the different noises that they create in the water below, all blending into one united echo of grace.

"Over there is the Argentina side," Marcos says to us, pointing across the river toward cliffs that are even higher than where we are standing on our side. "But I like this side more," he confirms. "This takes you *into* the falls."

"C'mon," Marcos says as he proceeds to walk down a winding, downhill path—into the rainforest and into the falls.

In wonder, we follow.

And then the waterfalls begin to talk to me. Just like those Blue Ridge Mountains in Roanoke.

———

"Welcome home, old friend," the waterfalls say.

"But I am far from home," my soul says. "And we are not old friends because I have never met you before. I've never seen anything like you before."

"Oh, but you have," the waterfalls respond. *"Keep walking...."*

I step out onto another lookout deck, one that is lower than the first, but still above the falls. It is easier to see the intricacies of the falls from here, simply because we are closer to them. In front of me, probably 300 yards away, across the river, is a rocky cliff. To my right, a number of short, meandering falling streams, flowing over rocks and bouncing off stones, pouring into a circular pool about halfway down the cliff, then bursting in unison from a single waterfall into the river below. To my left, a collection of waterfalls conspiring on a concave ledge, flowing *into* one another, their water becoming *one* by the time it crashes into the river. In the distance, at least a half mile away on a second tier, *more* waterfalls—at least one hundred of them draped over *another* stretching cliffside.

"What do you see?" the waterfalls ask.

"You are all so different," my soul responds.

"Very good," they affirm. *"Our love for humanity is revealed in many ways."*

"Your love for humanity?" my soul asks.

"Of course," they confirm. *"Why else would we be here? Keep walking...."*

The path flattens for the next several hundred feet, and though it still feels like we are above the waterfalls, it is taking us closer *to* them, into the bending river. Coatis—possum like rodents with long, striped tails—walk the railing, searching for their next meal, which is probably in a nearby trashcan. Human food.

Trees hang over the path, often blocking our view. We can hear the falls steadily growing louder. The sun bleeds through the trees, littering the path with speckled drops of light. At one point, there is a pocket in the trees where we can clearly see the two tiers of waterfalls. We stop on the path to gaze out beyond us. It is not a lookout deck, but it is still a splendid sight. Directly over the railing is a drop-off, replete with green foliage, as if the cliffside is wearing a coat. The cliffside across the river bends toward us, its waterfalls bursting over its edges. People hurry by us, excited to get to the next spot.

"What do you see *and* hear?*"* the waterfalls ask.

"I see both tiers of the falls, and I can hear the waterfalls from the first tier more clearly," my soul responds.

"Do not hurry through life," the waterfalls say, *"going from one thing to the next, accomplishing one thing after another. There are miracles all around you for you to observe, gifts for you to open. This life—wherever you go and, most importantly, wherever you are—is sprinkled with the divine. My power is always near. But sometimes you must slow down and look through the trees.*

"I said that you must slow down and look through the trees.

"Keep walking...."

The path branches outward, this time away from the cliffside, until it spits us out at an elevated lookout point at the turn of the river. Here, you can see directly down the throat of the river, like a doctor and her flashlight, and notice the convergence of multiple falls in the distance, creating a misty pit that rises like smoke into the sky.

We continue to walk. This time the path drifts back into the ravine and begins to slope downward, pulling us *into* the falls.

After multiple lookout points and a quarter-mile or so of walking, we feel the air begin to cool, the path becomes shaded, no longer by the hanging trees, but by the shadows of the cliffside. We eventually emerge from the rainforest, and, suddenly, we are *below* the falls, no longer on top of them. We are fifteen feet or so above the water and its tumbling, rocky, rapids.

The path is damp.

The air is misty.

We are literally standing in the gulley, surrounded by a half-circle of waterfalls, curving around us. We are *in* the throat, near the vocal cords; the resounding crashing of the falls is so loud that we almost have to yell to be understood by one another. In front of us is a path that arms its way even deeper into the falls, into the center of the gulley. The rapids tumble beneath the path. The circular platform at the end of the path actually hangs over *another* tier of waterfalls.

"What do you see *and* hear *and* feel?"

"I see the bottom of the falls, and I hear them crashing against the water," my soul says. "I can feel the mist on my skin, rising from the surface of the water."

"Why did you keep walking? Why did you not turn back from where you came from and go back to the bus?"

"Because I wanted to keep following the path. I wanted to see where it would go. It is too beautiful to turn back."

"You are beginning to get it. When you are filled with wonder and awe for the mysteries of life, you will always venture down the path. You will know no other way. Only the fearful or complacent turn back. Only the spiritually deaf and mystically blind will settle for a life of absolutes and solutions and formulas. They will remain on the previous platforms because they will think that they have already arrived at what is best. But the mystic must always walk down the path. However, to walk down the path, you must first recognize that all of life is a beautiful mystery that is to be discovered and enjoyed. Now go, be baptized."

"What?"

"I said to go, be baptized. Go. Keep walking...."

Marcos and I walk up the path that stretches over the rocky waters, the first time today that the path has branched outward like this at a ninety-degree angle. We arrive at the platform, and the hanging mist from the crashing falls around us is drenching our skin. It is as if we are back in the steam room again where we prayed together the night before.

Soaked.

Alive.

Touching heaven.

Oh, how all of life is a thin place! Like the waterfalls said to me, all we must do is recognize how thin—how mysterious, how heaven-soaked—life already is!

We look over the edge of the railed platform and find ourselves staring down the terrifying overflow of another waterfall, crashing into another tier of the river. And then, there it is, a rainbow—climbing up the waterfall, stretching and bending in front of us, then fading into the mist. This trip began with a rainbow. Here it is, ending with a rainbow. A promise. Not for prosperity. But a promise of presence. Here I am, just a writer with a restless mind and a wild heart, standing next to this man, an inspirational missionary. I am *in* the river *with* Marcos, just like the man in Naranjal who rushed into Marcos's arms to be baptized. And the presence of the divine is in Marcos and in me and in all these drenched people around us. And it is in these waterfalls and in the rocks, and, oh, it is as if I can hear them singing!

"What do you see *and* hear *and* feel *and* taste?*"

"You!" my soul shouts. "I *see* the falls and I *hear* the falls and I *feel* the falls and I can *taste* the falls! I am covered in the same water that tumbles down these cliffs! I am one with the most magnificent thing my body has ever seen and heard and tasted and felt!"

"At the center of Us, the ethos of the Triune dance, is a love that is to be experienced—experienced by you. To be seen. To be heard. To be felt. To be tasted. Now close your eyes."

"Okay," my soul says, surrendering.

"I baptize you in the name of Trinity—the Father and the Son and the Holy Spirit. Stand here as I drench you with my love and grace. Taste the kiss of the divine on your lips. And when you leave, do not forget that these waterfalls are only a metaphor for what already is of life—a mystery full of love and grace that is to be experienced."

47

VIOLET SKY

We are on a bus from Ciudad del Este to Asunción, the capital, where Nila and Ricardo will pick us up. It has been a good day but is not really worth writing about, as this was our "tourist day."

All we did after Iguazú Falls this morning was shop throughout the afternoon in Ciudad del Este, which was especially lively considering today was Paraguay's Independence Day. We will sleep in Asunción tonight, our final night in Paraguay, and then we will spend time with Nila and Ricardo tomorrow before they take us to the airport.

This bus ride has been entertaining thus far. Every thirty minutes or so, the bus will stop, and a vendor from the streets will board and walk up and down the aisles selling food and goods. A few minutes ago, a woman boarded the bus, carrying a gigantic basket of *chipas* (always *chipas!*) on her head.

"*Chipa? Chipa? Chipa?*" she kept saying incrementally, squawking like a bird.

And then, when she walked by Coach Briscoe, she took the big basket off her head and plopped it on his lap without forewarning. He kept peering over the basket, like a groundhog peeking from his hole, as she sold *chipas* from his lap.

I took a photo of him. I will call it "Groundhog Briscoe."

———

I am sitting in an aisle seat. Next to me is a stout Guarani mother in a bright pink shirt, making the journey to the capital with two of her children on her lap—an infant boy with damp, black, curly hair, and a girl who must be five or six or ten, with a laugh that sounds like music. Coach gave them a Clif bar.

I keep looking out the window at the splendor of the countryside off of Highway 7—the kaleidoscope of dark green flatlands, bronze brushlands, the light blue sky, and the dark shadows of distant trees—and smiling at the mother and her children next to me. What a beautiful country with such beautiful people. I cannot believe this trip has already come to an end. I do not want it to come to an end. I do not want to return to the chaos. The projections. The perceptions. The rat race. The drama. The dreams that taunt me throughout the day and wake me from my sleep. But I must return. You cannot run from your problems. You must live amongst them. Befriend them.

Scooting toward the aisle to my left, I pat the space between me and the mother to my right, offering the little girl a place to sit. This is a six-hour bus ride, after all, a long time for this mother to have two children in her arms. The mother smiles, but the girl remains on her lap. Maybe they are already as comfortable as they can possibly be. Close to one another.

———

The sun is setting outside our window.

I am in a reflective state this evening, thinking about the trip and all that has been revealed to me. The main thing that keeps rising to the forefront of my mind is how interesting it was to spend this particular week in Paraguay, leading up to the people's Independence Day, which is today. Each town and city we visited seemed to be clothed in red, white, and blue. People walking around selling flags. Banners slouching above those red-clay streets. Light poles wrapped in ribbon. It felt like we were back in America, a deep, yet plain, reminder, perhaps, that we are all more alike than we have dared to imagine.

Here I am, next to this middle-aged Guarani woman with two children on her lap, someone who lives a world away from my home in America, someone who speaks an entirely different language than me, someone who has an entirely different background, and, just as our countries share the same colors in their flags, we are also the same at the core of our beings, where the breath of the divine resides … and also the same in our identities, wrapped in the reality of Belovedness.

We are on a bus together.

Going to the same place.

Looking at the same sunset.

And perhaps the place is more than a bus station.

And maybe the sunset is more than this world.

Then, staring out the window with this mother whom I do not even know, her son cradled in her right arm, her daughter nestled in her left arm, both of them asleep, I see it, spelled out across the expanse: a violet sky, the red embers of the sun mixing with the whites of the clouds mixing with the blues of the heavens.

The blending of our countries' colors.

Oneness. Union. Fullness.

We are so different. Yet mysteriously the same. Mystically united.

My spirit breathes and glows.

My soul ventures out into the field and covers my dreams with the clay.

My body falls asleep.

Acknowledgments

Thank you, Dad, for your constant encouragement the past six years as I worked on this project, and to Mom, Katie, and Carrie; when faced with unknowing, I never felt like I was alone. Much gratitude to the Briscoes and the Kurrles for welcoming me into this story and allowing it to take me wherever it took me creatively.

Thanks, Bruce, for being first in the publishing world to believe in this project and sign me as your client, and then for your continued efforts as my guide and editor. Thanks, Morgan at two|pr, for getting this train moving. Thanks, David, for all of your advice about navigating the publishing sphere and my writing pursuits. Thanks, Lisa, for your wonderful edits and attention to detail, and to Sylvia, for always doing the same. Much gratitude to Morgan James Publishing for finding a home for this project, especially to Aubrey, David, Karen, Jim, Nickcole, their bookstore marketing team, and their talented design team. Thanks to all who took the time to catch the vision of the book and endorse it, including the ones who will come in after writing this; I'm deeply humbled.

Thanks to everyone who used their talents to support the book, gave their valuable time to read through rough drafts of the book, and donated their hard-earned resources to empower the launch. Those people are Dave, Brooke, Benny, Lauren, Cedric, Eli, Adam and Julianna, Josh and Becky, Aunt Chris, Brent and Amy, Grizel, Diane, Austin, Hep, Natalie, Neuhart, Knust, Mike, Dylan and his brilliant film crew of Elizabeth, TJ, and Jenice, and all the others who will come alongside me after this is published and support this message and story. Along the way there were so many lifelong influences in my creativity—like my godmother, grandparents, extended family members, teachers, and friends—and it would take me at least ten pages to name them all.

To Watershed Charlotte—my home—and its staff, where my belonging led to transformation. To my two therapists at Forest Hill Church's Care and Counseling, along with Dr. Browning, for guiding me inward, the journey of a lifetime. To Brett and Robert at *Sports Spectrum Magazine*, for giving me a start and a space to grow as a writer. Thanks to all of my incredible friends in Charlotte who met me where I was on my journey of spiritual deconstruction and discovery and all the wonderful conversations we had while I lived there; these conversations deeply influenced this book.

This book was mostly written at Amélie's French Bakery in NODA, Smelly Cat Coffeehouse, Birdsong Brewery, and Rush Espresso in Ballantyne; I'm so thankful for all the caffeine and the beer that helped me to plow through my self-doubt. While writing this book, I mostly listened to Bon Iver, Josh Garrels, Noah Gundersen, and Blind Pilot—music that inspired me to engage the complexity of my emotions and vulnerably share them.

Thank you for taking the time to read this book. It means the world to me, and I hope we have the chance to meet soon.

About The Author

Stephen Copeland is a writer and storyteller. Though an established collaborator, *Where the Colors Blend* is his first book in his own voice. He obtained a bachelor's degree in journalism and Bible from Grace College and is a member of the International Thomas Merton Society.

He is a former staff writer and columnist at Sports Spectrum Magazine, a national faith-based sports magazine, and has also been published in Christianity Today. Stephen resides in Nashville, Tennessee.

Donations to the Kurrle family's mission
work in Paraguay can be sent to:

Interstate Softball Tournament

P.O. Box 7851

Roanoke VA, 24019

(Donations are not tax deductible. If you have any questions, you can email Chad Briscoe at softballforareason@gmail.com.)

To connect with the author, you can send him an email at stephen@copelandwrites.com or message him on Twitter or Instagram (@steve_copeland).

Morgan James
Speakers Group

We connect Morgan James published authors with live and online events and audiences who will benefit from their expertise.

Morgan James makes all of our titles available
through the Library for All Charity Organization.

www.LibraryForAll.org